VANTAGE AT SEA

by the same author

*

RIVER OF GOLDEN SAND
IN GOOD COMPANY
MOANALUA

*

(editor)
BEST STORIES OF THE NAVY

Ship on the starboard tack. 1565

VANTAGE AT SEA

England's Emergence as an Oceanic Power

BY THOMAS WOODROOFFE

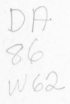

ST MARTIN'S PRESS
New York

To
G. FARIE
Commander, RN
who first taught the Sea
and the Royal Navy to a succession
of young Naval Officers, one of whom
was the author

Contents

*

NOTE ON THE CALENDAR

Dates are given according to the English Calendar, except in Chapters XII, XIII and XIV, where they are given 'New Style', or according to the Spanish Calendar. Thus, Medina-Sidonia sighted The Lizard on July 29, which the English called July 19.

Illustrations

*

ILLUSTRATIONS

Maps

*

CHAPTER I

Prologue

*

Towards the close of the fifteenth century most Courts in Europe had come to accept the theory that the best way of reaching India lay across the sea, but only the rulers of Spain and Portugal had sent out expeditions to prove it. In 1492, acting on a belief that he would find a short cut to the westward, Columbus happened upon the fringes of the New World for Spain; Portuguese navigators with surer instinct had for years past been feeling their way down the coast of Africa and were now round the Cape of Good Hope and were about to open the route to India and the Far East. The world was expanding fast; almost every year undreamed-of lands appeared out of the Ocean Sea, and the only two rivals upon it could not agree how to divide any future rich spoils. So each side went secretly to the Pope for his backing in the matter.

Here was a problem that might have given Solomon pause, but His Holiness Alexander VI rose to the occasion with a solution that was as simple as it was magnificent. He divided the world in two. All to the west of a given line was for Spain; all to the east for Portugal. In sonorous Latin the world was apportioned for ever; Ferdinand and Isabella of Spain, their heirs and successors, were granted 'all the firm lands and islands to be found to the west and south from the Pole Arctic to the Pole Antarctic, such as have not heretofore been possessed by any other Christian King or Prince'.

This award took no account of the aspirations of other Christian States and but little of geography. Nor did it satisfy King John of Portugal, who knew of the existence of South America and did not see why Spain should be given all lands to the south, a direction

11

which he considered the preserve of Portugal. In 1494 the disput-
ing parties met at the little town of Tordesillas in Castile to try to
decide how the line should run. This was not a simple matter; no
accurate method existed of determining longitude, how far east or
west one place might be of another, and no two charts produced in
argument were the same. So, when it was agreed that the line
should run vertically through a point situated some eleven hundred
miles west of the Cape Verde Islands, not even the most learned
geographer present could state precisely where this point lay. But
in spite of the speculative nature of the proceedings the envoys of
King John were able to ensure that Brazil should be included in
the sphere of Portugal. The question of what happened where west
met east on the other side of the world the negotiators wisely left
to be decided when anybody reached there.

One result of this haphazard partition of the world was to con-
fine the English to waters which bred a race of such consummate
seamen that in the end it was England who controlled those very
trade routes which Spain and Portugal were so busily dividing between them. For another, a Latin culture and the Catholic faith
prevail today from the Rio Grande to Cape Horn. But at the time
of its signing the implications of the Treaty seem to have been as
far beyond the grasp of its signatories as they were of the other
crowned heads of Europe. These practically ignored the Treaty,
and King Henry VII of England was so little moved by its provisions that only four years later he allowed an English ship to sail
out across the Atlantic to see what was on the other side.

Her captain hoped to find Cathay. John Cabot, a Venetian,
learned in Renaissance geography, persuaded eighteen merchants
of Bristol to share his belief that by sailing westwards from Europe
they would reach the shores of that fabled land. After fifty-two
days of crowded discomfort in a vessel named the *Matthew of
Bristol*, Cabot and his crew reached a heavily-wooded shore upon
which they planted the Royal Standard of England and took possession of the place under the impression that it was a part of the
territory of the Great Khan. Cabot's geography was a bit out, for
the place where they had landed was at the northern end of Cape
Breton Island. On the way home the crew of the *Matthew* varied

their diet by hauling basketsful of cod from the sea. They had stumbled upon the Newfoundland Banks, a discovery which in the long run was of more importance to England than the silks and spices of Cathay: deep sea fishing grounds provided the hard school for Tudor seamen. The only official comment recorded on the voyage is the laconic entry in the accounts of the Privy Purse that ten pounds were paid to 'him that found the New Isle'.

The Spanish Ambassador at once protested that Cabot's continent already belonged to his sovereign, but Henry VII would not consider the protest. From the first he had disregarded the Papal division of the world, although he had been prepared to recognize the rights of prior discovery, but now he announced that he would recognize actual possession and nothing else—a doctrine of which his grand-daughter Elizabeth was to make effective use.

Henry VII might stand up for a principle, but his England was only a minor power which could not afford large state-financed expeditions, and he did not dare to antagonize Spain. So while English ships confined their trading voyages to Europe, Spain and Portugal went unchallenged on their careers of discovery, each carrying out its own interpretation of the Award. For Spain this meant conquest and the spread of Christianity, with all the material benefits that went with them. The Portuguese were not so fervent: in their African possessions at least they worried less about the fate of the infidel in the next world and more about the benefits of trade in this. Nor did they spend their energy on conquest. Their possessions along the Guinea Coast and the Bight of Benin were no more than fortified trading posts, precarious footholds on the fringe of an unknown continent. For that dark hinterland out of which the natives appeared with their merchandise, the Portuguese cared little. It was only after they had reached India that the Portuguese set about the conquest of new discoveries and the spread of Christianity among the inhabitants. They pushed on to the Spice Islands and beyond, and soon their caravels were sailing up the Tagus laden with the exotic cargoes of the East, silks and ivory, sandalwood, cinnamon and cloves. Spain and Portugal kept to their own sides of the line, but within its sphere each claimed a monopoly of trade and conquest.

PROLOGUE

English merchants with ideas of poaching in these preserves soon found that their activities were limited by two factors: The Treaty of Alliance between Henry VII and the Spanish Crown confined their trading in the Atlantic to the Canaries, and if they looked to the East they had no English navigators capable of taking their ships towards those desirable markets. Even for their brief excursions into the Atlantic, English captains had to rely on foreign pilots—and this at a time when Albuquerque had made the Indian Ocean a Portuguese lake from Mozambique to the Moluccas, and St. Francis Xavier was preaching to the Samurai of Japan.

It was hardly to be expected that these foreign pilots would hire themselves for voyages into the Portuguese and Spanish preserves, or would give away the secrets of how the spices of the Moluccas or the silver of Peru might be reached, so English ships had to be content with coasting prosaically to the Baltic or sometimes as far as the Mediterranean. Although the reign of Henry VII was not one of outstanding achievement, it was a turning point in English history. England was emerging from the Middle Ages and those first changes began to appear which were to transform the Kingdom from a small unconsidered agricultural country into a thrusting oceanic power.

Until now wool had been England's chief export, which Europe found essential for the making of fine cloth. The Flemish weavers would use none other, and every year the Venetians sent round a galley fleet from the Mediterranean to fetch it for their looms. But during Henry's reign, for the first time in her history, England exported more of her own home-made cloth than of her raw wool. One day English ships would be scouring the seas of the world for markets for that cloth; and, as if in anticipation, the ocean-going ship made its first appearance. The clumsy medieval 'round ship' with a single mast, capable of going only where the wind took her, was giving place to the three-masted vessel which could beat against the wind and allowed her captain a wider choice of destination.

Henry encouraged the building of these sea-going ships by offering a bounty of so much a ton to the merchants who built them; for he was the first King of England to realize that seaborne trade

Medieval 'Round Ship' about 1470

was worth far more to the country and himself than costly and vainglorious military expeditions to the Continent. This was a notable departure from precedent, but when he came to build on his own account he was responsible for a more startling innovation; he built the first King's ship designed to fight rather than to be just another transport. His *Regent* with her 180 man-killing 'serpentines' was a significant advance in naval thought and construction, although her lines were not much of an improvement on those of the old round ship. Henry did not consider that he could afford a large fleet of King's ships in permanent commission; instead he prepared a framework upon which the whole maritime strength of the country could expand if need arose—which was possible when there was as yet little difference between a warship and a merchantman. In the first year of his reign he had forbidden any but English ships to carry wine to his country, a Navigation Act designed to build up a reserve of shipping. To arm this reserve quickly in time of war, he built new storehouses and depots at Greenwich and Woolwich and decided that not Southampton but Portsmouth should be a naval base. Here again he produced something new. Until then ships had been 'docked' by lying on the mud when the tide went out with a sort of stockade of brushwood built round them, a primitive and unsatisfactory expedient for working on a ship's bottom. While St. George's Chapel, Windsor, was still in process of building, the King instructed the architect, Sir Reginald Bray, to turn his attention from that work of art to the designing of a dry dock at Portsmouth. Bray seems to have been a man of parts, for his dock, built of wood, was a success; while its cost, £190 0s. 6¾d., is an indication of the exact accounting demanded by his shrewd and cautious sovereign.

Before Henry VII died a much-travelled Portuguese geographer had felt himself able to declare that North and South America made one vast continent—though he would not go so far as to say that its inhabitants were descended from Adam. English ships had visited the northern part of that continent and established a fishery off an island which they called the New-found-land. The cloth of England was seeking fresh markets and her merchants were established in Seville. There were the rudiments of a fighting navy.

PROLOGUE

The signs pointing to the future of England were directed towards the sea.

When Henry VIII came to the throne, the healthy state of the Royal Exchequer, impressions received during boyhood, and a new invention by one Hans Poppenruyter over in the Netherlands, all combined to influence the new King in leading his country further in this direction. As a boy at Greenwich Palace, the future Henry VIII had been allowed to run wild in the wonderland of the nearby Royal Dockyard, where he made friends with the sailors, learned to pull an oar with the best of them and even mastered the recondite art of piping upon the seaman's whistle. The magic of ships got into his blood, and now that he was King with all the money in the world he could build as many of these fascinating toys as he liked and better than his careful father had been able to afford. A gorgeous figure dressed in cloth of gold with bright scarlet hose and wearing a seaman's whistle on a gold chain round his neck was to be observed at the launch of each new ship; and officials soon discovered that the beady brown eyes of their new master missed very little of what went on in his dockyards, while the technical knowledge he had picked up as a boy allowed him to ask and expect answers to the most awkward questions. Only three years after he had come to the throne, an incident during the war with France led to the asking of one of these questions and the answer that was given led eventually to England's dominance as a naval power.

On a fine summer's day in 1512, when the English fleet came up with the French outside Brest, the English *Regent* and French *Cordelière*, the largest ships present, found themselves grappled together during the course of the engagement. After nearly three hours of bloody hand to hand fighting, 'suddenly the Caryke was one flaming fyre and lykewyse the Regent within the turning of one hand.' Both ships sank.

Although he gave a present of ten pounds to the messenger who brought him the news of the 'drownding' of the Carrack, Henry VIII was not the sort of man who would relish losing one of his own ships each time an enemy was sunk. There must be some better way of dealing with an enemy ship, and here—although it is impossible to say for certain that he did—it is likely that he suddenly remembered those great guns which he had bought from Hans Poppenruyter for his army and fortifications. They were great, powerful things which would blow a ship to pieces in no time, as he knew from experiments that he himself had carried out. Also they had other advantages.

The medieval gun was built up of strips of metal bound together and loaded at the breech end. Even when the guns did not explode on being fired, the gunners had to wait anything up to half a day for the breech-block to cool off before they could reload. The new guns of Hans Poppenruyter, on the other hand, were cast in one piece and loaded at the muzzle which allowed for a more destructive rate of fire. Why not mount them in his new ships? A question like this from Henry VIII was apt to be regarded as a command and his master shipwright, James Baker, soon found an answer. The new guns were so heavy that they would have to be mounted low down in the ship, therefore the ship's sides would have to be pierced for them to be fired through it. Whether the King deserves all the credit for the idea or not, he was very much the master of his own navy and the fact remains that within three years of the loss of the *Regent*, the first ship in the world with rows of gunports gaping in her sides was launched. When the *Mary Rose* ran down the slipway she decided the pattern of naval warfare for the next 400 years. The era of the broadside had arrived.

With the output from his own yards and by the conversion of merchantmen bought from the Hansa towns or in Italy, Henry VIII built up the most powerful fleet in the world. It was not long before his navy turned out to be a sound investment, and a shocked ambassador was reporting to his master, Charles V of Spain, 'the King has no respect or fear for anyone in the world'. As long as his navy held command of the Channel, Henry could defy Pope and Emperor from the safety of his own realm where no one could get at him. Because of his policy the Navy had a restricted function: it was designed for use in Home waters, not for operations out of soundings: and there is no record during the whole reign of a King's ship having cruised to the westward of the Scillies. Henry needed his navy close to his own shores, to repel attack from France, to help in the invasion of Scotland and to protect his

European trade. In 1545 the Navy foiled an attempted French invasion, and later on the inhabitants of Edinburgh were taken by surprise when his sailors in their green and white jackets swarmed ashore from their ships to pillage and then burn Leith. The Navy was so strong that it was called upon to do very little actual fighting. Having by its mere potential gained command of the Channel, its squadrons were employed in the protection of trade against pirates and privateers. So instead of using their broadsides in fleet actions, Henry's ships were chiefly employed in guarding the herring fleet, escorting the wool and wine fleets to Calais or Bordeaux, or in providing a Channel guard during the winter months. The ships themselves were squat and ugly, very broad in the beam and 'built loftie'—floating fortresses crammed with soldiers and sailors, but just what was needed for operations in which no squadron was ever more than a few days' sail from a home port.

Although the Royal Navy was not yet oceanic, it had demonstrated off the Isle of Wight that England's best defence lay not in archers and pikemen drawn up along her shores, but in ships out upon the sea, while its command of the Channel made Englishmen appreciate for the first time the excellent strategic position of their island at the gateway to Europe. The peoples of Northern and Central Europe were crying out for the products of the East, the silks and pearls and damasks, but above all for the pepper and spices which alone could make a diet that in winter consisted largely of salt fish and putrid meat at all palatable. On its way to Antwerp and the Baltic all this rich traffic had to pass within sight of the shores of England. Owing to the new discoveries the main trade routes of the world had shifted from the land-locked Mediterranean to the broad oceans, and England, as well as Spain and Portugal, faced the Atlantic. Why should these two latter countries hold a monopoly of its use? In their imagination Englishmen saw their own ships sailing halcyon seas to the bazaars at the ends of the earth, and what beckoned them was not conquest or evangelism—it was trade.

Henry was hoping for new markets when, in 1527, he sent John Rut to find a western passage to Cathay; but soon after this attempt had failed, the King became too much concerned with his own

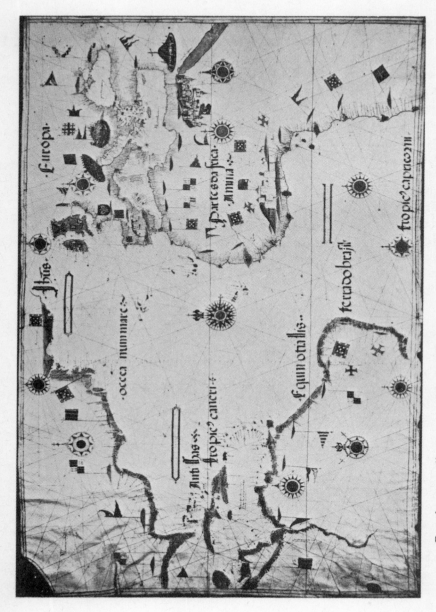

Portolan on vellum 31 x 48 inches by the Portuguese cartographer Jorge Reinel. 1540.

domestic affairs to be interested in further excursions overseas. However, without waiting for official encouragement, certain of his subjects decided to tap at their source some of the riches pouring up the Channel. Swarthy and gesticulating Portuguese sailors in the alehouses of our southern ports had given away many of the secrets of their voyages to West Africa and Brazil, and a solid merchant of Plymouth, William Hawkins, thought he would try his luck on a voyage to the southward. His mixed cargo of combs, hatchets, knives and brass bangles, strangely included nineteen dozen nightcaps. But he must have studied his market for he returned, after calling on the coast of what is now Liberia and then crossing to Brazil, with a valuable cargo of "olyphante's tethe' and 'Brasilwood', which was used in dyeing cloth. Although the Court was mildly interested to see the ivory, Hawkins had not brought back any gold, and his voyages caused little stir. In fact, men soon found a much quicker and easier way of obtaining West African products: they turned privateer and took them off the Portuguese ships sailing up the Channel.

The spices of the East and how to come by them was a question exercising the minds of worthier men than those prowling in the Channel, and a pair of English merchants living in Seville made a special study of the subject. The great Casa de Contratacion, or House of Trade of the Indies, from which all Spanish overseas trade and exploration were directed, was situated in Seville, so that these well-to-do Englishmen were in a good position to learn some of the closely-guarded secrets of Spanish discovery and even to get unofficial copies of confidential charts of the Far East. They may have caught more than one glimpse of the great 'Padron Real' or Master Map of the world kept up to date by the Cosmographer Royal, but they did more than pry and keep their ears open. Robert Thorne actually managed to place his friend Roger Barlow in a Spanish expedition bound for the Moluccas via the Straits of Magellan; and though the Squadron got no farther than South America, Barlow returned with much valuable information and a knowledge of the latest Spanish methods of navigation. Barlow included an account of his experiences in a translation he had made of a sort of Spanish explorer's handbook, and, with the title of 'A Brief Summe of Geographie' forwarded the result to Henry VIII.

Robert Thorne was too delicate a man to go voyaging overseas, but ideas conceived in the seclusion of a study often have more influence on the course of events than the exploits of men of action. Thorne was a man with an original mind; centuries before his time he thought in terms of the globe instead of the map, and he worked out to his own satisfaction that the shortest way from England to the Spice Islands lay Northabout, over the Pole. He wrote to his King urging him to encourage discovery to the northward, the only direction left for England, for all to the south was either a Spanish or a Portuguese monopoly, but he received no reply to his reasoned suggestion. Some years later he returned to the attack in an answer to a number of questions from Dr. Lee, the King's Almoner, on the subject of the 'Spiceries'. It is by this letter that Thorne is chiefly remembered, for his long and prosy geographical treatise was suddenly illumined by a phrase which crystallized into one sentence the heroic temper of an age to come: 'So I judge there is no land unhabitable or sea innavigable.'

While Barlow and Thorne were alive no one but the King had a chance of studying their submissions, and when he had read them the papers went to join countless other yellowing bundles in the Royal Archives. Thorne's two letters lay forgotten until Hakluyt printed them in his *Traffiques and Discoveries* in 1589. Roger Barlow had to wait even longer to get into print; it was not until this century that any of his countrymen could read the descriptions of flying-fish, humming-birds and cannibals as observed in the Estuary of the Plate by an Englishman 400 years ago. But this keen and interested pair must have shared their secrets and theories with the growing circle of those interested in geography; and there is evidence that Thorne's conclusions influenced the direction of an important voyage of exploration, although it was not until after his death and in the next reign that Englishmen sailed to the northward.

In 1553, a number of London merchants who wanted wider markets for English cloth were granted a Royal Charter for the 'Discoverie of Regions, Dominions, Islands and Places Unknown'.

PROLOGUE

Their real purpose was to reach Cathay by sailing eastwards along the top of the world. The Life Governor of this 'Company of Merchant Adventurers of England for the Discovery of Lands unknown' was Sebastian Cabot, now a very old man, who had sailed as a boy with his father John in the *Matthew* and on other voyages. They had failed to discover a north-west passage, but now Sebastian was optimistic about this new direction By this time they were able to employ an English pilot for the expedition. A number of capable navigators had learned their art on trading voyages to Barbary or the Levant and of these the company chose Richard Chancellor. As it turned out, they could not have made a better choice, for in addition to being a navigator with the unusual accomplishment of making his own instruments, Chancellor was an exceptional man in other ways. A soldier, Sir Hugh Willoughby, was given command of the expedition, for which three ships, the largest being 120 tons, had been specially built and provisioned for eighteen months. On a fine May morning in 1553, the *Good Hope*, the *Edward Bonaventure* and the *Confidence* dropped down from Radcliffe on the ebb in tow of their own boats, and the citizens of London were able to admire the new suits of sky-blue cloth worn by the ships' companies and the excellent pulling of the boats' crews. At Greenwich all the courtiers came running out of the Palace to mix with the crowds of common people on the bank, while sedate and bearded members of the Privy Council peered over each other's shoulders from an upper window. The crews manned the yards, the guns fired, the sailors cheered—and only the young King who lay dying within his palace missed the show.

After a month of delays on the east coast, towards the end of June, Sir Hugh Willoughby's ships at last spread their sails before a fresh south-westerly wind and were soon hull down on their voyage into the unknown. After calling at the Lofoten Islands, where they found the inhabitants kind and hospitable, the ships sailed on to the North Cape. Here on a fearsome day of swirling mist and wild gale the ships became separated. When the weather cleared Richard Chancellor in the *Edward Bonaventure* found himself alone, and so, 'very pensive, heavie and sorrowful', he and his little company sailed on under the eerie light of the midnight sun.

PROLOGUE

Spray froze on the rigging; metal seared naked flesh as if it were red hot; the winds screaming across the tumbling wastes seemed to freeze the very spirit of a man; the seamen had no charts to show them where they were, but under Chancellor they sailed on 'resolute to make proofe and triall of all adventures'. After many days of dread of the unknown that was more paralysing than any cold, they came to the large inlet, known today as the White Sea, and discovered from some fishermen that the name of the country was Russia or Muscovy. On anchoring, Chancellor found that, although the local Governor was personally keen to trade, he dared not until he had first got permission from Moscow. Eventually Chancellor and a few companions made the journey by sled all the way from the Arctic to Moscow through the plains and pine forests of a sparsely-populated country. But the journey was worth the trouble. The Emperor, Ivan the Terrible, was so taken by Chancellor's demeanour that, after a banquet of such huge proportions and length and with so much to drink that after it the only course the English could remember was the first—a roasted swan on a golden platter—he gave permission to start trading. The Emperor then handed Chancellor cordial letters to his own sovereign and he returned to England. Thus was founded the Muscovy Company which opened up trade with Russia, outflanking the Hansa League in the Baltic. For the first English representative to Moscow the company sent one George Killingworth, who was, appropriately, a draper.

In 1555 Chancellor made his second visit to Russia and learned at last what had become of Willoughby and the other two ships. They had wintered on the desolate coast of Lapland and there in their ships all had died of cold. Chancellor spent the summer in Moscow, learning all he could about the country and organizing trade with the Emperor, but on the return journey the ship was driven ashore and broke up near Aberdeen. Chancellor was drowned, though the Russian Ambassador, who accompanied him, was saved.

Richard Chancellor was the first of that long line of gifted seamen who have served their country well. Skilled and efficient on his own element, he also had a way with men: he could gain the

22

confidence of a few Russian fishermen terrified at the size of his ship, deal as an equal with a barbaric potentate in the splendour of his own court, and, what was even more of an achievement, lead a company of ignorant and superstitious English sailors through the perils and hardships of an Arctic voyage. His contemporaries called him 'the incomparable Richard Chancellor'. It is his epitaph.

The Muscovy Company started trading in earnest with Russia and even when they sent out further expeditions to try to reach Cathay by the northern route, Philip, who was now on the throne with Mary, made no objection. He did not seem to mind as long as they confined themselves to northern waters, but he forbade any more Guinea voyages, which is not to say that they ceased, for English merchants sturdily refused to be restrained from trading wherever they could find markets.

The English were beginning to chafe at what they considered an unwarrantable partition of the world. Maps of the world were losing their mystery; they really meant something to a growing circle of learned men in London. Dr. Dee, a mathematician with a European reputation, could correspond on equal terms with the master geographers of the Continent. A country which until 1550 had produced hardly any geographical works of note was now printing Dee's *Perfect Art of Navigation* and Eden's *Treatise of the Newe India*. England had her own pilots now, using navigational instruments made by English craftsmen. The accurate fixing of longitude was still impossible, though it was realized that it could be determined by means of an accurate timepiece; and some navigators knew enough to sail on a great circle, thanks to the indefatigable Dr. Dee. The horizon had cleared and the time had come when Englishmen under the patronage of Elizabeth were to sail towards it and far beyond.

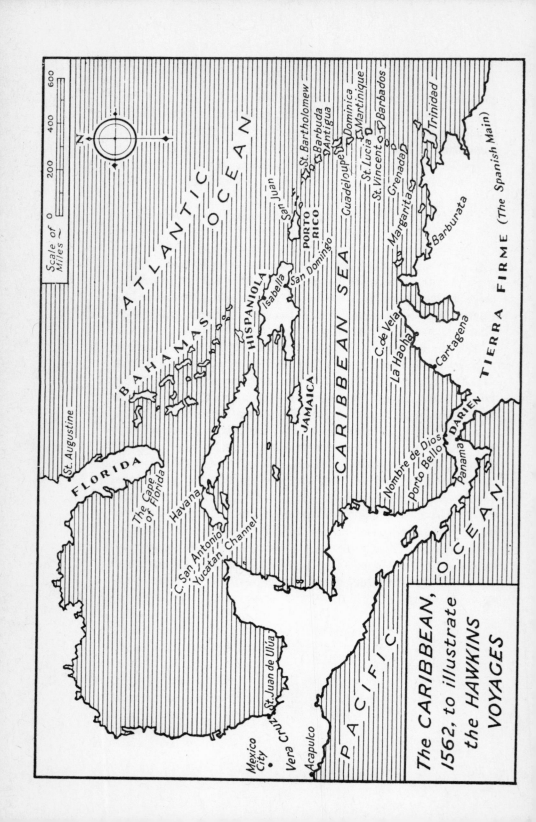

The CARIBBEAN, 1562, to illustrate the HAWKINS VOYAGES

CHAPTER II

Beyond the 'Line'

★

The old order books of the Plantin Press in Amsterdam, which published the maps of Mercator and other leading European cartographers, prove that during the first few years of Elizabeth's reign London booksellers were doing a brisk trade in maps of the world. This may seem surprising in the citizens of a country which by continental standards was poor and backward, but it shows what Englishmen were thinking about. Now that Calais, the last European distraction, had gone, the thoughts and ambitions of Englishmen were focused on the oceans. No longer did a young man with a hankering for adventure go off to the wars across the Channel; instead he went to sea on a voyage to Guinea or Barbary, where he found just as much adventure and was likely to return with something in his pocket. The Treasury was empty, Henry II of France had one foot in Leith and the other in Calais, and England might appear to be in a bad way, but those observers on the Continent who gave Elizabeth no more than a couple of years on the throne were reckoning without the character of the Queen or the temper of her subjects. If those wiseacres in Antwerp had but realized it the cause of England's recovery and expansion was there before their eyes—in those bales of English cloth being unloaded at the quays.

English sheep and wool were the finest in the world and more than three-quarters of England's wealth came from the export of cloth and woollens. This bald statistic, so unromantic in itself, largely explains England's rapid growth into a great sea power, because the search for markets for this cloth forced English traders to the far corners of the earth, wherever there was water to float a ship. But there was something more compelling even than the hope of profit—a state of mind. Elizabethans had a wistful urge to see what lay on the far side of the horizon and this curiosity worked like a ferment in their minds. It lured them out from their sheltered island to find, some fame, a few riches, but the largest number lonely deaths in strange seas.

The trouble was that as likely as not the far side of that horizon was either a Spanish or a Portuguese monopoly. English voyages to the Guinea Coast had continued under Elizabeth (she had actually taken shares in some of them herself), and her traders were now bringing back gold dust from the Gold Coast beyond Cape Verde. A succession of Portuguese envoys arrived in England to protest at these infringements, but they could not back their protests with threats of force. Portugal's most valuable trade route from the Far East with spices for Antwerp and Central Europe passed up the Channel, so that Portugal could not afford to declare war on England. Elizabeth, who was just as much aware of this as the ambassadors, was quite prepared to argue the matter; she would not recognize the rights of prior discovery or the Bull 'Inter Caetera' of 1493—only effective occupation. Did a couple of forts hundreds of miles apart on the coast constitute effective occupation? Of course not. As long as her subjects kept away from the fort and traded with independent negro chiefs they had every right to do so and were infringing no monopoly. She waved these protestors away. Successive envoys retired disconsolate, though one, impressed perhaps by those shapely jewelled fingers, sent the Queen ten pairs of gloves from Paris on his way home.

There were no such pleasant exchanges with Spain when in 1561 Cecil bluntly told the Spanish ambassador that the Pope had no right to partition the earth and award kingdoms. So far only the Portuguese monopoly had been infringed, but Spain realized that before long England would be pushing into the Spanish sphere also, and after a most unsatisfactory conversation with Cecil an exasperated Spanish ambassador warned his King: 'Nothing will bring these people to their senses. They claim to have a right to go to all lands or provinces belonging to friendly states without exception.'

BEYOND THE 'LINE'

These words were the cue for the appearance in history of a good-looking young sea captain trading out of Plymouth. This man was far above the ordinary run of bluff and uncouth Elizabethan mariners, for he had been well educated, was always dressed in good taste, and invariably softly spoken. But he was more than a personable young man; he had a charm of manner and subtlety of brain that would have made him a successful diplomat. Being also a leader of men and a fine seaman, he followed in the direct succession of Richard Chancellor. He was the first Englishman to break the Spanish monopoly in the West, and if thereby he was in some measure responsible for the quarrel with Spain he also had a larger hand in the defeat of the Armada than any other of the Queen's subjects. The name of this young sailor was John Hawkins and he was the son of that William who brought home the 'Olyphante's tethe' in the time of the Queen's father.

On voyages down to the coast of Africa or Brazil, John Hawkins, like any other captain in that trade, had been in the habit of calling at the Canary Islands as a sort of half-way house. But on the visits he made Hawkins took in more than fresh water and provisions. By making friends of the Spaniards he dealt with he came to learn a great deal about the Spanish colonies in the West—that close preserve with which all trade was forbidden. For the Canary Islands lay also on the Spanish route across the Atlantic. Ships from Seville, outward bound, first dropped down to the Canaries where they watered, then picked up the north-east trades which took them right into the Caribbean. There was little, therefore, that those Spanish friends of Hawkins's, and especially one, Pedro de Ponte, could not tell him about conditions in the Spanish colonies.

The only traffic permitted the colonies with the outside world consisted of an escorted convoy from Spain, the 'Flota', twice a year; independent Spanish voyages were forbidden.

Hides and sugar cane, therefore, which could have been exchanged for the imported goods the colonists so badly needed, lay rotting in the storehouses. Lack of shipping was only one of the handicaps which cramped the development of the colonies; another was a chronic shortage of labour. When the natives of the area proved to be of no use as slaves, negroes were imported from

27

Africa, and the Spanish Crown allowed foreigners, chiefly Portuguese, to carry slaves to the Caribbean under licence. The duty per slave imported legally was fixed so high that few slaves were imported legally—instead a thriving 'black market' in slaves and island produce grew up along the unpatrolled coasts of those distant settlements.

Philip kept no permanent naval squadron in the Indies, and did not hold local command of the sea. Instead of gaining that first, he issued a whole series of regulations to restrict trade, immigration and commerce. But laws are only workable when they are backed by public opinion, and no one in the colonies saw anything morally wrong in breaking the regulations, especially as it paid so well. Landowners and merchants, governors and their officials, all were in the swindle together, although the officials, in order to clear their own yardarms at any subsequent investigation, insisted that an elaborate farce should be staged to disguise what really happened.

While the absence of a naval force in the Caribbean allowed the Colonists to break the law with profit and impunity, it had most unpleasant results in another way. French privateers from La Rochelle were free to cruise like sharks in the waters of the Caribbean. The settlements were widely separated one from another by water, and usually were badly fortified, with no regular garrisons. When a strange sail was sighted in the offing, the church bell rang, women, children and valuables were carted off inland, while a few terrified volunteers put up a token resistance before joining the women and children, and the French privateers could loot and burn as the fancy took them. The settlements lived in dread and terror of these rough 'Lutherans' as the Colonists called anyone not a Catholic; and local governors, at the risk of losing their own pickings from illicit trade, wrote urgently, but in vain, to their King for protection.

All this Hawkins gathered from his friends in the Canary Islands, but, more important than these broad outlines, he picked up that local information without which no mariner even today likes to approach a foreign port. As he sipped their wine ashore or entertained his Spanish friends in the great cabin of his own ship, his charm extracted all he needed to know about the West Indies: what goods were in most demand, authentic information about harbours and prevailing winds, and how to treat with the touchy but dishonest officials. For Hawkins had determined to take a hand himself in the lucrative West Indian commerce, and it was as a peaceful trader that the first Englishman appeared in the Caribbean.

Hawkins should be honoured as the first man to test the monopoly of Spain beyond the line, but his fame has become tarnished because the chief commodity in which he chose to trade was not good English cloth or even nightcaps, but human beings—woolly-pated African negroes. A man can only fairly be judged by the standards of his own time and England's conscience in this matter did not start to worry her until over two hundred years later. Hawkins saw nothing disreputable in his venture nor did anyone else at that time, least of all Elizabeth and her council who were only too eager, after the first had been a success, to take shares in his subsequent voyages. Hawkins was not starting anything new, what was new was the sudden appearance of English ships in a flourishing and established trade. King Philip of Spain considered that Hawkins had committed a crime, not in slaving, but in poaching on preserves awarded forever to Spain by Almighty God in the person of His Vicar upon earth, Pope Alexander VI.

Knowing a good deal more of what actually went on in those preserves than did the King of Spain himself, Hawkins went to London where he raised the financial backing for a slaving voyage from, amongst other subscribers, such estimable citizens as the Lord Mayor, the Treasurer of the Navy and two governors of the Russia Company. In an odour of complete respectability, therefore, Hawkins sailed out of Plymouth Sound in October, 1562, with four small ships and a company of only 100 men all told. He was the first English sailor to recognize that overcrowding at sea could be more deadly than any human foe. With small crews he could keep his ships clean and wholesome and provide generous rations for all. John Hawkins once wrote that he always 'desired the name of an orderly person and had always hated folly', an astonishing confession in that age of slapdash flamboyance. Although he believed in careful planning, his caution did not make the audacity of his undertakings any the less—instead it made them successful. He had thought everything out for this, his first, journey into an unknown sea. He had a company of picked men, well cared for, and had timed his sailing so as to be well clear of the Caribbean before the start of the hurricane season. Hawkins's friend, Pedro de Ponte, had a Spanish pilot for the West Indies waiting at the Canaries, and had also warned his own agents in Hispaniola to expect an English trader. Hawkins knew that no foreigner was allowed to trade in the Indies without a licence or even to go there, and that the bills of lading of all goods to be sold in the Colonies had to be examined by the Casa de Contratacion at Seville. But he intended to break these laws openly—there was to be no hole-and-corner business for him—and he was sure that if he appeared as a peaceful trader, a one-time subject of King Philip and, most important of all, carrying the goods the colonies could not get from Spain, that the local authorities would allow him to trade. But this was not his only object, his ultimate aim was to break down the monopoly and open up a regular trade between England and the Spanish dominions overseas.

After picking up the pilot, one Juan Martinez, at Tenerife, Hawkins coasted along the west of Africa, until he came to what is now Senegal, between Cape Verde and Sierra Leone, where he either captured ashore or bought from Portuguese ships or traders some four hundred negroes. He embarked these in three of his ships and, after loading the fourth with a cargo of local products, pepper, wax and ivory, he sént her back to England.

Then in the *Saloman* as his flagship, with the *Swallow*, the *Jonas* and a chartered Portuguese vessel in company, Hawkins stood out into the Atlantic until he picked up the north-east trades which carried him swiftly to the forbidden Caribbean. He was making for Hispaniola, the modern Haiti, where at Santo Domingo, on the south coast, the Government of the Islands and the Spanish Main was situated. His idea was that, if he were accepted here at headquarters, he would have no trouble anywhere else. He was expected by the officials and colonists of Santo Domingo, but his appearance there would have been too blatant, and so it had been arranged through Pedro de Ponte for him to go to the smaller settlements on the north coast. In April, 1563, his squadron anchored off the minor port of La Isabella which his crews found a welcome change from West Africa. Instead of the pounding surf and steamy heat of the Guinea coast, the ships were swung to a pleasant easterly breeze off a strip of golden beach under wooded hills, while far inland ranges of distant mountain peaks lost themselves in curtains of writhing mist.

Hawkins at once set up booths ashore and started trading; the burghers flocked in with hides and sugar, pearls and even gold to exchange for the negroes, cloth, linen, taffetas and manufactured metal goods which the English had to offer—for all trading was done by barter, no money being used.

As the word went round that, unlike the Portuguese contra-bandists, these English gave good value, the settlers hurried down from the countryside or from other settlements on the coast and the trading was in full swing when a certain Lorenzo Bernaldez appeared on the scene. This man was a Jewish lawyer who had been sent from the capital, Santo Domingo, on the difficult cross-country journey to La Isabella with orders to collect some men on the way and arrest the English. Not that the council really wished to stop the trading, nor had Bernaldez the smallest intention of carrying out his orders literally—this was merely a face-saving expedient so that when awkward questions were asked from Spain the local authorities would be able to protest that they had done all they could to enforce the law. Hawkins, who had been well coached in the rules of the game, handed over one hundred negroes to Bernaldez, received a written permission to trade in return (which both men knew the Spaniard was not empowered to give) and the bartering went on as merrily as ever. After loading his own three ships to capacity, Hawkins had enough hides and sugar left over to load two more, the Portuguese slaver he had brought from Guinea and another vessel which he chartered locally from relations of the Spanish pilot. He placed his second-in-command, Thomas Hampton, in charge of the Spanish ship and ordered them both to Seville, of all places in the world, consigning the goods to Hugh Tipton, a prominent English merchant. Haw-

kins never vouchsafed his reasons for this singular action, but
whatever he expected, he got nothing from it. The Portuguese
crew took their ship into Lisbon which was the end of that cargo;
while the chartered Spanish vessel, not surprisingly, was seized
with her contents by the customs at San Lucar on her arrival in
Spain. Thomas Hampton just managed to escape arrest while the
unfortunate Tipton was taken off to gaol.

After sending these two ships to Spain, Hawkins sailed for
England; and, while his deeply-laden squadron was rolling home
before the westerlies of the North Atlantic, the ladies of Hispaniola
were preening themselves in their new silks and taffetas and apprehensive officials sat down to try to explain to their King in long,
unconvincing letters just how the events of the past few weeks had
come about. A rather lame effort by the President of the Council at
Santo Domingo ended with a timely request to be employed in
some other post where he might serve His Majesty better; but it
was the lawyer, Bernaldez, who showed to what heights the imagination of a Spanish colonial official could rise when it came to explaining away irregularities. On reaching the north coast after
great hardships, so Bernaldez wrote, he had captured two Englishmen. When he saw, however, that the ships of the 'Lutheran Corsairs' were ready for action and well armed, he thought it wise, in
order to prevent the corsairs from doing damage, to accept 105
negroes on behalf of His Majesty in exchange for the two English
prisoners. After 'kissing His Majesty's royal feet' this humble
vassal signed himself 'Lorenzo Bernaldez, Licentiate', and hoped
for the best, conveniently failing to mention that he had sold the
105 negroes to the local planters and pocketed the proceeds. This
plea of yielding to *force majeure* was to become the stereotyped
defence put forward by officials after Hawkins's later voyages.
Unfortunately for Bernaldez and the President, one Echegoyan, a
disgruntled colleague who either suffered from scruples or who had
not been paid enough to keep quiet, gave the whole game away
in letters to the King and the House of Trade in Seville. This
affected Hawkins too, because the cargo he had sent to Spain,
which otherwise had had a good chance of getting through, was
confiscated.

Why Hawkins consigned those cargoes to Seville will never be known for certain, but he generally had a pretty good reason for everything he did and this may have been part of a larger plan. Already Hawkins could say that he had traded freely and openly in Hispaniola with the good will of the authorities, and if he could have said further that two cargoes had been allowed through by the Casa de Contratacion at Seville, then a precedent for English ships being employed in the West Indian trade would have been established. It had been well worth trying because all Hawkins stood to lose were two cargoes which he could well afford. The plan failed because King Philip, quite understandably, refused to change his policy for a heretic who had broken Spain's laws on three counts—and there, so far as the King was concerned, was an end of the matter. But not for Hawkins.

CHAPTER III

The Spanish Main

*

The first voyage was so much of a success that there had to be another, but with a difference. What had been the private venture of an enterprising trader of Plymouth now developed into a full-blown official expedition. Most of the Privy Council took shares, Cecil helped in the preparations, the Queen lent one of her ships, the *Jesus of Lubeck*, and John Hawkins sailed as an officer of the Queen. If he had been left to himself Hawkins would never have chosen the *Jesus of Lubeck* for a tropical voyage. She was one of the ships Henry VIII had bought from the Hanseatic League more than twenty years before, and through years of neglect she was barely seaworthy, also her build was out of date, for she was high-charged with towering poop and forecastle. However, this gave her an imposing appearance alongside the snug and seaworthy little Elizabethan ships, and she was cheap and well armed—altogether a majestic old hulk which would add to the prestige of the squadron so long as no one inquired too closely into the condition of her timbers. The *Jesus of Lubeck*, 700 tons, was flagship and with her sailed three of the Hawkins's ships: the *Saloman*, 130 tons, flagship on the first voyage, the *Tiger*, fifty tons, which had been a privateer, and the tiny *Swallow*, thirty tons, which could be used up creeks or for sounding ahead of the larger ships when approaching an unknown coast.

During the spring and summer of 1564, these ships were fitted to accommodate some five hundred negroes—and there was so much general talk of the expedition that the Spanish Ambassador soon knew all about it, the details of its equipment and even its aims, all of which he reported to King Philip in July, adding that

The *Minion*

The *Jesus of Lubeck*

he could get no satisfaction from the Queen when he complained. In October the ships took in stores: dried beans and peas for the negroes, bacon, biscuits, dried fish, beer and cider for the ships' companies, with forty butts of malmsey wine for the great cabin; and when all was ready Hawkins was summoned to a farewell audience of the Queen at Enfield. The modest trader of Plymouth had become an instrument of the high policy of the realm.

When Hawkins led his squadron out of Plymouth Sound on October 10th the Royal Standard was fluttering bravely at the main of his flagship and all ships flew the Cross of St. George, for this was an 'Armada of Her Queen's Majesty of England' as he was later to describe it. They were no sooner out of sight of land than they came up with two ships from London making the Guinea voyage, the *John the Baptist* and another Queen's ship, the *Minion*. Crossing the Bay the *Jesus of Lubeck* sprung her mainmast and the squadron became separated in a gale, but Hawkins picked them up again and, because the wind was against him, put into Ferrol on the north coast of Spain. During a stay there of five days Hawkins issued his detailed sailing orders for the voyage, orders which were summed up in terse sentences of a biblical simplicity: 'Serve God daily, love one another, preserve your victuals, beware of fire, keep good companie'. This was not an order produced for the benefit of posterity—something which would look well in the history books. It meant precisely what it said and in those sentences of three words each no more was needed for a voyage in Elizabethan times, when sailors were quarrelsome, improvident and careless. In each of Hawkins's ships prayers were said every day to the whole ship's company, and any man who dodged them got twenty-four hours in irons; while that gale in the Bay had shown the need of good station-keeping. On October 30th Hawkins sailed from Ferrol, and in a week the squadron had raised the snow-capped peak of Tenerife. Hawkins at once got into touch with his friend Pedro de Ponte and, while he was making arrangements for his second visit to the Caribbean, the squadron was employed watering or taking in fresh provisions, and the decrepit *Jesus of Lubeck* took the opportunity of setting up her mainmast.

From Tenerife Hawkins shaped a course for Cape Blanco, but

as he sailed down the African coast he found that negroes were much harder to come by than on the first voyage. The *Minion* which had passed along here some weeks before on her way to Guinea had carelessly spread the word of his coming so that the negroes had become wary and, in the words of one of his officers, 'did avoide the snares we laid for them'. They even laid snares of their own and when the *Tiger's* carpenter foolishly went ashore unarmed to gather fruit he had his throat cut. The sailors had no satisfactory results until late in December when they came to the mouth of the Callousa River and learned that a number of Portuguese caravels were trading some sixty miles up-river. Leaving his flagship and the *Saloman* anchored at the mouth, Hawkins went up with the *Tiger, the Swallow* and the larger of the other ship's boats. He returned on Christmas Day with two caravels loaded with negroes which he had bought from Portuguese slavers who most probably got a better price from Hawkins than they did from their own employers. The next batch of negroes was obtained at an exorbitant price. The Portuguese recommended a negro town where it might be possible to capture a hundred negroes, and Hawkins landed with forty of his men. The negroes fled on his approach, but instead of sticking together his men scattered in ones and twos looking for gold in the native huts. The negroes saw their chance and attacked fiercely. Hawkins, with a dozen men, only just managed to prevent a massacre of the entire landing party. As it was, the captain of the *Saloman* and six men were killed and many others wounded, which was the cost of ten negroes captured.

For the next month the squadron worked down the coast to Sierra Leone and on January 29th, 1565, Hawkins sailed for the West Indies with 400 negroes below hatches. For eighteen days, unable to make headway against the Guinea Current, the squadron sweltered in calms and fluky winds so that it began to look as if the water might run out. But at last, in the words of an officer in the *Jesus of Lubeck*, 'God, who never suffereth his elect to suffer, sent us the Ordinary Brise the sixteenth of Februarie', which was his way of saying that when they were far enough to the northward they picked up the north-east trades.

The favourable wind bore the squadron across the Atlantic to

Dominica, where the luck still held. For this was an island inhabited solely by intractable cannibals who only a couple of months before had eaten the entire crew of a Spanish caravel which had called there for water. But Hawkins struck a deserted part of the coast where no cannibals swooped down on his sailors as they filled their casks; and he sailed the next evening. He steered to the southward because this time he was going to try a new market; on the first voyage he had touched only at the Island of Hispaniola—now he was bound for the mainland, the north coast of South America. The starlit nights were pleasantly cool as they sailed on, and by day from a cloudless sky the sun glittered off a smooth blue Caribbean. After a while they came to another island, Margarita, where a friendly mayor supplied them with fresh beef and mutton; but the Governor of the island forbade any further trade and refused to meet Hawkins or supply him with a pilot. The squadron proceeded with no idea of what landmarks to look for or how they might be set by the local currents, and even if they had possessed charts of the coast, these would have added little to their knowledge. On sighting land Hawkins himself went on ahead in his flagship's pinnace and eventually brought his squadron safely to anchor in twenty fathoms off Cumana in what is now the Republic of Venezuela. They had reached the Spanish Main.

For a coast which was later to figure so luridly in history and romance, Englishmen's first introduction to it was tranquil enough. A few friendly Indians appeared on the foreshore with samples of their local produce to trade. In exchange for 'beades, pewter whistles, glasses, knives and other trifles' the natives handed over chickens, a corn called maise, unfamiliar to the strangers, all kinds of delicious tropical fruit, and a certain root vegetable. An Englishman then ate his first potato and pronounced it to be of infinitely better flavour than his own parsnips or carrots; from which one may safely conclude that it must have been a sweet potato, a variety which had been cultivated for centuries in South America.

Hawkins's men were far more interested in these naked Indians than they had been in the equally undressed negroes of the African coast. Perhaps the South Americans with their long black hair were more comely; they were something entirely new and most of

the sailors had seen negroes before. Anyhow, the English studied
the habits and customs of this unfamiliar people with all the enthusiasm of professional anthropologists. They noted the dress, or
the lack of it, the details of toilet and diet, how the arrows were
poisoned, and even those customs which had to do with the bearing of children. John Sparke, a practically-minded officer in the
flagship, took particular note of the beds woven of different
coloured cottons which 'the natives carry about with them when
they travel, and, making the same fast to two trees, lie therein,
they and their women'. The advantages of a bed which could be
stretched between two uprights no doubt appealed to men who
slept how they could on the hard planking of the mess deck and,
whether or not as a result of Sparke's observation, hammocks were
adopted by the Royal Navy during the reign of Elizabeth. Generation after generation of sailors, in sailing ship or ironclad on all
the oceans of the world have slept snugly in hammocks these last
few hundred years, as indeed, surrounded by all the latest inven-
tions of modern science, they do still. For comfort and con-
venience in a warship at sea no one has been able to improve upon
this form of bed. The hammock of the Royal Navy, however, is
made, not of prettily dyed cotton, but of stout unbleached canvas
—and it holds only one.

From Cumana the squadron coasted westwards until Hawkins,
still in his pinnace, brought them to a Spanish settlement of some
importance, the town of Burburata, which was the seat of government of a province. The Governor here turned out to be one,
Alonso Bernaldez, who was a nephew of that Lorenzo Bernaldez
of the first voyage to Hispaniola; the uncle appears to have given a
few tips on administration to his nephew and told him about
Hawkins. When the Governor arrived back from a tour inland,
Hawkins blandly explained the presence of his squadron in the
roadstead by saying that while on a voyage to Guinea he had been
blown off his course and landed up here quite by accident. Bernaldez did not even question this statement; he knew that he was
not meant to believe it; that it had only been made to provide him
with an excuse when he came to make an official report on the
visit. The interview then proceeded almost according to an accep-

ted formula. Hawkins declared that his ships were full of unpaid and hungry soldiers, that he needed food and money to keep them quiet and therefore he asked leave to trade to provide them with these necessities, or there was no knowing what they might do. Hawkins added that he and his ships were at the Governor's disposal for his protection against pirates. As the population of Burburata, led by the Governor, generally left the town and headed for the mountains whenever a sail was sighted in the offing, this must have had a strong appeal, though not so strong as the thought of negroes to be sold. Bernaldez and his council put their heads together and, after arranging for a number of witnesses to swear on oath before a notary that the Governor and his associates had only traded with Hawkins very much against their will, he gave the necessary permission.

Booths were set up in the church square and the bartering proceeded, but Bernaldez was too grasping. The Governor demanded a duty for each slave which Hawkins very well knew was far above the legal rate. But that was quickly settled. Hawkins landed an armed party and threatened that, if the Spaniards did not accept the customary duty, 'he would displease them'. After that he paid the legal duty and before he left was given a certificate to the effect that he was an honest and fair trader. Shortly before the squadron sailed, a Frenchman, Captain Jean Bontemps, in the *Green Dragon* of Newhaven arrived in harbour and the news he brought was significant. He reported that he had been driven off the Guinea coast by Portuguese galleys and that the same, if not worse, had happened to the *Minion* and her consort. The Portuguese authorities were clearly tightening up the protection of their monopoly in Africa and it looked as if the old days of easy slaving were over. But trade was brisk at Burburata, the sun shone, the food was good, and after the manner of sailors in any age, no one in the squadron, except perhaps Hawkins, bothered his head about something which only affected the future. And on May 4th, the town and neighbourhood of Burburata having bought all it could afford, Hawkins made off north-westwards on the look out for a low-lying island a couple of days' sail along the coast.

The island of Curaçao was nothing more than a huge cattle

39

ranch. In one field John Sparke counted 100 carcasses laid out in a row, their skins and tongues removed, just left to rot or be picked clean by the clouds of raucous fighting seabirds. The holding ground was so bad here that, instead of anchoring, the squadron had to lie off backing and filling all day while they loaded hides, sail well clear of the shore at nightfall with a long beat back next morning. Although the sailors gorged themselves on fresh beef, turning up their noses at mutton or even lamb, everyone, from Hawkins downwards, was thankful when they had completed loading after ten days of this anxious work.

Hawkins now coasted down a peninsula, often stopping to ask the way, until he reached Rio de la Hacha, the centre of a pearl fishery. The Governor of the place refused to allow trade on the grounds that he had just received orders from Santo Domingo forbidding it. Hawkins replied with the usual yarn of having been driven off his course and proceeded to give the Governor an excellent excuse for trading. On the morning of May 21st he fired a culverin, then manned and armed boats and made for the beach. The townsmen put on a brave show with drums beating and flags flying as they marched towards the landing place. Anyone less experienced than Hawkins would have thought them about to resist his landing to the last man, but he guessed rightly that this was all bluff, and when he fired a couple of shots from the small guns in the bows of his boats over the heads of the advancing Spaniards they lay flat on their faces. The show was over, a token resistance to clear the Governor had been made and trading could now begin. Instead of resenting this unconventional behaviour by a visiting trader, the Spaniards gave Hawkins a glowing certificate of good conduct. From its wording it is clear that the discipline of the squadron was exceptional—Elizabethan sailors were not regulars, they joined for the voyage and what they could make out of it. Yet at three o'clock in the afternoon of May 30th Hernando de Heredia, the Clerk of the Council, sat down to write this: 'The said Captain (Hawkins) and his men have traded and transacted business with all the people in the town, maintaining the peace and not disturbing it, and working no harm to any person of any quality or condition'. And at 4 p.m. after a courteous exchange of salutes, the remarkable man who had evoked this testimonial led his ships out of harbour and stood away to the northward.

Hawkins had decided to call at Hispaniola on the way home to fill his remaining cargo space with yet more hides. But having no pilot to warn him, he did not allow enough for the strong current setting to the westward, so that he missed that island completely and fetched up instead somewhere off the middle of Jamaica. As its hills and valleys slowly took shape under a blanket of low cloud, the conduct of a Spanish passenger began to attract notice. He appeared on deck in a brand-new suit of clothes and, with a magnificent gesture, threw his old ones over the side. Then, hopping excitedly about the poop, he began to point out landmarks as if he really recognized them. But the Spanish merchant was a landsman to whom this view of Jamaica from the seaward was something entirely new and, in fact, he had no idea of where the ship was. Instead of saying so, he pretended to recognize each new headland as it glided by, always promising a good anchorage just round the next one. Soon there were no more headlands to point to, only the open sea—the squadron had been carried down to leeward and missed Jamaica too.

The Spaniard was hardly to be blamed for his excitement because he lived in Jamaica and this was his first sight of it after three years spent as a prisoner of the negroes in Guinea where he had been captured when he was on a trading voyage. Hawkins rescued him and offered him a passage home, and the prospect of rejoining his wife and family after all this time was rather too much for him. But he got little sympathy from John Sparke, who observes with some justification, 'This man was a plague not only to the Captain but to himself'. Hawkins lost the chance of £2,000 worth of hides, while the Spaniard, after being in sight of home, was carried on to England in his Sunday best. He is not mentioned again in the account of the voyage, there is no record of what eventually became of him, and we are left wondering if he was ever restored to the family waiting for him in his island home. We do not know even his name.

The prevailing trade winds and that same current which had carried him past Jamaica prevented Hawkins from getting his hides in Cuba either; and by the middle of June the squadron was in soundings, cautiously feeling its way among the shoals off the coast of Florida. By day the ships' companies amused themselves fishing for bonito, and each night the squadron anchored off a monotonous, low green shore. As the ships moved slowly north-wards with the Gulf Stream helping them, Hawkins kept close in shore in his pinnace, exploring the creeks and lagoons of that deceptive coastline. He was looking for fresh water, also he did not want to risk overshooting the French colony which lately had been planted in Florida. Before leaving England he had been given orders to investigate rumours which had reached London of the great mineral wealth of the country and he was to see if it were suitable for settlement by Englishmen.

The Florida Channel was the only way out of the Caribbean for the Plate Fleets on their homeward passage and, with an early appreciation of oceanic strategy, the English Government pre-ferred that if anyone were to be established in a strong position athwart the homeward route of laden treasure fleets it should be themselves. Hawkins seems to have taken Sparke with him in the pinnace, and that officer's observant eye noticed at once that the country was good cattle country but that there was no great mineral wealth. He found time, too, to note the habits and cus-toms of these natives, as he did of those at every place they touched at. He was interested to observe that the 'Floridians' of both sexes painted and tattooed their bodies with weird designs—a fashion which did not subsequently spread to Europe; but he also noted a habit which did: the natives enjoyed sucking the smoke of a 'Kinde of dried herbe' through a cane with an earthen cup at its end.

When at last Hawkins came upon the French, he found them established in a fort some miles up a river. Their commander, Laudonnière, told him that they had been there a year without relief and were short of food. Sparke at once put his finger on the weakness of the French position. The natives grew only enough food for themselves with no disposable surplus and the French, being soldiers, would not demean themselves by tilling the soil and growing food for themselves; they expected the natives to do it. As the garrison had to eat, they robbed the natives, with the result

Letter from John Hawkins to the Queen dated September 20
1565 at Padstow

that the French had a hostile countryside to contend with. After supplying the French with food, which he could ill spare, from his own remaining stores, Hawkins offered the entire garrison passage to France in the squadron.

This was not only generosity on his part, it would have paid him if they had accepted. The English Government would like the French clear of Florida, while the King of Spain would have been overjoyed to see them go, and more, he would have been under an obligation to Hawkins. At the back of Hawkins's mind there was always the hope that if only the King could be persuaded that it would pay him to do so, then he would allow the English to trade in the Western colonies. But Laudonnière was no fool, he saw through Hawkins's plan and replied that it was his duty to stay where he was. Hawkins sold him a fifty-ton ship which was paid for partly in gunpowder, while for the balance he accepted a promissory note which, twenty years later, was still owing. But Hawkins was too humane and honourable a man to take advantage of the Frenchmen in their extremity, 'wherein', wrote Laudonnière, 'doubtless he has won the reputation of a good and charitable man, deserving to be esteemed as much of us all as if he had saved our lives'.

Consoled for his rebuff by these courteous phrases, Hawkins moved on to the northward and after a month reached the Banks of Newfoundland, where he replenished his very scanty stocks of food by catching great quantities of cod. Three weeks later, on September 20th, 1665, the squadron arrived safely at Padstow in Cornwall. As soon as the ships were berthed Hawkins sat down to report his arrival to the Queen in a letter that was both short and modest. 'Pleaseth it your Majesty', he wrote in his cultured, readable hand, 'to be informed that the 20th day of September I arrived in a port of Cornwall called Padstow with Your Majesty's ship the *Jesus* in good safety. Thanks be to God our voyage being reasonably well accomplished according to our pretence'.

The backers of the voyage received a profit of sixty per cent on the money they risked, or so the Spanish Ambassador reported to King Philip, who must have wondered how on earth Hawkins managed it. The truth was that the Hawkins voyages were made in well handled ships commanded by a man who knew his business. The greater amount of profit on this venture came not from the slaves but from the hides, which could be picked up for a song in the West Indies and sold at a good price in Europe. But when Spain tried the same thing nearly all the profit on West Indian produce was swallowed up in the cost of transporting it. The Flota system, whereby all traffic was handled in one convoy, caused delays, official dues were heavy and the rate of insurance prohibitive. For not only had the risk of French corsairs to be insured against, but the way Spanish ships were handled increased the hazard. Though they were larger and could carry more than English ships, they were cumbersome and unwieldy. Even more important than the ships were the men who sailed them. Except for those from Biscay, Spanish sailors could not compare with the skilled Elizabethan seamen. As long ago as the sixteenth century it was shown that when it came to shipping, a top-heavy bureaucracy could not hope to compete against seamen free of red tape and regulations. On those first two voyages John Hawkins led the way, and because of its efficiency English shipping has had the largest part of the world's carrying trade ever since.

About a year after his arrival at Padstow, Hawkins had organized an expedition at Plymouth all ready to sail for the Spanish Main, where he had orders to fulfil which he had booked in 1565 at Rio de la Hacha. But his second voyage had created such a stir that he was the subject of sharp diplomatic exchanges between Spain and England; and after the Spanish Ambassador had served an ultimatum on the Queen she gave Hawkins orders that he was not to leave the country. Instead of sailing himself, therefore, Hawkins dispatched four ships on the round voyage to Guinea and the Caribbean under the command of a Captain John Lovell. The voyage was not a great success and no more is known of this seaman, but of a young man who sailed with him much was to be heard. His name was Francis Drake.

While Lovell was away Hawkins had prepared another expedition of his own, which, by a good deal of staunch lying, the Queen and Cecil had managed to persuade the Spanish Ambassador was intended for Africa. Although the Ambassador was not too happy when he learned what the ships were loading he was at last re-assured. For the ships had been taking in quantities of beans which were used for feeding slaves, as well as fine cloths and linens, wares to tempt the Spanish planters in the Indies. The Queen lent two warships and in the summer of 1567 gave Hawkins his orders for the voyage that was to be the most fateful of them all.

CHAPTER IV

San Juan de Ulua. 'The Troublesome Voyage'

*

The old *Jesus of Lubeck* had been so badly strained on the previous trip that even the £500 that was spent on refitting her in the Medway could not have made this rotting hulk seaworthy. Yet now she was brought out again and only his great sense of duty can have persuaded Hawkins to accept her for the second time as his flagship. The other Queen's ship, the *Minion*, was not much better. She was even older than the *Jesus*, dating from 1536, and she had been employed for years in making voyage after voyage to Guinea during which she had acquired a sinister reputation. In later ages she would have been called an 'unlucky' ship and seamen would have avoided her like the plague. She seems to have formed the habit on those Guinea voyages of killing off her crews; time and again she had come limping home with a handful of starving, fever-crazed wretches, who were all that remained of a company that had sailed so bravely with flags flying out of the Port of London. Her latest exploit of this kind had been a couple of years before, when she had been reported at the Azores with all her victuals finished, most of her crew dead and a few survivors patching her up for the voyage back. That was the last anyone expected to hear of her, but only a month later she crept into the Thames with a rich cargo of gold and ivory. The old *Minion* had struggled home again. Somehow she always did.

After embarking their guns and ammunition at the Tower of London the two warships sailed round to Plymouth, where the remainder of the expedition, made up of ships belonging to the Hawkins brothers, was lying in the Cattewater: the *William and John* 150 tons, the *Swallow* 100, the *Judith* 50 and the *Angel* 33.

46

SAN JUAN DE ULUA. 'THE TROUBLESOME VOYAGE'

Quite a number of old hands joined before they sailed, some turning straight over from Lovell's expedition which had got back in September. In the *Jesus* Hawkins had as master Robert Barrett, who could speak good Spanish, George FitzWilliam, who had sailed in the flagship on the second voyage, and young Francis Drake, fresh home from his first Caribbean voyage. Thomas Hampton, Captain of the *Swallow* on the first voyage, now commanded the *Minion*, while James Ranse, who had been out with Lovell, was going straight back again as master of the *William and John*. During September, merchants came down from London with their goods and the ships loaded a cargo which could only be for the West Indies as the Spanish Ambassador quickly recognized: Woollen cloth, linens, cottons and taffetas, tinware and swords—not to mention beans for the slaves. Then the merchants jogged slowly back to London, their minds filled with thoughts of profit, and on October 2nd, 1567, the wind becoming fair, Hawkins made the signal to weigh and proceed. With the *Jesus of Lubeck* proudly wearing the Royal Standard and the other ships all sporting brand-new sets of flags, the fleet wound slowly by the crowds of sightseers on the Hoe and on past St. Nicholas Island until their sails filled off the wooded hump of Mt. Edgecumbe. Hopes were high as they ran free out of Plymouth Sound, but for the greater number of the 408 men and boys who sailed on that crisp October day it was their last sight of the red earth and green fields of Devon.

Trouble was not long in coming. Only four days out the *Jesus of Lubeck* was very nearly lost with all hands when the fleet ran into a full gale in the Bay just north of Finisterre. When the gale struck them the *Minion*, the *Swallow* and the *Jesus* each lost the boat she was towing astern; proper station-keeping was impossible, the ships became separated and it was each one for herself. The old *Jesus* with her antiquated high poop and timbers strained in the previous voyage was soon in grave danger. She laboured so heavily in the towering seas that a seam in her stern opened up and the crew were able to stop the water pouring in only by plugging the leak with bolts of cloth taken from the cargo. The ship was so rotten that as soon as they had plugged one leak another started somewhere else. After a while, things looked so bad that Hawkins mustered the ship's company and told them that there was only one thing left to do—and that was to pray. After the manner of Elizabethans, 'no one', at this news 'could refraine his eyes from tears'. But if they wept and prayed they also got on with the job: they kept the pumps going and the carpenters never stopped their search for new leaks. After four days of tears, prayers and sweating at the pumps, the storm died down as suddenly as it had arisen; and at dawn on the fifth day 'the winde being northerlye and the wether faire' the *Jesus* with the *Angel* now in company, shaped a course for the pre-arranged rendezvous at Tenerife.

Picking up the *Judith* on the way, the *Jesus of Lubeck* and the *Angel* eventually sailed into the crowded roadstead of Santa Cruz in Tenerife. After a punctilious exchange of salutes with the Castle and a Spanish ship bound for the Indies anchored in the roads, Hawkins sent ashore to inform the Governor that he had come to pick up the rest of his fleet which had been dispersed by weather and that he wished to buy fresh provisions. In a cordial reply the Governor offered him all the facilities of the port. Hawkins then sent the usual presents ashore, and just as in the old days, a number of prominent citizens came off to be wined and dined in the great cabin of the flagship. On the surface his welcome had been as friendly and open as ever, but Hawkins sensed a subtle change in the atmosphere and when invited ashore in his turn, he excused himself on the plea that the Queen had forbidden such visits.

He was anchored within range of the guns of the fort and for the next few days, while Hawkins entertained the Spaniards, the boats of the English ships on their trips inshore threaded their way among a number of Spanish vessels that were anchored between the English and the fort, masking its fire. On the evening of the fourth day, Hawkins suddenly noticed that the Spanish ships were shifting berth so as to leave the guns of the fort a clear range of fire. At midnight he quietly made the signal to weigh, and when day dawned and the Spanish gunners ashore were looking to their pieces the English ships were anchored demurely some miles out, with their boats on the way in for water as if nothing had aroused their suspicions. After an exchange of civil letters with the baffled Governor, Hawkins recalled his boats and, giving the Castle a farewell salute as he sailed past, made for the nearby island of Gomera where he found the *Minion* and the other two ships. This incident at Santa Cruz was the first sign that times had changed, and not only in the Spanish possessions, as he was to discover soon on the coast of Africa.

After making his landfall on November 10th at Cape Blanco, Hawkins spent a thoroughly unsatisfactory three months on the African coast. His first raid on a native village at Cape Verde was a failure, only nine blacks being captured at a cost of twenty men, including Hawkins himself, wounded by arrows or darts which turned out to have been poisoned. Although Hawkins cleaned his own wound, his men laughed at their trifling scratches until, a couple of days later, they began to develop alarming symptoms and eight of them died from some form of lockjaw. Moving on south Hawkins came up with a number of Frenchmen who were combining trade with piracy and two joined his squadron, one of them, Captain Bland, in a stolen Portuguese fishing boat which piously he had named *The Grace of God*. After another abortive raid where the negroes were too wary to be caught, Robert Barrett tried to open up trade with some Portuguese caravels in the estuary of a river, but he was greeted only with 'oprobrious woordes'. This was too much for Barrett, who landed with 240 men to attack. The Portuguese combined with the negroes ashore and Barrett was driven off with four men killed. He got no slaves and a wigging from Hawkins.

While the *Jesus* lay off Sierra Leone, the lighter draught ships picked up a few negroes on various rivers along the coast, and the *Angel's* pinnace, while engaged on this duty, was holed and sunk by a hippopotamus. Of the twenty-eight men in the boat only two were lost, thanks to smart rescue work by another of that ship's boats. Up to date, Hawkins had obtained only 150 negroes. He was wondering what to do when a couple of negro chiefs asked for his help in a war against two other tribes. After some stiff fighting, with Robert Barrett again leading the landing party, though Hawkins himself took part in the final assault, the combined forces took by storm a strongly-fortified town on the River Tagarin. The English lost nine killed and had a great many wounded. The chiefs presented Hawkins with some three hundred prisoners, and these were the lucky ones—although their future was slavery. For there took place then, by the eerie, flickering light of burning huts, a scene which was a bit too much even for Elizabethans. Scores of the captured were slaughtered and cut up like cattle to be roasted and eaten then and there. Those the victors could not eat, over a thousand men, women and children, were herded in droves into the river to drown.

It was now the beginning of February and Hawkins had been too long on the coast. His men were dying of fever and he had to be out of the Caribbean before the start of the hurricane season. He had never before left things so late, but his sailing from England had been delayed a month and he had been longer than his usual custom on the African coast.

He now had about four hundred and fifty slaves and his fleet had been increased to nine ships, made up of his own six, a Portuguese fishing boat he had bought and the two Frenchmen who had joined him on the coast. Hawkins must have felt the need for hurry and on February 7th he sailed from Sierra Leone for the west; but luck was against him, he was delayed by bad weather, the trip across the Atlantic took him fifty-two days and it was only on March 27th, 1568, that he made his landfall at Dominica.

Although it was late spring when he arrived in the Caribbean, Hawkins seemed in no particular hurry as he coasted from place to place along the Spanish Main during the next few months. He found that, on the whole, new and stringent orders from their King had had little effect on the attitude of Spanish officials, so that in most ports he was able to enjoy 'reasonable trade and courteous entertainment'. He certainly received the latter from a convivial Governor of the island of Margarita who gave a series of official banquets; and the fleet was able to sit down to its first square meal for two months when the Governor supplied quantities of fresh beef and mutton in return for the usual trade goods.

Refreshed and rested after the passage across the Atlantic, the squadron arrived at Burburata on April 17th, Easter Saturday. Here for a month and more they lay at anchor, 'selling everye daye some wares', and, almost as important, refitting the ships' running gear which badly needed it after five months out from England.

In fact everything went smoothly until they arrived at the pearling centre of Rio de la Hacha, where Miguel de Castellanos, the Treasurer who had got the better of a deal with Captain Lovell the year before, now refused to have anything to do with Hawkins. His excuse was that trading with the English had become altogether too expensive a luxury because the last time he had granted a licence it had cost him 20,000 pesos by the time the Council had finished with him. This was not believed by Hawkins, who promptly landed in force and took the town, without, however, hurting any of its defenders, who fled after firing one volley. But de Castellanos still refused to parley, though strongly urged to do so by the merchants of the place to whom the sight of all those ships crammed with desirable goods out in the harbour was almost more than they could bear. It was all very well their recommending an interview with the English commander, de Castellanos objected, he was dealing now, not with a rather stupid sea captain, but with John Hawkins and 'he is such a man', so he explained ruefully to the merchants, 'that anyone talking to him hath no power to deny him anything he doth request'. But in the end the Treasurer was prevailed upon to parley, whereupon Hawkins got his licence and trading began. De Castellanos took his defeat very well and, far from bearing Hawkins any grudge, before the fleet sailed the pair of them were giving each other presents. Hawkins presented the Treasurer with a fur-lined velvet cloak with gold buttons and returned on board himself with a woman's girdle of pearls, 'a very rich thing' in the opinion of one of his officers. While negroes, cloth, silk, linens and other goods were being exchanged for gold, silver and pearls, to the satisfaction of both parties, the English sailors were finding their own amusement. One, Job Hartop, a gunner in the *Jesus*, and six others went crocodile fishing up the river in one of the flagship's boats. Using

51

a live dog as bait they soon got a bite and after an exciting and dangerous afternoon came alongside the flagship with a crocodile skin to add to their collection of curios. It was now the beginning of July, trading at Rio de la Hacha had been completed, and, after an exchange of salutes, the squadron proceeded along the coast.

There was no hitch, or even argument, at the next place, a tiny settlement of only forty-five houses named Santa Marta. All the Governor asked before granting a licence to trade was that he should be provided with an excuse for granting it. From his experience on the first two voyages, Hawkins knew exactly the kind of face-saving comedy to stage. While the ships fired a few harmless rounds well over the settlement, Hawkins landed in full armour at the head of 150 men and marched into the town. Then he solemnly burned the oldest and most tumbledown of the forty-five houses; a flag of truce now appeared, Hawkins repeated the well-worn story about having to sell a few negroes to pay for the expenses of the voyage, the Governor gave the licence to trade and then he and Hawkins went off to a banquet which was all ready waiting for them. Following their Governor's lead, the local Spaniards were extremely friendly, so that trade was brisk and the ships' companies feasted off fresh beef during the whole of their stay. Towards the end of July, after a fortnight in this congenial atmosphere, Hawkins sailed for Carthagena where no such pleasant reception awaited him.

Carthagena was the terminal port where the Plate Fleet, which collected the products of the Spanish Main and the silver from Peru, congregated before sailing for Spain. It was the only well-protected place in the Caribbean and had within its walls a garrison of about a thousand Spanish foot and horse soldiers backed by native levies of 6,000 armed Indians. Such a town was not to be awed by the threat of English culverins and, including Frenchmen, Hawkins had only 370 men in his fleet. When the Governor of Carthagena, therefore, refused to have any dealings whatever with the 'English General' and even returned his letters unopened, Hawkins gave up all hope of being able either to force or cajole the Governor into trading at what was to have been the fleet's last port of call before sailing for home. This was a double blow because he had hoped also to revictual here for the voyage. Watering as best he could at a small island, on 8th August he sailed out of Carthagena.

While becalmed for two days just off the port, Hawkins transferred to other vessels the crew of the Portuguese caravel he had obtained off Cape Blanco, stripped the ship of everything worth having and sank her because she was not in a fit condition to make the long voyage home. At this point one of the Frenchmen who had joined in West Africa, decided to try his luck on his own and sailed off. Captain Bland in his *Grace of God* stayed with Hawkins, and when they picked up a wind seven ships sailed north towards the Florida Channel.

The weather broke as they were coming up to Cape St. Anton, the western point of Cuba, and the fleet had to run before a violent gale which took them far into the Gulf of Mexico. As she laboured in the heavy following sea the *Jesus of Lubeck* nearly foundered; the seams on either side of her sternpost opened and the Caribbean poured in so freely that fish were actually swimming about above the ballast in her hold. By superb seamanship Hawkins managed to keep his old hulk of a flagship afloat; bolts of cloth were again brought out to plug the leaks, the pumps were manned day and night, and to reduce her topweight and let her ride more easily, much of her lofty upperworks above the stern were cut away and jettisoned. The *Jesus* came through, but on a wild, tempestuous evening the *William and John* lost touch with the fleet during an alteration of course. She was not seen again by the fleet but made her own way back, arriving in Ireland in February of the following year. Before Hawkins could think of trying to cross the Atlantic he had to find some place where he could patch up the *Jesus*, but he had no pilot and knew nothing of the Gulf of Mexico. He refused to abandon her because 'she was the Queen's Majestie's shipp and she should not perish under his hand'. However, another gale drove him south again when luckily he fell in with a Spanish merchantman bound, so she informed him, for the principal and only port in the Gulf, San Juan de Ulua. This was the port used by the 'Flota' serving 'New Spain' or

Mexico and the fleet was expected at about this time. Hawkins would much rather not have gone there, but he had no choice, he was short of food and water, his flagship was in a sinking condition, so, keeping the Spaniard in company, he made her show him the way to San Juan de Ulua.

As he approached the land, the *Jesus* sailed on ahead, and Hawkins ordered the other ships to strike their flags of St. George, while the flagship and the *Minion* wore the Royal Standard at the main, but the flags were so faded and weatherbeaten that no one could distinguish the lions and luces from any distance. Certainly the local mayor and other officials did not, for when the sails of the fleet were sighted, slanting in a long uneven line towards the port, they put out hurriedly in a small boat to welcome what they thought was the expected Flota from Spain. They only discovered their mistake when they arrived alongside the *Jesus* and were addressed in English. Hawkins ordered them on board and with his courteous manner quickly soothed their panic, explaining that all he wanted was food and water for which he would pay, and a chance to put his ships into a fit condition for the Atlantic crossing. With the officials on board he entered the harbour, receiving a salute of sixteen guns from the gunners ashore who were under the impression that they were greeting the 'Flota'.

San Juan de Ulua was not a good port. The only protection was given by a narrow strip of shingle a quarter of a mile from the mainland which acted as a sort of detached mole. The shingle was a couple of hundred yards long and only showed three feet above high water, but it was a slight protection against the prevalent northerlies. Ships had to lie in a row anchored by the stern with their bows secured to the island. The local officials were quite prepared to be friendly and co-operative, and all might have been well but for the arrival of the Seville fleet which changed the whole situation. For it was bringing a new Viceroy, Don Martin Enriquez and Captain General Don Francisco de Luxan. These were not colonial officials ready to flout the law and meet Hawkins half-way —they were Spaniards fresh from Spain with their careers at stake. They would insist upon a meticulous observance of Spanish law. Even if Hawkins could truthfully say that he was a mariner who had only put in for shelter, that did not affect the matter. By law he had no business or right to be in the New World at all. In their eyes he was outside the law.

Early next day the look-outs in the *Jesus* counted the sails of thirteen large ships gleaming pink under the rising sun from where they lay becalmed in the stillness of a tropic dawn outside the southern entrance to the harbour. It was the Plate Fleet from Spain. The wail of boatswain's whistles in the English ships brought the men tumbling up from down below and one Francisco de Bustamente, a Spanish official whom Hawkins held on board his flagship as a hostage, marvelled at the scene of orderly confusion as the English prepared for action. The gunners loaded their guns on the broadside then ran them out and built neat little piles of spare shot close at hand. Bowmen with stocks of arrows climbed up to the tops while other men brought pikes and arquebuses, breastplates and armour from the store-rooms down below and laid them out along the upper deck. Men were brought from the smaller ships to the flagship, while a party of fifty gunners hoisted guns over the ships' bows and dragged them across the shingle to augment the shore battery on the island, from which all Spaniards had fled. Whoever held the island commanded the harbour, and in a little over two hours, Hawkins was in possession of it, his fleet was ready for action and he was in a position to bargain with the newcomers.

The arrival of the Seville fleet faced Hawkins with an awkward problem. As he put it in his account: 'Now I am in two dangers and forced to receive one of them'. He could not possibly leave harbour himself for the first northerly would dash his fleet to pieces on a lee shore. If he meekly allowed the Spaniards to enter he was certain that 'with their accustomed treason' they would attack him at the first opportunity; for he knew very well that he had broken Spanish law and should not be in the Indies at all, let alone ensconced in San Juan de Ulua. On the other hand, if he prevented the Spaniards from entering their own port, which he was now able to do, it would be an act of war, and his commission did not allow him to go about starting wars on his own; furthermore, the Queen had expressly forbidden him to harm any of

King Philip's subjects. The Spanish fleet had nowhere else to go, if a northerly sprang up it might be wrecked, the two warships of the Indian Guard would certainly try to force an entrance. He had to choose between the probable destruction of his own fleet and the Queen's certain displeasure. But there was the faint hope that, holding the whiphand as he did, by adroit bargaining he might avoid an attack from the Spaniards if he allowed them to enter, and so, as he writes: 'I thought better to risk the uncertainty, and therefore, as choosing the least mischief, I proceeded to conditions'.

The Flota arrived off the port on a Friday and until Saturday evening negotiations continued between Hawkins in the harbour and the Viceroy Don Martin Enriquez in his flagship off the entrance. Finally it was agreed that Hawkins should be allowed to sell his wares, to buy victuals, and, most important, that he should remain in possession of the island which was the key to the whole position, and finally that ten hostages should be exchanged as a pledge. The best and most vivid account of the voyage to date ends abruptly at this point because the writer of it, George FitzWilliam, went as one of the English hostages. On Monday night, while the Spanish fleet still lay outside waiting for a favourable wind, several hundred soldiers whom the Viceroy had secretly summoned from Vera Cruz were embarked during darkness in the ships of the Flota. On Tuesday morning the Spaniards entered harbour, exchanging salutes with the English as they did so, and for the rest of that day and all Wednesday both fleets were busy getting the ships berthed, the English making as much room as they could. While these manœuvres were going on Englishmen and Spaniards were mixing freely on the island as they secured the ships, officers and men working together in the most friendly way. By Wednesday evening both fleets were berthed, the line being so crowded that there were only a few feet between ships. So far there had been no incident and it almost seemed as if Hawkins had brought off his gamble.

But on Thursday morning, September 23rd, he noticed a lot of unnecessary coming and going between the Spanish ships and he at once suspected that something was in the wind. Passing the word to the *Minion* which lay next to a large Spanish merchant-man to be ready to move at short notice, Hawkins sent Robert Barrett, the flagship's master who could speak good Spanish, in a boat over to the Viceroy to find out what all this activity was about. Then, while waiting for his master's return, Hawkins went in to dinner. But Robert Barrett never returned to his ship. On arrival on board the Spanish flagship he was bundled off down below and clapped in irons. Hawkins was just sitting down at table when the note of a trumpet call rang out clear over the congested harbour. The events which followed were rapid, bloody and confused. At the signal, the soldiers from Vera Cruz, who had been hidden in the Spanish ships since Monday night, leaped from the beakheads of their ships on to the island where they took the English gunners completely by surprise and killed all but a few. This well-executed *coup* gave the Spaniards the battle in the first few minutes, for they now had the island, and with it command of the harbour. Hawkins rushed on deck to find the Spanish merchantman hauling herself alongside the *Minion* and boarders pouring over her side with cries of 'Santiago' or 'St. James for Spain'. But the *Minion* was on the move; she had slipped her head-rope and was hauling herself clear by her stern anchor. She managed to repel the boarders and as she slipped out into the stream, the Spaniard surged alongside the *Jesus* and there was some sharp hand-to-hand fighting before the flagship also slipped from the island and hauled clear to join the *Minion*.

English men-of-war now engaged Spanish warships for the first time in the West. The *Jesus* and *Minion* fired at almost point-blank range into the high, yellow-painted sterns of the Spanish flagship and the other vessels lying in a convenient row. It was more than the Spanish sailors could stand, they jumped off their ships on to the island. And when an officer drove some back on board the flagship he found the Viceroy standing alone fully armed on the poop of a deserted vessel with the shot whizzing about his ears, too proud to take shelter below. The flagship was soon so badly holed that she was resting on the bottom, the other warship was on fire, one merchantman sunk and the others damaged. The English were getting the better of things. But at this moment the guns on the island came into action at a range of about two hundred yards and the *Jesus*, which was shielding the *Minion*, had soon lost her rigging, her masts were shot through and her hull so holed that there was no hope of saving her. The guns on the island had turned the day; the *Angel* was sunk, the *Swallow* taken, but Drake in the *Judith* had slipped out into the harbour. Hawkins ordered her and the *Minion* alongside the flagship to take off her men. The *Judith* complied, then lay off out of range, but while the *Minion* was alongside taking treasure and cargo from the *Jesus* the Spaniards fired one of their ships and sent her drifting towards the English. At the sight of her looming up through the smoke sputtering with flame, the crew of the *Minion* panicked. They cut their sails loose and let go their haw-sers. As she moved off the panic spread to the *Jesus* whose crew jumped for their lives, some missed and were drowned and many were left behind. Hawkins was one of the last to jump. The *Minion* and the *Judith* now withdrew out of range. The battle of San Juan de Ulua was over.

It was quite clear from the Spanish records that the Viceroy had not the slightest intention of honouring the agreement. Before his signature had been sanded, messengers were on their way to summon 1,000 soldiers from Vera Cruz. The Spanish Admiral made no bones about their treachery; he stated baldly that they fully intended to break the agreement when they made it. If the Spanish officials had any apology to make, it was not for having broken their pledged word, but for having had any dealings at all with a 'heretic corsair' who had broken Spanish law. As soon as the *Jesus* was abandoned, the Spaniards swarmed on board. They found no treasure, which had been transferred to the *Minion*, but they did find their hostages down below unharmed and they may have come upon a crocodile skin stuffed with straw, lately the property of Job Hartop, gunner in the flagship. The guns which he and his fellows had served were distributed among the towns of the Caribbean and years later a man who had been taken prisoner at San Juan recognized one in the Castle at Havana.

'So with the *Minion* only and the *Judith* a small bark of fifty ton, we escaped; which bark the same night forsook us in our great misery'. Thus Hawkins brings his account of the affair to an end. Drake in the *Judith* had slipped out that night leaving Hawkins anchored a mile from the island. On Saturday, overcrowded, short of food, damaged and leaking, the *Minion* sailed, just managing to claw off a leeshore in a rising northerly. For a fortnight they 'wandered in an unknown sea' making their way slowly up the coast of Mexico and as they sailed the food ran out and the pets on board were eaten one by one; cats, dogs, monkeys, parrots all found their way into the pot, and when they were gone the crew scoured the ship for rats. On October 8th Hawkins ran in towards the land hoping to find a harbour in which to repair the ship and get food, but he found neither. One hundred of the men asked to be put ashore here, preferring to take their chance with Indians in an unknown land to certain starvation on board. Hawkins landed the men, giving each one six yards of cloth and money if he asked for it. With the remaining 100 he sailed eastwards until at last on November 10th he got out through the Florida Strait and cleared the Bahamas into the Atlantic. The colder weather killed many of the starving men and every day a swirl on the water marked, just for a second, a grave, as a round shot took another down into the depths; but the ship sailed on. They were chewing hides in the cargo to stop their hunger; they were almost too weak to work the sails; their ship was leaking, but somehow Hawkins made them go on. Because the wind was against him, instead of steering for England Hawkins made for Northern Spain and on December 31st put in to Vigo. Here many of those who had survived hardship and starvation at sea died within the sight of green hills; they gorged themselves on fresh meat, and being starving, the unaccustomed food killed them. At last on January 25th, 1569, a scarred and battered ship, her sails worked awkwardly by fifteen emaciated scarecrows, crept slowly into Mount's Bay in Cornwall and dropped anchor.

For the last time the *Minion* had struggled home.

CHAPTER V

Spanish Treasure in the Caribbean

*

When Hawkins and Drake got home with the full story of San Juan de Ulua, 'Seafaring men', so a contemporary recorded, 'fretted and desired war with Spain, but the Queen shut her ears against them'. There was a rising of the nobles in the North: England was not united and she was too weak to fight Spain. And there was nothing to be gained from a war because Elizabeth had so far got much of what she wanted; she had been able to behave like a spoiled child, not, as she fondly imagined, owing to her skill in diplomacy, but because she happened to be the keystone of Philip's European policy. The Guise family in France was violently anti-Spanish and, as long as they remained so, it paid Philip to keep Elizabeth on her throne. For it was the aim of the Guise family to replace her by their relative, Mary Queen of Scots, and thus, with Ireland and France, to form a powerful combination opposed to Spain. The only obstacle in the way of this ambition was Elizabeth; and while the Guise policy remained what it was she could do almost as she liked. She took full advantage of an ironical situation in which his Most Catholic Majesty King Philip had to put up with almost any insult or provocation from the heretic Queen Elizabeth.

If the two sovereigns were at one in avoiding war, a number of their subjects were not. There might be uneasy peace in Europe, but it was war, open, savage and unrelenting, 'beyond the Line'. The voyages of John Hawkins had impressed his countrymen with the possibilities of the Caribbean, but the affair at San Juan de Ulua changed the character and purpose of English activities in those waters. Where Hawkins had gone to establish peaceful trade with the Spanish colonies, most of his successors went only for what they could take by force. They talked righteously about being 'revenged for injury', or 'seeking recompence and amends for loss and wrongs received', but all they were after was loot.

For some thirty years the French had been roving the Caribbean with no thought of trade, and now English adventurers joined them in the sport of 'Flota hunting'. The glittering prize which attracted French and English alike was the annual homeward-bound treasure or Plate Fleet, laden with the riches of the New World. These English adventurers were pirates, nothing less; and though at first there was not a strategic purpose behind their attacks, they were striking Spain at her most vulnerable point, her sea communications.

For Spain was the first country in the world to depend on oceanic trade and the only country in history to try to carry on such a trade without a navy to keep the sea routes open. The imports consisted mostly of bullion, small in bulk, great in value, and without this annual transfusion of riches, Spain had not the resources to maintain her position in the world. Silver from the mines of Peru paid the Spanish infantryman in the Netherlands; passing secretly from hand to hand it fomented civil war in France; it penetrated the Baltic in exchange for masts and rope and ships to bring over more silver; it paid the interest on the huge loans which European financiers had made to Philip and his father. The Spanish Empire, the schemes and ambitions of King Philip, the very life of Spain itself depended upon the punctual arrival of the Plate Fleet from the West Indies.

All traffic with the Western colonies was restricted to the one port of Seville, an arrangement which dated from the days of Ferdinand and Isabella. Seville was hardly a convenient port because no ship of over 200 tons could cross the bar at San Lucar and cargoes had to be transhipped for passage up the Guadalquivir. All trade and treasure shipments were controlled by the Casa de Contratacion of Seville, which had grown from a small affair of three officials, who met twice every day except holidays, into a vast organization which dealt with every detail of the commerce and its ramifications and ordered the times of sailing and courses for ships from Chile or the Philippines. The members of the Casa de Contratacion or, as they might be known to-day, 'The Commissioners for the Indian Trade', answered to no one but the King; except on political questions they even gave orders to West Indian governors. The Casa had its own courts and prison. It maintained a training college for pilots and even ran its own gunnery school. The Commissioners framed innumerable regulations governing passengers, cargoes and ships —regulations which ranged from the prohibition of unmarried women as passengers to how the cargo should be stowed and the number of guns and anchors to be carried by each vessel— and they maintained an army of Visitors and Inspectors to see that these instructions were carried out.

On paper, the West Indian trade was admirably organized, but the dead hand of Spanish officialdom could not operate the machine it had created. People broke the regulations regardless of the penalties. In fact, one of the major industries of Seville was the forging of papers and certificates, of which the price went up every time the punishment for forgery was increased. It could not greatly affect the volume of trade if a shipmaster sailed with a prohibited passenger or two on board, or short of the proper number of guns. The trouble was inherent in the system itself—a vast soulless monopoly. Seaborne trade, affected by so many quickly-changing factors is too sensitive to run efficiently under a multiplicity of cast-iron regulations. More was lost through delays than through smuggling.

Moreover no regulations can make badly-designed ships seaworthy. The Spanish ships of the treasure fleets had too short a keel for the length of hull with its towering superstructures. Spanish shipwrights knew little of and cared less for the scientific principles of shipbuilding; their vessels were weakly constructed. Their light draught and breadth of beam made them cranky and difficult to sail to windward. But worst of all they were dangerously over-masted, with over-heavy spars and weak standing rigging, badly set up. They could bowl along before the south-east trades, but the losses were tragic whenever a Flota met a hurricane or norther in the Caribbean, or even an average Atlantic gale on the homeward passage. The fact remains that notwithstanding privateers and pirates, inefficient administration and bad ships, the Flotas went out and back and treasure flowed into Seville in fantastic amounts over a number of years, enough, as one Spanish writer said, to have paved the city of Seville with flagstones of gold and silver.

The French privateers had put an end to independent sailings to the West Indies years before, and ever since 1526 ships had sailed in convoy. Luckily for the Spaniards, and incidentally for Columbus, the prevailing winds in the Atlantic made it almost impossible to miss the West Indies if the Canaries were the point of departure; so the wind regulated the courses of the plate fleets out and home. After leaving Seville with only a fortnight's stores the fleet dropped down to the Canaries, where it completed with provisions at Tenerife or Grand Canary before steering south until it picked up the north-east trades. After that it was only a matter of running before a steady breeze over a sun-lit sea with the weather getting warmer every day. At night the fleet shortened sail, which gave them a daily run of some 150 miles, so that after a month's wallowing in the long Atlantic swell a small green dot appeared on the horizon which was the prescribed landfall of Deseada, if the pilot had been up to the mark, but as often as not it was Dominica or Martinique, also islands in the Antilles. After single ships had been detached for various ports the great concourse split in two. The section for New Spain or Mexico, properly known as the 'Armada', parted company and entered the Caribbean between Deseada and Montserrat by what became known as the 'Galleons Channel'. Then from landfall to landfall as laid down in the sailing directions issued by the Casa, this fleet made its way through the Caribbean—Santa Cruz, Puerto Rico, Hispaniola; from Cape Tiburon up to the Isle of Pines just south of Cuba. From Cuba's western point, Cape San Antonio, the course led them clear of dangers off the coast of Yucatan to a point to windward of San Juan de Ulua, which they entered by the North Channel, just as Hawkins had

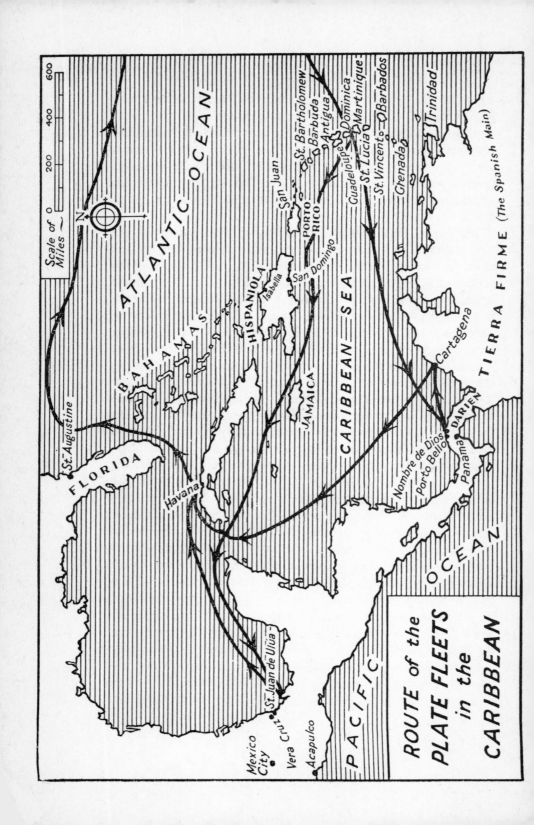

Scale of Miles
600
400
200
0

N.

ATLANTIC OCEAN

St. Augustine
FLORIDA
BAHAMAS
HISPANIOLA
Isabella
San Domingo
Havana
JAMAICA
San Juan
PORTO RICO
CARIBBEAN SEA
St. Bartholomew
Barbuda
Antigua
Guadeloupe
Dominica
Martinique
St. Lucia
St. Vincent
Barbados
Grenada
Trinidad

Cartagena
Nombre de Dios
Porto Bello
Panamá
DARIEN
TIERRA FIRME (The Spanish Main)

PACIFIC OCEAN

St. Juan de Ulúa
Mexico City
Vera Cruz
Acapulco

ROUTE of the
PLATE FLEETS
in the
CARIBBEAN

seen them enter on that fateful Wednesday morning during his third voyage.

Meanwhile the other section, which was bound for the Spanish Main and was known as the 'Flota', steered down for Cape de la Vela in Venezuela. After sighting the mainland—and still with the same wind it had picked up off the Canaries—the fleet proceeded cautiously along the coast, keeping to the dark blue water outside the forty-fathom line, until at last the clumsy galleons dropped anchor in Nombre de Dios Bay. Fast advice boats from the Canaries which had overtaken the fleet had already warned the authorities ashore of the Flota's probable time of arrival and the little settlement, normally half deserted, had come suddenly to life. For the next few weeks it was crowded and busy. Merchants from along the Spanish Main had arrived there by sea, to be joined by others who had made the long journey up from remote parts of South America and across the Isthmus, until every room and hovel in the place was taken. The heavily-barred treasure house for these few weeks in the year was crammed with riches. Jewels and precious metals, bullion and specie lay ready for the Plate Fleet; pearls from Venezuela, gold from Chile, emeralds from Bolivia, shining ingots of silver from the new mines at Potosi in Peru, had all been brought immense distances to this fever-stricken little settlement on the Caribbean.

The treasure from the west coast of South America travelled up to Panama in unarmed ships, because no one but the Spaniards had so far found a way into the Pacific and they trusted that no one else ever would. At Panama it was loaded on to pack-mules for the journey across the Isthmus. Long pack trains, travelling by night to avoid the heat, wound slowly across the Isthmus. The track twisted and turned, now zigzagging down a steep hill, now swerving aside to avoid a fallen tree or large boulder. The clip-clop of hooves and the bells of the mules made a comforting music for the muleteers against the stealthy noises of a forest at night. About half-way across the Isthmus the trains arrived at the small settlement of Venta Cruces. Here the bulkier goods and any passengers were embarked in shallow-draught boats for passage down the Chagres River to the coast. The more valuable freight

SPANISH TREASURE IN THE CARIBBEAN

—and always the Royal Quinto or fifth, His Majesty's revenues—
continued by pack train until long strings of mules halted at last
outside the Treasure House in Nombre de Dios.

The movement of treasure was made to conform with the
position of the outward-bound fleet: it was not even started from
Peru until the expected time of arrival of the Flota was known,
nothing began to move from Panama until the Flota actually
had arrived. Then for a time Nombre de Dios was a busy and
animated settlement. The galleons unloaded their cargoes; casks
of Spanish wine; velvets from Italy, silks, damasks and taffetas
for the ladies of distant Lima, perhaps a sword or two of superb
craftsmanship, bearing the trade mark of a small dog from the
workshop of Julian del Rei in Toledo, for the wealthier settlers;
illuminated missals for their wives. All the heavier goods went up
as far as Venta by water, to proceed from there by mule train to
Panama; but the lighter, more valuable packages did the whole
crossing by mule. Down in Nombre de Dios the merchants,
assembled from all of the Caribbean region and Spanish America,
bullied, chaffered and sweated, while all day the sun beat down.
When in the evening it disappeared behind the distant blue hills
inland, the stars brought no cooling breeze but only mosquitoes.

The Plate Fleets were strictly forbidden to touch anywhere on
the homeward passage, so that after embarking the treasure they
sailed provisioned for eighty days. Advice boats raced back to
Seville with the news of their sailing, while the settlements of
Nombre de Dios and San Juan de Ulua went back to sleep again
until the following year. Flota and Armada had to meet at Havana
for the homeward run and both were dead to leeward of the rendezvous. The Flota from Nombre de Dios used an eastward-
running coastal eddy to fetch Carthagena where it was well to
windward of the dangers off the coast of Nicaragua. From here it
had a soldier's wind to take it through the Yucatan Channel, where
again it used coastal eddies along the north coast of Cuba (of
which Hawkins had been unaware) to take it to Havana. The
armada from San Juan de Ulua worked up into the Gulf of Mexico
until it picked up a northerly wind and so made the rendezvous.
From Havana, the combined Plate Fleets, a great concourse of

66

galleons laden with gold and silver, with jewels and even with silks from China which had crossed the Pacific to Mexico, spread their sails for home. Helped by the Gulf Stream they left the Caribbean by the Florida Channel; and in summer, keeping to the westward, sailed round the north of Bermuda where they picked up the prevailing westerlies for the Azores. Here extra ships of the 'Indian Guard' were awaiting them to strengthen the escort for the final lap. The last landfall was St. Vincent, and so on to San Lucar where the officials of the Casa boarded and inspected all ships before the cargoes were taken up to Seville.

The 'avisos' or advice boats, handy little craft of some twenty-five tons, ran constantly to and fro across the Atlantic, down to the Canaries and between ports in the Caribbean. They carried orders from the King, dispatches from his governors, sometimes an important passenger or an especially valuable cargo. They brought news of the movements of the Plate Fleets and, racing from port to port in the Caribbean, the latest intelligence of foreign corsairs. Being good sea boats which stood up to the weather far better than the galleons, these tiny craft maintained the communications which enabled King Philip to run an empire from a cell in the Escorial.

The great galleons lumbered out across the Atlantic and back the following year, unarmed ships sailed unescorted up the Pacific coast of South America. The deep-toned bells of the mule trains rang through the silent forests of Darien or echoed mournfully across the high sierras of Mexico. So it was that a Spanish infantryman paid for his drink in a Flemish tavern with a silver piece minted in Peru; a Castilian grandee dined off porcelain from the valley of the Yangtze; or an emerald from the jungle of South America set off the dark loveliness of a court beauty in Vienna.

So far in the development of the Spanish colonies no real threat to the communications between Peru and Spain had come from the outside world. The colonial authorities were inclined on the whole to welcome rather than to fear illicit traders. Even the French privateers, those 'Thieves by sea' as the Spaniards called them, were no more than a tiresome, if persistent, nuisance. The sack of some defenceless seaboard village, the capture here and there of an inter-colony trading vessel, the interception of an occasional advice boat from Seville—however disturbing for the individuals concerned—could not seriously affect the main stream of that vast South American treasure which flowed through Nombre de Dios. Privateers kept well clear of the armed galleons of the Flotas, and the pickings of the average corsair were so small and uncertain that Hawkins probably made more on one of his voyages than a privateer did on several. But about the year 1570 the French privateers started new tactics which greatly perturbed the colonial authorities. For the first time they directly attacked the Spanish communications, not from any strategic idea, but simply because it was an easier and quicker way of getting rich. They ranged along the Darien coast off Nombre de Dios; they appeared in oared pinnaces up the Chagres River and robbed the bark traffic plying between Nombre de Dios and Venta Cruces. But of more serious import for Spain than the looting of silks and wine from a bark belonging to the merchant Baltazar de Melo by these French privateers was the presence among them of an English ship, for she was commanded by Francis Drake.

Drake had returned to the Caribbean to retrieve the fortune he considered he had been robbed of at San Juan de Ulua, and he was not particular how he made it. In this he was no different from other Englishmen who were in the Caribbean at this time not as traders but openly as pirates. Although Spanish dispatches spoke of Drake merely as 'an English corsair', he was very different from the ordinary run of privateer, French or English, as the Spaniards were soon to discover, for Drake's ambition soared far above river barks or coasting vessels. He could not be content with cargoes of wine or merchandise, he wanted the treasure itself and if he was not strong enough to take it off the galleons, then he would remove it from the King's Treasure House at Nombre de Dios before ever it was loaded on to the Flota.

On his first exploratory voyage he had not gained the fortune he had hoped for, but he had learned enough of local conditions to enable him to make it next time and he reached England with the means to fit out an expedition of his own. In his prospecting along the coast of Darien he had discovered a good anchorage, sheltered and remote from any Spanish settlement. Also he had noted the need for pinnaces in that sea of frequent calms. Under oars, pinnaces had mobility whatever the state of wind, and, more important, they had the power to manœuvre at night in a hostile roadstead. Drake made his plans carefully and in detail; he had pinnaces built in sections and obtained the arms best suited to an attack by night: small cannon for the boats, muskets, bows and arrows, pikes and fire pikes for the landing party and even 'two drums and two trumpets' so that by splitting his party he could give the impression to Spaniards still half asleep that he was in greater force than he actually was. Then, collecting seventy-three men, including two of his own brothers, all he thought necessary for this hazardous undertaking, in the *Pasco* of seventy tons and the *Swan* of twenty-five, on May 24th, 1572, he cleared from Plymouth to seize the fortune which the Spaniards owed him.

After a quick passage out (twenty-three days to Guadelupe), unperceived by any Spaniard, he reached the hidden anchorage of Port Pheasant, as he had named it, and at once set about assembling the sectioned pinnaces. While this work was proceeding under the direction of Tom Moon, his carpenter, two ships ghosted in through the narrow entrance. The first was commanded by James Ranse, once an officer under Hawkins, who had since turned from trading to piracy, the other was a Spanish advice boat from Seville which he had captured off Nombre de Dios. Ranse and Drake joined forces and within a week the pinnaces had been launched, their masts stepped, provisions loaded and all was ready. Next morning the little fleet of three ships with four pinnaces, which included one belonging to Ranse, sailed for an island off the coast which Drake had chosen as a convenient advanced base for the attack on Nombre de Dios.

With fifty-three of his own men and twenty of Ranse's, all volunteers, Drake sailed away with the pinnaces, leaving Ranse in charge of the ships. Just after sunset the raiding force anchored close under the land six miles from the town, but during the long wait in the darkness the difficulty of the enterprise began to prey upon the nerves of the men who most probably had never before

69

given a thought to its implications. As the moon rose, therefore, Drake gave the order to weigh and the little force rowed hard along the coast through the darkness until, at about three o'clock in the morning, the pinnaces rounded a point and there before them, pale and silent under the moon, lay Nombre de Dios, with a high church steeple standing out above the houses. There also, with lights about her decks as she stowed away her sails, lay a Spanish merchantman which had just arrived. On sighting four pinnaces under oars come suddenly foaming round the point her captain sent his boat in shore to give the alarm, but the pinnaces were too fast and easily cut it off, so that the English landed without opposition in a sandy bay just outside the town. Unfortunately a solitary Spaniard happened to be on guard and awake at the very spot where they beached, and without waiting to give a challenge he bolted for the town. In a few moments the night was full of wild clamour. As they formed up in the moonlight the English could hear the cries of frightened women and children being hurried to the Panama Gate, the beat of drums round the streets calling the townsmen to arms and loud above all the frenzied ringing of the church bell.

Leaving a dozen men as boat-keepers, Drake wasted some precious time climbing a small hill to see if a battery which he had heard of the year before was in position, but though the earthworks had been prepared he found no guns. By the time he was ready to advance the first panic in the town had subsided, the local militia, having been raided lately by bands of escaped slaves from the jungle were at their posts with their arms ready. The English force was divided in two with Drake leading one section, his brother and John Oxenham the other. Then with trumpets sounding and drums beating the two sections entered the town from different directions. When Drake's party advancing up the main street came to the market place they were met by 'a jolly hot volley of shot'. Many of Drake's men were wounded and the trumpet suddenly stopped in the middle of a note. The English fired back and without waiting to reload their muskets used their bows and the arrows which Drake had had specially made in England.

Although several were wounded and their trumpeter lay stretched out dead on the market square, Drake's party followed up their arrows with a charge. The Spaniards were standing firm until suddenly there came the rat-tat-tat of a drum from the other side of the square, and looking round over their shoulders the townsmen saw John Oxenham and the other party bearing down upon them. For the little band of shopkeepers defending their town, this was enough. They broke and fled. Drake and forty men were in possession of one end of Spain's lifeline, but they were not concerned with that. They had come for treasure, and after failing to stop that insistent church bell which was getting on their nerves, they grabbed a Spaniard who led them to the building where the mule trains unloaded. By the light of a guttering candle, Drake, Oxenham and a few other Englishmen peered into the shadow expecting to see fantastic riches heaped before them, the dull gleam of gold and silver, the coloured fire of precious stones. But all they saw was a bare floor and a few bars of silver stacked against the wall. Drake had arrived too late. The Flota had sailed six weeks before and that year's treasure was out of the Caribbean by now and well into the Atlantic. The 'intelligence' Drake had gleaned the year before was either false or had been wrongly interpreted. He should have known that his plan had never had the slightest chance of succeeding because the bullion was only in Nombre de Dios when the harbour was full of galleons, the town crowded with soldiers and the treasure itself under strong guard. Drake had miscalculated, and here he was now with a mere handful of Englishmen in a hostile town where the enemy might soon rally after the first surprise. He ordered his men to stand to their arms outside the building. What his feelings were at this moment has not been recorded, but the men with him were getting restive.

It was not long before dawn when a man's courage is at its lowest, many were wounded and all were exhausted. At this juncture their last sparks of enterprise and courage were dowsed by a sudden tropical downpour which soaked them to the skin. Drake had persuaded himself that there must be treasure somewhere and he wanted to explore the town; he tried to encourage his dispirited men by urging them not to give up now when he had brought them to the 'Mouth of the treasure of the World'. Just then they preferred their boats and said so. The waverers saw their chance when Drake suddenly fainted through loss of blood from a wound which he had concealed until now, and they carried their Captain down to the waiting boats.

As the crimson ball of the sun came up from the Caribbean they sailed out of Nombre de Dios Bay, pausing only to take with them 'for the more comfort of our campanie' the unfortunate merchantman which had arrived from Europe a few hours before. She was more suitable for the wounded than the crowded pinnaces and they discovered in her hold a cargo of Canary wines, a poor substitute for the 'treasure of the World', but a capture which no doubt allowed the raiding party to forget their troubles on the trip back to the Isle of Pines. Soon after they reached the ships Ranse decided that he had had enough of Drake's wild schemes and sailed away to go roving on his own account.

Drake's situation was now precarious. He and a number of his men were wounded. They were alone on an enemy coast thousands of miles from home and entirely dependent for supplies on what they could take by force. But as he tossed and turned on his sick bed in the steamy heat of the Darien coast, Drake's mind was busy with new plans. If he were to have any future on the sea he had somehow or other to 'make' this voyage. For Drake was not yet the legendary figure he was to become in his own lifetime, when he had only to 'stamp his foot in the West country' to get as many men as he liked. He was just one of many West country captains— all of whom could hold out the prospect of easy and quick riches. Drake had no constituted authority over his men except that given to the captain of a ship according to the immemorial usage of the sea, and if things went badly the sailor on an independent voyage cared little enough for that. The Elizabethan sailor accepted discipline when it clearly paid him to do so: in times of common danger or at the prospect of loot. He was not quite the heroic figure which looms so romantically through the mists of time. While his daring often verged on madness and he would cheerfully stand appalling hardship, he was also capable of sudden cowardice

72

or mutiny. Drake's volunteers were not sweating in the Caribbean for love of their country or to further the cause of the Reformation—they were there simply for what they could get out of it. So far they had got precious little, but whatever their fortunes on this voyage they always responded to that indefinable magnetism in Drake which all great leaders of men possess.

During the following months when there was no great enterprise in the offing to keep his men interested, to make them forget their loneliness and hardship, Francis Drake needed all his qualities as a leader. It was a time of waiting when Drake himself seems to have had no very clear idea of what to do next, so he kept his company too busy to brood upon their grievances. One need was urgent if he were to stay out here until the voyage was 'made' —he must have a secure base. But before that he tried something even more harebrained than the attack on Nombre de Dios. He thought he might take the walled city of Carthagena by surprise attack. Carthagena, however, had been warned, and as soon as Drake appeared at the entrance to the inner harbour, the church bells rang out, heavy guns fired and horse and foot mustered on the foreshore. Obviously there was nothing to be hoped for from Carthagena and all Drake got from this excursion was an empty cargo ship which he picked up in the outer harbour on his way back to the open sea. Next morning he captured an advice boat which was carrying letters to all ports warning them to prepare well against 'Captain Drake'. No more was he an anonymous English corsair. He now made his way along the coast until he came to where the Isthmus makes a sudden dip before swelling out into the continent of South America and here, up the Gulf of Uraba, 'in a convenient road out of all trade', as he described it, Drake started on his base.

He got the best out of his men by making this task a mixture of hard work and holiday. He divided the company into two watches, working them day on and day off. So that while one lot cleared the jungle, built huts and refitted the pinnaces, the others enjoyed the simple games they had last played on their village greens in England, bowls, quoits and skittles, and the ship's fletcher was kept busy providing arrows for those who fancied themselves at the butts. For a fortnight the ring of axes and clang of the anvil mingled with shouts and laughter on a strip of land between the dark green forest and the glittering sea as these west country men worked and played, their failure so far, their danger and their isolation forgotten. Before arriving at the Gulf of Uraba, Drake had one night persuaded Thomas Moon, the carpenter, to scuttle the *Swan*, so that the pinnaces would be fully manned for his next venture.

As soon as they were refitted, Drake sailed with two pinnaces, each with a full crew, leaving his brother John in charge of the ship with orders to follow. Drake first sailed back along the Isthmus to the mouth of the Maddalena River to get in touch with the band of escaped slaves and outlaws whose leader he had first met when he lay wounded on the Isle of Pines. These outlaws, known as Cimaroons, who infested the hinterland and knew their way about the jungle had first given him the idea for a venture more desperate and extravagant than any he had yet thought of. If there was nothing to be had from Nombre de Dios and he could not attack the Flota itself, then he would lift the treasure on its way across the Isthmus. The Cimaroons, who were always ready for anything which would annoy the Spanish authorities, took him to a new lair up the Gulf of San Blas, more conveniently placed for setting off inland than distant Uraba, and from them he now learned what he had failed to discover on his previous voyage —movements of the Flota, which could not be expected until the end of the rainy season, a wait of four months. Every evening, while staying at a camp ashore prepared by the hospitable Cimaroons, and especially after one of the frequent thunderstorms, the crews of the pinnaces were maddened by 'a kind of flies, like our gnattes', until the Cimaroons taught them to get relief from the bites by smearing themselves with lemon juice. When John Drake arrived at this new base, Drake sailed off to fill in time by preying on inter-colony trade and, in his need to 'make' the voyage, even tried to do some ordinary trading at Carthagena where he offered English cloth amongst other things. He cannot have been too surprised when Carthagena would have none of him. So he sailed along the Main as far east as Curaçao but was unable to land anywhere, the Spaniards were ready for him. After two months away, the weather being bad, provisions low and the men in the second pinnace beginning to murmur, Drake returned to the Gulf of San Blas.

He was greeted with the news that John Drake had been killed in an attack on a Spanish merchantman. Six weeks later his brother Joseph died of a mysterious illness which had already taken off a number of his dwindling company. In order to find out what this malady was, Drake ordered the surgeon to carry out a post-mortem. The chronicler of the expedition recorded the finding of that gruesome operation performed under a tropic sun, 'the liver swollen, the heart sodden, but the guts all faire', which left no one any the wiser about the cause of death. 'This was the first and last experiment', adds the writer, 'that our captain made of Anatomy in this voyage'. The epidemic continued. One after the other twenty-eight men complained of headache, the shivers, then vomiting, and after a delirium sank into a coma from which none awoke: for the 'flies' which so annoyed them were not 'English gnattes'—they were mosquitoes carrying the germs of yellow fever.

When no more than a couple of dozen Englishmen were left alive, the Cimaroons reported that the Flota had at last arrived in Nombre de Dios; and when a pinnace which Drake at once dispatched confirmed this news, he and the Cimaroons made their final preparations for a journey towards the great capital city of Panama. Drake's men had been watching their shipmates go down like ninepins, all he had given them so far had been failure, hardship and death, yet when their Captain called upon them for an enterprise more daring than any he had yet suggested, they were ready to follow him. And so, on a day early in January, 1573, Francis Drake and seventeen other Englishmen stepped forth into the twilight of the jungle on Darien.

Drake could never have considered such an undertaking if thirty of his negro allies had not volunteered to accompany him: these men led the expedition by secret ways through the jungle, they carried the provisions, made camp every evening and kept the pot filled with game shot with their bows and arrows. Before sunrise every morning this oddly-assorted band was on the march. About a mile ahead four expert Cimaroon guides blazed the trail, then came an advance guard of a dozen blacks on the look-out for Spaniards, and after them the English in a body, wearing armour over their rough canvas clothes, shouldering clumsy firearms or trailing pikes, and each man slung about with spare pairs of shoes. The white men were surprised to find it pleasantly cool in the shade of the great forest, but the going was hard on men who had never marched like this in their lives. After four days of blundering over roots and the tough lianas across their path, of climbing hills and wading rivers, they arrived on a clear, breezy day at the summit of a high range of hills.

It was ten o'clock on the morning of February 11th, 1573, when the leader of the Cimaroons took Drake by the hand and 'prayed him to follow him, if he was desirous to see at once the two Seas, which he had so long longed for'. And with that he led Drake up to a platform built at the top of one of the giant trees. Over his shoulder Drake could see the sharp blue line of the Caribbean horizon, but he had seen that often enough from the deck of a ship. He gazed out ahead. Far beyond the hazy ridges and furrows of forest a faint greenish line merged imperceptibly into the sky—the great South Sea. On stepping down from the tree, and in front of all his men Drake fell upon his knees. After a solemn pause he got up and not until then did he tell his men of what he had seen, adding that he had 'prayed Almightie God of his goodness to give him life and leave to sayle once in an English ship upon that sea'. John Oxenham seems to have been the only one of the company to feel the high drama of that moment, for he alone jumped forward asking leave to accompany his leader. But, as it so transpired, it was Oxenham who first sailed an English craft on the Pacific.

After a while their way led them out of the forest into rolling grassland and they had their first glimpse of distant Panama. For the next three days it seemed to the Englishmen as if the city were only just beyond the next rise, but always, when they reached the crest, there it was as far away as ever. The time came at last when they could count the ships lying in the harbour, ships even now perhaps unloading the treasure they had come so far to capture. From here the whole company marched in silence, dodging cautiously from cover to cover until they halted in a grove of trees not far outside the town. They peered through the trees at Panama with its fine buildings, broad streets and its great cathedral glowing in the afternoon sun—tantalizing sight as the 'faire citie' lay all quiet and unsuspecting. A negro who had once been a slave in Panama was sent in to find out what he could about the movement of treasure, and this brave man returned with heartening news. The Governor of Lima, on his way back to Spain, was setting out for Nombre de Dios that very night with a string of mules, eight of which were laden with gold and one with jewels. Drake and the negro leader did not wait for any more. The party set out at once on a forced march of twelve miles to a place on the route, which the negroes had chosen as the best position for an ambush, just short of Venta Cruces.

The invaluable Cimaroons had supplied Drake with detailed local knowledge so that the plan for this attack had been carefully worked out. While Drake with half his men took one side of the track, Oxenham and the remainder took the other, with the parties spaced some distance apart along the road. The idea was that when the mule train was neatly between them the trap would close; Drake's men grabbing the leading mule and Oxenham's the hindmost, the animals being tied head-to-tail for the march would not be able to stampede into the forest. The English wore their shirts over their armour so that friend and foe could be distinguished in the confusion and darkness. Drake gave strict orders that trains from Venta Cruces towards Panama were to be allowed to pass because they would only be carrying merchandise, and he was after gold. When all had received their orders for this practically foolproof plan and all were in position, they lay down well hidden in the long grass just off the highway. It was a still, quiet night with nothing to be heard but the mysterious rustlings and murmurs of the forest. An hour went by, and then, far away in the distance they heard the deep-toned bells of a mule train making its leisurely way from Panama. The

English had only to wait a little longer for the voyage to be well and truly 'made'.

Just at this moment they heard another sound, trotting hooves coming along the road from the direction of Venta Cruces and as they peered through the grass they saw a horseman going quietly along, a page-boy at his stirrup. At this, Robert Pike, who had spent the time of waiting in drinking neat brandy, forgot his orders and jumped to his feet. The sound of the hooves changed suddenly from a sedate trot to a gallop and disappeared into the distance, and after a while the bells were silent. Drake and his men lay wondering what this meant, but after some time the bells started again. They looked to their weapons and in a few minutes the trap closed on a mule train, but the mules were loaded only with food and odd bales of merchandise. On being warned by the horseman that there was something suspicious going on a little way back along the highway, the Treasurer had held up his own train and sent on another carrying nothing of any value. 'Thus', the chronicler of this voyage remarks, 'wee were disappointed of a most rich bootie', adding the pious reflection that no doubt God had not intended this particular haul to be captured. Drake learned from the head muleteer of the captured train that on seeing that ghostly apparition suddenly arise by the side of the highway, the horseman had guessed that the Englishman Drake was somewhere about. Now that his presence on the highway was known Drake's only course was to get back to his base, and he chose the shortest way there—through Venta Cruces. But that night was not to be without an example of the punctilio of those days, though the time was after midnight and the place the thick of a tropical jungle. Just outside Venta Cruces the English were challenged by a party of Spanish soldiers. Their commander called upon the raiders to surrender in the name of the King of Spain, his master, promising on the word of a gentleman to treat them with all courtesy if they did. Out of the darkness came Drake's reply: 'For the honour of the Queene, my Mistresse, I must have passage this way'—then a shot from his pistol. In the brisk skirmish which followed one Englishman was killed and others wounded, but the rest fought their way through, bursting into the terrified little settlement with hoarse shouts of 'Gold, gold'. But no gold was here, only some clothing and merchandise which Drake gave to his allies.

The raiders were limping, dispirited and weary but Drake kept his little band going, 'encouraging his companie with such example and speech that the way seemed much shorter'. He had failed again, yet 'he marched most cheerfully and assured us that he doubted not but ere he left the coast we should be bountifully paid and recompensed for all those paines taken'. Such was Drake's personal magnetism that his men believed him, even now. Helping along those who had worn out their shoes and buoying up all with his own determination, 'after marching many daies with hungry stomackes', Drake brought his men to the sea.

This raid disturbed the Spanish authorities not so much for the damage it had caused as for what it might portend. Being unaware—or unable to appreciate—that Drake's voyage was an unofficial venture, Panama, Nombre de Dios and the Commander of the Flota all reported to the King that it was a reconnaissance before the English came out in strength to occupy the Isthmus. And with a strategic insight hardly to be expected of a committee of harassed colonial officials, the Council of Panama demanded not soldiers as protection, but warships in the Caribbean, 'for if the sea is safe', they wrote, 'we shall be safe on land'.

While these despatches were racing back across the Atlantic, and just when it seemed to the English that nothing could now 'make' their voyage, Captain Le Testu, a Huguenot privateer well known on the coast, turned up at the anchorage in need of fresh water. Here, perhaps, was their last chance; and as they listened politely to his account of the latest happenings in France and his protestations of friendship, they were wondering if they could trust him far enough to invite him to join them in another go at the mule trains. He had a well-armed ship with a company of fit men four times as numerous as Drake and his scarecrows. After talking the matter over Drake invited Le Testu to bring twenty of his men and join with the English under Drake's leadership in an attack on the mule trains. Although the English would only provide eighteen men, it was their project and Le

Testu, rather surprisingly, agreed to go equal shares in any booty. The Cimaroons were ready for anything and said they knew of a place much nearer Nombre de Dios because the Flota was nearly loaded and the movement of treasure would soon stop for the season.

After moving along the coast in pinnaces the party, led by the negroes, entered the forest, where the English who were now old hands at the game astonished their talkative French allies by marching in dead silence. Along secret ways the Cimaroons brought the raiders to a spot on the Panama road not far from Nombre de Dios, and hidden in the long grass the party sat down to wait. It was a calm, still night and they were so close to Nombre de Dios that they could hear the carpenters hammering as they worked through the night getting the galleons ready for sea. But Drake and his men were listening for something else and not long before dawn they heard it—the faint sound of those deep-toned bells. In the eerie quiet of that windless night they could hear the music from far off. But as it came slowly nearer the Cimaroons excitedly pointed out that it was a whole multitude of bells meaning a long succession of mule trains, and the raiders looked to their arms and tensed themselves in readiness. Now they could distinguish the clack of hoof against stone, the creaking of harness and the chatter of the muleteers, then the first train was passing them. Each train had its guard of soldiers, but being on the last lap of the journey and so near home, the guards were shambling carelessly along keeping no sort of a lookout, for after all, they too could hear the carpenters at work by now, and how could an attack be possible so near to Nombre de Dios? Drake let a couple of trains carrying ordinary merchandise go past, but when one laden with gold and silver came by the raiders pounced. A couple of shots rang out as soldiers fired wildly and Captain Le Testu fell, badly wounded in the stomach, and one negro was killed. But the surprised guards and drivers soon took to their heels in the direction of the town, leaving the French and English to rip open the cases and make off with what they could carry. They hid most of the silver in the woods and concentrated on the gold, for they could hear bugles sounding and drums beating as the alarm was given in the town. When the Spaniards streamed out of

Nombre de Dios a storm broke and the rain came down in sheets. Leaving Captain Le Testu and about ten tons of silver in the forest, but clutching their gold in quoits and bars the raiders floundered through the mud and at last reached their boats.

On reaching his ship Drake had to have his little joke. He gave the impression that the raid had been another failure, and then 'tooke out of his bosome a Quoit of Gold, thanking God that our voyage was made'. So it may have been, but at that very moment the head of his partner, Le Testu, was gracing the market square of Nombre de Dios on the end of a pike. In the excitement of dividing up the spoil no one had time to think of him, yet from the moment of his arrival Drake's fortune had changed and from now on nothing seemed able to go wrong. Even the Frenchmen with their powerful ship gave no trouble; when they might easily have had their own share of the gold as well as Drake's, they took only their half and sailed at once for France. And John Oxenham, on revisiting the scene of the ambush with some of the negroes, returned with thirteen bars of silver and a few quoits of gold. It was time to be getting home. As a parting present Drake gave his faithful Cimaroons what they valued far above gold and silver, the ironwork from the pinnaces, and some silks and linens for their wives. And not only the Cimaroons were content. With some £20,000 (equivalent to ten times that amount in our currency) to share between them his men had in truth been 'bountifully paid and recompensed for all paines taken'. Even the manner of their departure from the coast had the same dreamlike quality which the voyage had had from the moment of Le Testu's arrival. By this time the Flota had reached Carthagena where it was taking in stores for the long journey back to Spain, and as he was borne along on the coastal eddy Drake made a point of passing in full view of the anchored fleet, the flag of St. George fluttering proudly at his main and every flag and streamer blowing out as he came 'sayling forward with a large wind'.

On his way up past Cuba through the Yucatan channel, Drake picked up some pleasing additions to the booty in the valuable cargoes of several hapless inter-colony traders they encountered. At last, with the voyage well and truly 'made', he left the Caribbean by the Florida Channel to raise the Scillies after a quick passage of twenty-three days. Two of his brothers and more than half the company with whom he had set out had been left in their graves in a strange land, but even they were forgotten as one familiar headland after another showed up through the summer haze, and instead of the dank blue-green vegetation of the tropics they saw the tidy golden fields of England, while the breeze at evening carried on it the almost forgotten fragrance of their own land. The long nightmare was over and they were home at last. On Sunday, August 9th, 1573, Drake anchored in the Cattewater at Plymouth 'about sermon time' to the dismay of the preacher who was left looking down on rows of empty pews. For when the word sped round that Drake was back, 'all hastened to see the evidence of God's love and blessing towards our gracious Queene and Countreye by the fruite of our Captaine's labour and successe'. And on that pious note the chronicler ends his account of the voyage. But Drake's arrival at this precise moment was more of an embarrassment than a blessing to his Queen, for England and Spain were in the middle of delicate negotiations to resume normal trade, and they were haggling over damages. The tension and excitement after San Juan de Ulua had died away, relations between the two countries were improving and the sudden return of Drake, his hold bulging with loot, was hardly calculated to assist the English Council in claims for damages. Drake was hurried away out of sight. He was told to make himself scarce, so with great tact he went to serve his Queen more directly and less profitably in Ireland, leaving the Caribbean to lesser men.

Only a year after Drake had come sailing past the anchored treasure fleet with all flags flying, a certain John Noble arrived off the coast of Nicaragua on a voyage that was the occasion for one of the few cheerful dispatches from the Caribbean at this time. For Noble was evidently not of the stuff of which successful corsairs are made. He was doing fairly well up and down the coast when his ship was attacked by a Spanish 'frigate' sent from Nombre de Dios. This vessel carried no guns, only thirty soldiers with arquebuses, while Noble's ship carried four cannon. Instead of replying with their artillery to this feeble small arms fire the

English panicked, abandoned ship and made for the shore in the ship's launch. No one of her company of twenty-five escaped to tell what had caused this unusual behaviour, and as the Spaniards did not bother to inquire, we shall never know. The two ship's boys were condemned to the galleys for life and all the others were killed. John Noble himself and two companions were hanged at Nombre de Dios, 'Which has occasioned great joy and animated all', the magistrate of Panama reported to his King. 'And the realm is entirely quiet', he concluded his dispatch.

But not for long. The Governor of Veragua was soon complaining that his province was 'much vexed by corsairs' who were attracted by the gold. The trouble this time was Gilbert Horseley, a different proposition altogether from the ineffectual Noble. For sheer effrontery Horseley's raid compares with anything Drake attempted, because Horseley's was done on the cheap. He sailed from Plymouth with twenty-five men in the tiny *John* of eighteen tons, not much larger than one of Drake's pinnaces, which carried fewer than six guns, the largest of which was a three-pounder. Yet, after losing eight men in an encounter with a well-armed Spanish ship in the Caribbean, he sailed up the San Juan River into the interior of what is now called Nicaragua. He attacked isolated settlements perpetrating atrocities on the defenceless inhabitants which were considered shocking even in those days. Besides robbing them of merchandise and gold and silver in bars and bullion he held a rich citizen to ransom for 3,000 pesos. After a trip of only a few months Horseley sailed for England where he arrived unobtrusively at Arundel in June, 1575, having completed a voyage that must hold the record for speed in execution and return for money laid out on the venture.

Horseley had no sooner come and gone than there appeared in the Caribbean one of the few Englishmen who might be considered to have had some justification for robbing Spaniards. This was Andrew Barker, a Bristol merchant, who had sent a ship and cargo to the Canaries in all good faith, when Anglo-Spanish trading had been officially resumed, only to have both confiscated by the authorities. With no hope of getting satisfaction by lawful means he decided to try force and set out from England with two vessels, the *Ragged Staff* having Philip Roche as master and the *Bear* with William Coxe. For a time it must have looked to Barker as if he would recoup himself and more for his confiscated ship; the Flota was in Nombre de Dios, therefore treasure was on the move, and all the ships he captured as he worked along the Main were carrying packets of valuables. He even had the satisfaction of capturing a Spanish frigate which had been dispatched against him from the Flota and making her his flagship instead of the *Ragged Staff*. But that was the end of Barker's success; he could not get on with Roche and Coxe who finally mutinied and put Barker and twelve of his friends ashore on an island off the coast of Nicaragua. Here he and his party were surprised by the local commander, a certain Captain Lopez, who sent twelve heads and a hand to his superiors at Truxillo as ocular proof of his vigilance and efficiency. In reporting this exploit to his King, Captain Lopez modestly claimed no other reward than to be allowed to add twelve heads and a hand to his coat of arms. While Barker's head was on its way to Truxillo and Captain Lopez was writing for the macabre addition to his coat of arms (which, incidentally, he was not awarded) Roche and Coxe began the journey back to England, but only after many losses and mishaps Coxe and eighteen men reached England in June, 1578. Barker's brother prosecuted them for having procured Andrew's death and they 'shortly after came to miserable ends'.

In considering these English voyages one might gain the impression that they did great harm to Spain; but the sum total of the losses due to these raids—for that is all they were—was barely perceptible in the records of the specie that was reaching Spain. It was not the monetary loss which exercised the Spanish authorities on both sides of the Atlantic, but the inherent weakness of Spain's position which they exposed. Spain could not protect the trade routes along which her treasure flowed, she had not even local command of the sea in the Eastern Caribbean and she was learning painfully that an overseas empire cannot be enjoyed without sea power. If the colonial authorities were anxious about the situation in the Caribbean they were soon to be vastly more perturbed by events on the other side of the Isthmus of Darien.

CHAPTER VI

Spanish Treasure in the Pacific

*

Early on a February morning in 1577 when those faint breaths of air which come before the dawn were scarcely ruffling the glassy surface of the Gulf of Panama, Diego de Sotomayor and his family were fast asleep in his house on the largest of the Pearl Islands, not far from the great port of Panama. He was a well-to-do dealer in pearls, a good family man and a devout Catholic. Although tales of the fearful deeds of corsairs in the Caribbean had reached him and his slaves, none considered for a moment that such things could happen here in the Pacific, and Don Diego was enjoying the sound sleep of a man whose house is secure and conscience clear. But suddenly a wild barking from the watchdogs in his yard roused a slave woman who shuffled drowsily to the door, and after one horrified glance at what she saw there slammed it shut and ran to her mistress crying that the French were upon them.

But these unshaven ruffians were not French; they were the first Englishmen to reach the Pacific and their leader was John Oxenham. They broke down the door, seized Don Diego and made him produce all the gold, silver and pearls he had in the place, then proceeded to ransack the house, tearing religious pictures from the walls, strewing about the contents of cupboards and trunks, even trampling on the children's toys until that neat and tidy house looked as if it had been visited by a troop of monkeys. After a while they came upon the altar and vestments which Don Diego kept on the premises so that Mass could be celebrated in his house whenever he was visited by a priest. Oxenham's sailors smashed the altar to bits, their cook danced round in an alb,

85

that robe of white linen which a priest wears under his vestments, and ended by tucking its skirts into his trousers and using it for a shirt—the cleanest that he had had on for months.

While the English were behaving like schoolboys on the spree, declaring with gusto all the while that they were 'good Lutherans', a Franciscan friar whose job it was to minister to the slaves arrived on the island; and in Fray Miguel de Los Angeles these English sailors came up against something which they could not understand. This friar cannot have been one of the brighter lights of his community or he would not have had the duty of ministering only to slaves. In the peace and quiet of the cloister he had read daily of the lives and deaths of martyrs, but the last thing he can have expected this Monday morning was to face martyrdom himself during a routine Lenten visit. Yet this obscure and humble man was given that day a serene courage worthy of the old tradition.

He had landed with an official the English would have been only too delighted to manhandle, a commissary of the Holy Inquisition, but they ignored this man because he was not tonsured. As soon as they noticed Fray Miguel's tonsure they set about him, striking him in the face and crowning him with a chamber pot. Then they showed him a large wooden cross and asked him what it was. The account of an eye-witness, his companion, goes on: 'He answered that it was the image and likeness of the cross upon which Christ was crucified. "So", replied the English, "that is where we will hang you and burn you before we go." To which the friar answered that he did not merit so much honour. And at this they left him.' No more is heard of Fray Miguel who no doubt hurried back as soon as his duties allowed him to the comforting obscurity of the cloister after his brief excursion into the glare of history.

This sudden appearance of Oxenham in the Pacific was the outcome of that morning on Darien when he and Drake each had vowed to sail an English ship in that sea, and now Oxenham had the satisfaction of getting there first. He used the money he had made out of the 1572 voyage to fit out a ship of his own, but he had obtained neither leave nor licence to make a voyage; and in the spring of 1576 he slipped quietly out of Plymouth on his un-official venture with a company of fifty-seven men. He had chosen for his second-in-command one John Butler who spoke fluent Spanish with a Portuguese accent and who, like Oxenham, had first-hand knowledge of the state of affairs in Central America. It was this knowledge which led them to contemplate something far more ambitious than the usual raid in and out of the Carib-bean; they intended to seize control of the Isthmus itself, though precisely what was to happen if they succeeded they do not seem to have considered. The idea was not quite as mad as it sounds. The terminal ports of Nombre de Dios and Panama were only lightly held, while the link between them was precarious. There were too few soldiers even to guard the mule trains efficiently, let alone deal with the well-disciplined Cimaroons who controlled large tracts of the hinterland and were ready to ally themselves with anyone against the Spaniards. Oxenham's plan was strate-gically unsound, even if it were possible tactically. He was pro-posing to seize enemy territory many thousands of miles from any possible support; moreover, he was attacking a tender spot which would make the Spaniards react violently, and they could always bring stronger forces to the area more quickly than could the English. England was in no position to support any large-scale distant adventure, and in the long run it is perhaps lucky that Oxenham's daring *coup* failed, or she might have been tempted to embark on something far beyond her strength. And Oxenham failed because he had not enough men for the job they were ex-pected to do; because he was careless over details, particularly over what today we should call 'security'; but above all he failed because there happened to be in Panama at the time a most unusual official as President of the Council. Gabriel de Loarte was alert, energetic and more, he acted first and asked permission afterwards.

When Oxenham appeared off what is now the coast of Nicara-gua the Flota had arrived at Nombre de Dios, so that treasure was on the move and he had soon intercepted several richly laden local vessels. A prisoner from one of these spent some days on board Oxenham's ship listening to the very free boasting of the crew who told him of their plans, how with the help of the Cimaroons they intended a descent on the Pacific, and they even talked about the secret anchorage they were bound for on the Acla coast. Then this intelligent Spaniard was either released ashore or escaped. His report soon reached de Loarte at Panama, who now learned that there was an English captain on the coast who had taken part in the attack on Nombre de Dios, that these English were planning an attack across the Isthmus on shipping in the Pacific and that the captain, whom at first he thought was Drake, was lying up in his secret anchorage. Gabriel de Loarte at once ordered a force out from Nombre de Dios to scour the north coast, while he organized a search from Panama of likely bays and estuaries on the Pacific side. He came across nothing suspicious, but the party from Nombre de Dios discovered the secret English base. Here they missed the two pinnaces which Oxenham had brought out from England in sections, but found a prize which Oxenham was using as a store ship. This store ship held his spare cannon and culverins, ammunition, a stock of small arms and all the trade goods he needed for paying the Cimaroons who had no use for gold or silver but demanded instead cloth, linen or tools and weapons made of iron.

Oxenham was up-country negotiating with the Cimaroons when this disaster occurred. It left him in an awkward, wellnigh hopeless, position in which a less determined man would have sailed straight back to England, yet the search party had not discovered his original ship. Perhaps his dream of being the first Englishman to sail the Pacific lured him on. Here he was then, far out of reach of any help, with no artillery—only twenty arquebuses, very little ammunition, and nothing with which to pay the Cimaroons. To get their help he had to promise that all negro slaves taken would be given to them and all Spaniards killed. Oxenham at this time was forty-two, and it says a lot for his force of character that in spite of every pressure from his allies and even when he was in desperate straits no Spanish prisoner was killed. He now ordered the iron and cordage which he would need for new construction on the Pacific to be removed from the ship which had brought him out and the hulk to be burned.

Some of the ironwork went as part payment to the Cimaroons and the remainder he transported across the Isthmus to a lonely water-shed inland from the Gulf of San Miguel. Now the ring of English axes sounded in the forest. Cedar trees which were plentiful hereabouts toppled, fell, were sawn into planks and slowly the boat took shape. For the next few months and working in a moist, enervating heat, fifty Englishmen, 'fearing neither God nor Your Majesty', as a Spanish dispatch put it, laboriously fashioned a shallow-draught pinnace, forty-five feet in length and fitted for twelve oars a side. Once the ship was built they had to get her to the sea, and, manhandling her for a great part of the way, they floated her at last on the water of the Pacific Ocean. Then, with the Cimaroon chief as their pilot, they emerged from the Bay of San Miguel into the shimmering Gulf of Panama and made straight for some faint specks on the horizon far to the north-west. So it was that John Oxenham and his men, who had sailed out of Plymouth less than a year before, set the watchdogs barking outside a house on the Pearl Islands.

Whatever his feeling of exaltation when he landed Oxenham must have known that his position was desperate: he had no re-serves or resources, restive allies and not even a ship to sail home in from the north coast if ever he reached there. It was unfortunate that he allowed his men, who were intoxicated at the feeling of being at large in the Pacific, to get out of hand. Their behaviour was not typical of English sailors at the time, and certainly Haw-kins would not have allowed anything of the sort. The Spanish authorities were half inclined to admire Oxenham's bravery, but what upset them more than anything else was the behaviour of his sailors on first landing on Chapera. From the moment the altar was kicked to pieces and the cook danced round in church vestments, Oxenham and his men were doomed. The Council of Panama expressed the general feeling: 'What is felt most deeply, being cause for tears', so ran a dispatch, 'is the little reverence they show for the saints and the worship of God. They broke up crucifixes, insulted the Pope and committed many other insults for which God give us due vengeance in defending His honour by Your Majesty's unconquerable arms'.

That the Council were given their revenge so quickly was due less to Providence than to the negligence of the English themselves. Oxenham had given orders on arrival in the Pearl Islands that all boats were to be rendered unseaworthy and then proceeded to loot the islands at his leisure. A great number of boats were burned or had their bottoms stove in, but his sailors overlooked one canoe. A brave man sneaked away in this by night to reach Panama with the news of the raiders—and Oxenham had lost the advantage of surprise. Although de Loarte had been half expecting the English, and had lost a lot of sleep making plans when the first reports reached him, he had no idea that the English had been at large in the Pacific for the last three weeks. He now acted with energy. A vessel raced away to warn and detain all shipping coming up from the south. A detachment of soldiers set off inland deep into Cimaroon territory to intercept the raiders should they make back for the north coast. He organized and armed a militia for the defence of Panama; and within a week had equipped a striking force of six small vessels carrying two hundred armed men. And as well, though he cannot have relished doing so, he applied urgently to the Viceroy of Peru for help. Altogether, with the resources at his disposal, de Loarte had done far more than could normally be expected of the Spanish colonial official of those days.

After a pleasant and lucrative couple of weeks in the Pearl Islands, and still blissfully unaware of the measures which were being taken against him, Oxenham thought it time to be after bigger game. His pinnace appeared off Panama in the cool of the evening of March 7th just when the local defence force was holding its parade before nightfall, and, alarmed by this unexpected martial activity Oxenham sheered off to tackle something easier. No shipping in the Pacific was armed, the crews were not even issued with weapons and at this moment vast riches in defenceless ships were moving up to Panama as the Flota in Nombre de Dios was shortly due to sail. When a bark from Guayaquil, all unsuspecting, hove in sight in the Gulf of Panama, Oxenham with his oared pinnace quickly ranged alongside and she fell to him like a ripe plum. She turned out to be a prize worth taking, for in addition to 70,000 pesos in gold, she carried what was of far more value to Oxenham at the time: a store of food, including cheese and bacon, shoes and a stock of powder. He had some trouble with the Cimaroons who wanted to hold him to his promise that all Spaniards would be killed. But he let her go, and with no one on board any the worse, but considerably lightened, she arrived in Panama reporting that the leader of the raiders was 'a man of grave demeanour, much feared and respected by his soldiers'.

That is an estimate made by men still astonished at being alive and unhurt after a horde of cut-throats had come swarming over their side, and it does not help us learn what sort of man this John Oxenham really was nor what was in his mind. No account of his expedition from a survivor ever reached England, and all we have to go by are the Spanish dispatches and the report of his interrogation by men who were not in the least interested in the subtleties of his character—they only wanted to know how he had reached the Pacific and what really lay behind it all. For while Oxenham was in the Pacific, Andrew Barker was roving along the Atlantic coast and the Spanish authorities feared that the two voyages were connected as part of some larger English scheme of conquest. Actually each was a separate undertaking and both were entirely unofficial. This much we do know of Oxenham: he had been an officer in whom Drake placed great trust: at Nombre de Dios he led one party through the town, and he was in charge of one-half of the men in the attacks on the mule trains; from his actions he was a brave man, all the Spanish accounts agree upon that; he was reckless enough of consequences to defy his own Queen and to invade the dominions of the most powerful monarch in the world; so far he had done brilliantly in bringing off the apparently impossible. But he remains a puzzle: was he hopelessly casual by nature, or did his nerve suddenly fail him, leaving a sort of paralysis?

It would seem so from the way he behaved after this first success when, so far as he knew, everything was going well. With no attempt at disguising his movements Oxenham made straight for the Gulf of San Miguel, a fact which the plundered Guayaquil bark reported on arrival at Panama. He then went up a river, and with his shallow-draught launch—it drew only about a foot—

was able to get far up into Vallano, the territory of the Cimaroons. The gold Oxenham had taken from that one ship in the Pacific was itself worth more than all Drake had gained on his voyage in 1572, and perhaps Oxenham had decided that his voyage was 'made' and was on his way to the north coast in order to capture a Spanish ship which would get him to England. If this was his idea he does not seem to have been in any particular hurry over it, for he sauntered along as if he believed that the Spanish authorities must be all asleep. But they were not: the energetic Gabriel de Loarte had set things moving. Pedro de Ortega, the Inspector of the Royal Treasury at Panama, who had a personal interest in retrieving the gold taken from the bark because some of it belonged to the King, sailed in command of the flotilla with two hundred soldiers for the Gulf of San Miguel.

After wasting a lot of time up several of the rivers which flowed into the Gulf without having any luck, Ortega's perseverance was at last rewarded; he was 'guided by the Divine Majesty' to the Chucunaque River. De Ortega made his way up this until there was no more water for his boats, then leaving these under guard, he set out on foot with sixty soldiers following the course of the river and beating the thickly-wooded hills through which it flowed. After four days of this he picked up the trail on the river bank where the English had carelessly left pork rinds and biscuit strewn about after a meal. Ortega and his men pressed on until the morning of Tuesday in Holy Week when the sound of two shots halted them. Peering round trees the Spaniards saw the English lightheartedly breakfasting in the shade of a canvas awning without having troubled to post sentries. A few men were unloading the cedarwood pinnace because there was not enough water to float her, and they had to make the rest of their way to the Atlantic coast on foot. But they went no further as an organized body of men. A sudden volley from a few yards range took them completely by surprise. And there on the bank of a tropical stream with the pinnace grating gently on the gravel bottom, John Oxenham's expedition came to its end. A few English lay dead beside their unfinished breakfasts, others ran off into the forest, but de Ortega took a couple of prisoners from whom he learned that Oxenham was at a negro village a few miles away.

The Spaniards took the village without loss, for the English were so short of firearms and ammunition that some were using bows and arrows. Oxenham, though wounded, escaped into the bush with Butler and a few survivors. Three ship's boys did not get away and one of these 'after pressure' told where Oxenham had buried his Pacific loot. This was on Easter Sunday: it was only at the beginning of Lent that Oxenham had landed on the Pearl Islands. De Ortega knew that if he went campaigning with all these valuables he would lose more from his own soldiers than he had so far from the English, so he returned to Panama with treasure and prisoners, and when an inventory had been made it was found that not only had the entire amount taken from the treasure ship been recovered, but also the jewels and small sums of money which had been taken from Diego de Sotomayor and others on the islands. Pedro de Ortega now decided that he had done quite enough; and to make quite sure that he was suitably rewarded for his services he departed for Spain to make his report to the King in person. The same ship's boy, no doubt after further pressure, now confessed that he knew where Oxenham's two pinnaces were hidden and where more loot taken in the Caribbean had been buried. So de Loarte sent another officer and fifty soldiers with the lad across to the Atlantic coast. And there, just as the boy had said they would be, hidden up a creek with their decks awash were Oxenham's two sea-going pinnaces—and with them went his last hope of rescuing anything out of this disastrous voyage, even his own life. For Oxenham was now a wounded man on the run in a tropical forest during the rainy season, living off bananas; his men were scattered, his booty lost, all his craft gone and his allies were turning against him. It is small wonder then that even the energetic de Loarte was ready to let the negroes and the climate finish off what English were left alive, and he wrote to the Viceroy of Peru informing him that the campaign was over and that his help was no longer needed.

Unfortunately for the relations between the representatives of the King in Panama and Peru, an officer arrived in Panama at this moment with very different ideas on the subject. This Diego de Frias was a tactless individual who informed de Loarte that he had his orders from the Viceroy to punish the Cimaroons and make war on the 'English Lutherans', and whatever the authorities in Panama might feel about it he was there to carry them out. All this got de Frias was a delay of two months, for de Loarte's dignity had been offended at what he considered interference with his authority by the Viceroy issuing orders for a campaign in the territory under Panama's jurisdiction. After weeks of bickering and obstruction de Frias at last set off in August. A month later one of his columns ran Oxenham to earth in a banana grove. Oxenham was armed only with a lance and when he was covered by a soldier with an arquebus he saw that the game was up and he surrendered. In December de Frias rounded up Butler, his young brother Henry, the ship's master and fifteen other English. He also recovered about one thousand pesos in silver from a hiding place on the Acla coast, and in April, 1578, by which time his own troops were in rags, suffering from fever and physically exhausted, de Frias returned in triumph to Panama with nineteen English including their leaders and forty marketable negroes. De Loarte was mercifully spared the humiliation of having to welcome this bumptious officer for he had died while the expedition was up-country. Fifteen English sailors were executed out of hand as pirates, the ship's boys were spared and sent to Spain, while on orders from the Viceroy who considered them his game, John Oxenham and his officers were to be shipped to Peru. The ship which took them there, ironically enough, was one which Oxenham had narrowly missed capturing the year before when she was nearing Panama laden with treasure. On arrival, John Oxenham, John Butler, his young brother Henry and the ship's master were thrown into the prison for common criminals at Lima.

Some months later while they were still in gaol, on September 6th, 1578, Oxenham's old captain, Francis Drake, sailed out of the Straits of Magellan into the 'Great South Sea'. Following the *Golden Hind* were John Winter in the *Elizabeth* and John Thomas in the tiny *Marigold*. They had made a fast passage of only sixteen days from the Atlantic, but after victualling with penguins they met a wild north-easterly gale during which the *Marigold* disappeared, never to be heard of again, and the *Elizabeth* lost touch with the flagship, eventually making her way back to England through the Straits.

This left Drake in the *Golden Hind*, a lone English ship on the Pacific coast of South America, and as she sailed north for the next few weeks through sunlit waters the voyage became more and more like a dream. On a warm summer's evening when he ghosted into the harbour of Valparaiso the galleon *Los Reyes* beat drums to welcome in the strange vessel, and her crew hospitably brought a jar of Chilean wine up on deck, never imagining for a moment that a ship on this coast could be anything but Spanish. Then came the shock of incredulous surprise. One of the newcomers started to behave most queerly: he suddenly laid about him with the flat of his sword, shouting 'Down dog' in Spanish. This was Thomas Moon, the carpenter, who had scuttled the *Swan* for Drake long ago on the coast of Darien. There was something supernatural about this sudden visitation to the unfortunate crew, who were still crossing themselves as they were hustled down below, all except one man of sterner fibre who leaped overboard and swam ashore to give the alarm. The mean little settlement of nine houses was deserted when the English landed, but they discovered an acceptable store of wine in a warehouse, and removed the altar cloth and Communion Plate from a chapel near the quay. The *Los Reyes* herself yielded a rich haul of gold, and something even more valuable just then, a chart of this unknown coast and its harbours. After this auspicious start in King Philip's South American dominions the *Golden Hind* sailed away from the 'Valley of Paradise' to the northward, now standing well out to sea, now running in towards the dusty shore with its backcloth of towering blue mountains; and almost every day brought that little company of Englishmen some fantastic new adventure.

The routine job of landing for water was never dull and it could be dangerous, as on the day when a sailor named Richard Miniver was killed while standing up alone against two hundred Spaniards to give his companions time to man their boat and escape. But it could also be wildly farcical, when on another occasion the delighted party came across a Spaniard fast asleep on the foreshore alongside thirteen bars of silver, and, tiptoeing up to him, 'we took the silver and left the man', as the officer in charge tersely reported. And as if that were not enough for one forenoon, after leaving the snoring Spaniard they met an Indian boy 'driving eight sheep of Peru, which are as big as asses; every of which sheep had on his back two bags of leather, each bag containing fifty pounds weight of fine silver'. This is the only recorded instance of a watering party returning to the ship with eight llamas and half a ton of silver.

The *Golden Hind* which sailed forward through those forbidden waters was about the size of a modern Thames sailing barge; she was of 100 tons and mounted a broadside of nine guns. She was the only armed vessel on the whole length of coast, so that for some weeks Drake held local command of the sea in an area where none but Spaniards had ever been before, many thousands of miles from his own land. She was a good sailer with the legs of anything she was likely to meet, and her well-disciplined crew, after months of working together, were far more of a team than any of the scratch crews in the Spanish coasting vessels. On Sundays, she put on a show for her own benefit by hoisting all her flags and streamers, so that the Cross of St. George and the green and white of the Tudors crackled in a fresh Pacific breeze. She was a proud ship, and the man that had made her so paced up and down her freshly-scrubbed quarterdeck before church. On his head he wore a gold embroidered 'sea capp' which the Queen herself had given him, and round his neck a green silk scarf on which her Maids of Honour had embroidered, 'The Lord guide and preserve thee until the ende'. For Drake was not the desperate adventurer he had been seven years before: he now held the Queen's Commission which he would show with a naïve pride to the captains of ships he captured. One of these Spaniards has described Drake as a short, stocky man with a reddish beard, crafty, yet still somehow boyish, direct of speech and with a liking for effect—a typical west-countryman in fact. He received this captain on the quarterdeck of the *Golden Hind* with the words,

'Accept with patience what is the usage of war'. That their two countries were at peace seems to have escaped the notice of both. But it was the gesture rather than the words themselves which mattered, for Drake had blossomed out into a magnifico, and the courteous speech accompanied by the doffing of his casque and a bow were all as much a part of his new role as the state he kept on board. At church on Sundays he knelt on an embroidered cushion, while his chaplain, Master Fletcher, with a fine disregard for liturgical propriety set out the altar cloth and silver plate which had been in use a short time before in the little Catholic church by the quay at Valparaiso. Later, the ship's trumpeters sounded off to announce the dinner hour, and after rinsing his hands in scented water held up by a kneeling page, Drake took his seat at the table in his great cabin, and only then did his waiting officers pull out their chairs. The viols started up, their music only faintly marred by the creaking from the leather thongs of the steering gear, and so Drake and his officers dined in state. The youngest son of a poor Bible reader had come a long way since he had tightened his belt like the rest of his famished men as they trudged back through the forest after his first unsuccessful attack on the mule trains outside Panama.

He was always ready to do the same again and his men knew it: trumpets might summon him to the meal during that first awful month of storm in the Pacific, but all he dined off in his great cabin was putrid penguin like the rest of them. Though he was strict and never overlooked a fault, 'he treated his men with affection and they treated him with respect', as an observant Spanish gentleman noted, unconsciously describing the type of discipline which was to obtain in the ships of another Queen Elizabeth nearly four hundred years later. The *Golden Hind* which sailed on through sparkling blue seas was a taut and therefore a happy ship, where every man of his own accord kept his arquebus clean because he would have been ashamed not to. After the Doughty affair in San Julian Bay over on the Atlantic coast the year before Drake was sure of himself and of his company. After the execution of Doughty for mutiny he had moulded officers and men into a team. 'I must have the gentlemen to haul and draw with the mariners, and the mariners with the gentlemen', he told them after the execution. 'What, let us show ourselves to be all of a company.' And a company they had become. At times he would hold a council in his great cabin when he would listen carefully to what each of his officers had to say, and when all had spoken Drake announced what he had decided to do—and after that there was no more discussion or argument. He kept a couple of textbooks for navigators and an account of Magellan's voyage in his cabin; but lying out on the table where all could see it was *Foxe's Book of Martyrs*—hardly light reading for a voyage round the world, nor was it meant to be; to Drake it came second only to the Bible. 'It is a very good book', he told a Spanish priest. 'Look at it. You will see here those who were martyred in Castile', showing him the gruesome and fanciful woodcuts, many of which his young nephew had coloured with his paints. In his spare time Drake and this nephew made water-colour sketches of prominent features along the coastline and of the harbours they entered, a hobby which troubled the Spaniards, for until now this whole coast had been a well-kept secret.

Communication by land between the settlements dotted huge distances apart along that coastline was difficult and slow and in places impossible, so that the Spaniards had to rely upon the sea; Drake was therefore able to keep ahead of the news of his arrival by making sure that he left no seaworthy vessel behind him before sailing on. He even found time to give the *Golden Hind* a short refit, which he had to do whenever he saw a chance because he could not tell when he would get another. So in a secluded bay the ship was careened and tallowed, the extra guns in her hold were mounted, and, as he had done before in the Caribbean, Thomas Moon, the carpenter, set up and rigged a pinnace which had been carried out in sections. Before the end of January, 1579, Drake was off again, drawing a blank in one port but in others picking up such booty as a few dozen bars of silver, 'each of them the fashion and bigness of a brickbat', and at each place he either disabled the shipping or towed it crewless out to sea and set it adrift. Silver brickbats might keep his men interested and happy, but all he had taken so far was small change compared to what

Drake was after: the voyage would not be 'made' until he had taken a fully-laden treasure ship, and at his next port of call he heard news of just such a vessel.

Early on the night of February 13th the *Golden Hind*, with all her sails drawing in the landward breeze, was heading for a high mass of land, hazy and indistinct in the moonlight, which marked the entrance to Callao, the principal harbour in Peru and the port of Lima, the capital. 'We found there', wrote an eyewitness in the *Golden Hind*, 'about twelve sail of ships lying fast moored at an anchor, having all their sails carried on shore; for the masters and merchants were most secure, having never been assaulted by enemies and at this time feared the approach of none such as we were'. Again surprise was complete and the crew of the *Golden Hind* were able to ransack at their leisure every ship in the main port of Peru. When it came to searching a hold nothing very much escaped those lynx-eyed men, but these ships had not yet been loaded and, apart from a few trifles, all they picked up here was news of another ship, *Nuestra Señora de la Concepcion*, a vessel loaded with a fabulous amount of treasure which had sailed with a long start for Payta, a port farther up the coast. 'Whereupon', notes the eyewitness, 'we stayed no longer here, but cutting the cables of the ships in the haven with all speed we followed her to Payta'.

Messengers had raced off to Lima eight miles away, and at about one in the morning, when Drake was working his ship out through the narrow entrance, word reached the Viceroy in his palace that something very odd was going on down in Callao. At first Don Francisco de Toledo was under the impression that some sort of a revolution had occurred in Chile and that ships from there had attacked Callao, but whatever the trouble was 'the Captain General of those realms' was going out to meet it. The bells of the Cathedral rang out over the sleeping city, messengers hurried from door to door calling upon the citizens to muster in the Cathedral Square, while Don Francisco hurriedly buckled on his armour and rode through the moonlit streets to the Square carrying the Royal Standard. With the light from blazing torches glinting from his armour he made an impressive figure as he sat his horse, holding the standard aloft only a few yards from where Francisco Pizarro the Conquistador lay in his tomb in the gloom of the Cathedral. Yawning citizens, some still pulling on their clothes, gathered round their Governor, and he had just started a rousing speech calling upon the people to rally to the standard of Philip their King, when news arrived by a more coherent messenger that the raiders at Callao were not Chileans but English corsairs. At this most of the citizens went back to bed again, but not so the Viceroy. He sent Captain Diego de Frias galloping down to Callao with a troop of horse, but when they drew rein at the waterfront they saw Drake's ship, a ghostly shape in the moonlight, already gliding past the headland out to sea. As he had shown before, de Frias was not the man to give up easily when he was on the trail of English pirates. He managed somehow to get the sails bent in the 'ship of Miguel Angel' (the very one which had brought Oxenham to Lima), and, though she was unarmed, embarked his soldiers and put to sea after the *Golden Hind*. It was a gallant effort, but stupid, and very luckily for him the ship was becalmed in the lee of a headland just outside the entrance, and when the sun rose he could discern the *Golden Hind* well out to sea with all sail set bowling away to the northward. Instead of being massacred by Drake's guns, therefore, de Frias and his men got out the sweeps and arrived back in harbour in time for breakfast.

Meanwhile, the Viceroy had had an idea: on two occasions now these English had appeared suddenly out of nowhere and each time the one thing he had desperately needed he did not possess on the whole length of the coast—an armed ship. Perhaps his English prisoners, who were very resourceful men, knew how to make cannon, which he could cast locally and so be ready for the next visitation which he was sure would come. Some days later, while Drake with the Humboldt Current under him and a cloud of seabirds screaming round the ship was moving swiftly northward over a sparkling sea, Oxenham and his companions were being taken singly down the long, dark corridors of the Inquisition building at Lima, for by now they had been moved from the city gaol. But instead of receiving their usual forenoon instruction in the Catholic faith they were taken one by one to a room in which three officials, all unknown to them, were sitting. This was to be an interrogation but with nothing terrifying about it; the Spaniards were suave and polite and the proceedings were almost friendly. Having been sworn to tell the truth, there came the first astonishing question: 'Are you familiar with the process of casting cannon?' Each prisoner in his turn answered, most probably truthfully, that he knew nothing at all of the subject. On further questioning each man owned to having made 'fire wings with nails', burning heads for arrows, and other devices for setting ships on fire.

But the Spaniards were not interested in these tricks, and the Englishman must have been wondering what on earth all this was about when a question was put which set his heart beating with a wild surge of hope: did he know whether the Queen intended fitting out vessels to come to the South Sea, and did he know of any Englishman who had entered the Straits of Magellan. At the next question one can imagine the gasp of surprise and joy, instantly suppressed; did he know one Francis Drake. Whatever the prisoners felt about this, they one and all gave guarded replies, but it was clear now that Drake was on the coast, and, to judge from the rumpus a few nights ago, not far away. If perhaps they felt that they might be mistaken in their guesses, all their doubts were removed when a little while later John Butler was summoned to translate into Spanish a safe-conduct in English given to the Captain of the *Señora de la Concepcion*, addressed to John Winter. It was signed 'Francis Drake'. We shall never know what dreams and hopes these prisoners tried to keep alive as the excitement died away and they dropped back into the old dreary routine which seemed eternal. But the months crawled slowly by, the rains came then gave way to fine weather, and they must have realized at last that rescue was not for them. All we do know is that a month after Drake had arrived safely back at Plymouth, gibbets were erected in the Square of the Inquisition, and when death came to three of them on a summer's day, John Oxenham, John Butler and the ship's master met it like men in the brilliance of a South American sun.

About a week after the interrogation on the making of cannon, and at a time when the hope of rescue must still have been running high among the English prisoners at Lima, Drake reached Payta only to find that his quarry had sailed and was still ahead of him. If he was to capture the treasure ship at all he must take her on this coast before she reached the traffic in the Gulf or the safety of Panama; but whatever the urgency Drake could not resist picking up a small coaster which he met just about on the Equator making her way south. At first sight it looked to be a waste of time, for her cargo was ropes and tackle and only such expert searchers as a *Golden Hind* boarding party would have discovered in amongst all this junk eighty pounds weight of gold and a large processional cross studded with emeralds the size of pigeons' eggs which had been consigned to one of the religious orders in Lima. Then Drake hurried on as best he could, keeping close in to the coast until he had rounded the westernmost point of South America, when he promised a golden chain to the man who first sighted the treasure ship, not that his crew needed any encouragement to keep a good look-out—the chase was on, and they had talked of little else since they had left the hump of Callao astern.

On Sunday, March 1st, the *Golden Hind* was off Cape Francisco, where the land starts to fall away to form the Gulf of Panama. At three o'clock in the afternoon—whether it was his watch or whether he was only after a breath of cool air we do not know—Drake's nephew climbed up to the maintop and won the golden chain: some way ahead and to seaward of them he sighted a ship which, from her size and appearance, could only be the *Nuestra Señora de la Concepcion*. The Spaniard shortened sail as if he were glad of company and waited courteously for the stranger to come up with him. This did not suit Drake who intended to make his sudden pounce after sundown and not in the full glare of day. The *Golden Hind* was overhauling the other and as he could not very well take in sail without giving his game away, he used the old dodge of reducing his speed by towing casks astern; and at the same time he stationed the pinnace out of sight close under his starboard quarter. So all through that grilling afternoon the two ships crept slowly northward until the sun dipped into the sea and the sudden tropic night came down. Then Drake cut the casks adrift and the *Golden Hind* forged quickly ahead.

His gunners were at their stations, their slowmatch hidden out of sight, his archers were at the ready as Drake came within hailing distance. At first the Spanish captain, San Juan de Anton, could not believe his ears as a summons to surrender came across the water; but when this was followed by the whistle of arrows, the flash and roar of cannon and his mizzen came down, he surrendered—he had not a weapon of any kind in his ship so there was little else that he could do. The pinnace surged up alongside and soon Englishmen were swarming over his decks, working his sails and taking over the helm. All three vessels headed for the open sea to get well clear of the coastal traffic route. But de Anton's surprises for the evening were not yet over: he was taken on board the English vessel where a short bearded man, removing his casque with a bow, greeted him in quite good Spanish with the words, 'Accept with patience what is the usage of war', as if nothing very much out of the ordinary had occurred; then this well-mannered stranger led the bewildered Spaniard to his own quarters. In the morning Drake explored his prize and during the next six days, in the utter loneliness of the ocean, her precious cargo was transferred; gold and jewels, great chests of bright, newly-minted coin and Peruvian silver by the ton were duly tallied and struck down into the hold of the *Golden Hind*—362,000 pesos worth of treasure so the Spanish authorities reported to their King. The voyage was 'made'. All this time Drake had entertained de Anton as an honoured guest in the great cabin; and indeed the whole operation seems to have been carried out with good humour on both sides for the Spanish pilot was cracking jokes as he said good-bye. Drake handed de Anton a safe-conduct addressed to John Winter and gave him a message for the Viceroy threatening reprisals if Oxenham and his officers were put to death. Then the empty treasure ship sheered off and de Anton's last sight of the *Golden Hind* was of a tiny ship, the Cross of St. George at her masthead showing bravely against the sky, as she stood away to the northward.

SPANISH TREASURE IN THE PACIFIC

Drake wanted to keep well clear of the Gulf of Panama with its calms and light airs, for he guessed that any ships dispatched from Lima would make straight for the Gulf. And that is where the Viceroy's punitive expedition went looking for him, against the advice of the most experienced seaman in it who wanted to make a cast to the northward along the coast of New Spain, or what are now Guatemala and Nicaragua. As that is where Drake had gone the expedition returned empty-handed and Diego de Frias, amongst others, was heavily fined for inefficiency. While this ineffectual search was in progress Drake was in Nicaraguan waters where, in the moonlight before the dawn of April 4th, 1579, the keen eyes of the *Golden Hind's* look-out sighted a ship ahead. At that hour of the night everyone on board the stranger except the helmsman was fast asleep, so she was taken without a shot being fired. Her captain and owner turned out to be a Spanish gentleman of high birth and culture, Don Francisco de Zarate, with whom Drake was only too glad to be friendly. The captain of any ship is a lonely man and in de Zarate Drake met someone to whom he could talk openly on matters which he could not discuss with his officers; and from their conversations it is clear that Drake had kept bottled up a number of things that had been troubling him. First there was the longing to be considered respectable; he was at great pains to show that he was an honest sailor carrying out his Queen's orders and no pirate, that all he had done on the American coast was justified because of the harm Spaniards had done to the Queen's subjects, that he and Hawkins had been robbed of over a million at San Juan de Ulua; and that reminded him, did de Zarate by any chance know Don Francisco Enriquez, Governor of Mexico? De Zarate did, though he thought it wiser not to add that he was a close friend. 'Well', declared Drake with that touch of the theatre he could never resist, 'it would give me greater pleasure to come across him than all the gold and silver of the Indies'. And so, pacing the deck of de Zarate's ship or sitting at ease in the great cabin of the *Golden Hind*, Drake went on to talk of the Doughty affair, wondering if he had handled it correctly and asking his friend what he thought. De Zarate told Drake that under the circumstances Drake could

104

not have done anything else, even if it was drastic. The Spaniard was not the sort of man who would lie out of politeness or policy even to one who had him in his power. He wore the Order of St. James and was cousin to that Duke of Medina-Sidonia whose fleet Drake and others were to encounter nine years later in the English Channel.

For two whole days and more the self-made Englishman and the aristocratic Spaniard, who could recognize genius when he met it, enjoyed each other's company in the remote waters off Guatemala. Perhaps the nature of the cargo had something to do with their accord for it consisted of Chinese linen, silks and porcelain, too bulky to be worth the taking, if indeed there were any space left in the tiny hold of the *Golden Hind*, and after giving it a thorough looking-over Drake took none of it. But when he came to de Zarate's personal possessions he chose some rolls of silk and a few pieces of porcelain, explaining with many apologies that he wanted to take home a little present for his wife; then, having borrowed de Zarate's pilot to show him where to water, he gave a handful of money to each member of the Spanish crew and said good-bye to his friend. The pilot took Drake into the minute settlement of Guatulco where he watered and victualled, and Thomas Moon relieved a portly official, whom he met hurrying out of the town, of a golden chain.

Drake's luck held the whole of his time in Spanish American waters and his last capture was both timely and valuable. Two Pacific pilots with all their charts and sailing directions were on their way to Panama in a small coasting vessel to take over a ship bound for the Philippines when Drake captured them and took their charts. Then, in the words of one of Drake's officers, 'Our General at this place and time, thinking himself both in respect of his private injuries received from the Spaniards as also of their contempts and indignities offered to our country and prince in general, sufficiently satisfied and revenged, proposed to continue no longer upon the Spanish coast, but began to consider and consult the best way to our country'. In other words, having got all he could out of this part of the world, Drake thought it time to be on his way home. And whatever his officers may have advised he had already decided to go by way of the Moluccas and the Indian Ocean.

On April 16th, 1579, Drake left Spanish American waters, his ship deep in the water with the weight of treasure, after a raid which had again shown the Spaniards the futility of trying to carry on seaborne trade with no fighting ships to protect the seaways. He had taken a King's ransom, he had brought all Spanish coastal trade in the Pacific to a standstill for months, but from that evening when he sailed into Valparaiso to the morning when he sailed away from Guatemala he had not taken a single Spanish life. As he made his way northwards against baffling winds a stream of dispatches ranging from the reports of Viceroys to the depositions of humble sailors were on their way in fast dispatch boats across the Atlantic to King Philip of Spain. Whether from Viceroy or petty local official, military commander or dignitary of the Church, ship's captain or sailor the tone of each was the same: sober, objective with no sensation or wild abuse of Drake. Four hundred years later they are a commentary upon the type of man who carried on the affairs of the King in his South American dominions. When each had been studied and annotated, sometimes by the King's own hand, it was marked, 'To be put with what concerns Drake', or as they would say today in Whitehall, 'File under Drake'. It was a file that for the next seventeen years was to be in continual use.

Early in June Drake sailed into a good harbour on the coast of what is now California. Here he proceeded to give the *Golden Hind* a thorough refit which she needed badly. The local natives turned out to be so friendly that he did not need the fort he had built to protect his stores and treasure when the ship was cleared for her refit. He took formal possession of the country for his Queen naming it New Albion because its white cliffs reminded him of England, then, leaving a sixpenny piece nailed to a post as proof of ownership, at the end of July he set out into the Pacific and was soon in the north-east trades. For week after week the *Golden Hind* sailed on, a tiny speck in the immensity of sea and sky, where only the flying-fish twittering away from her bows or an occasional albatross soaring across her wake knew of her intrusion. After two months they sighted the Pelew group of islands in the Philippine Sea, and as the typhoon season was past they arrived safely in November at Ternate, one of the Spice Islands—the home of the clove.

The housewife who so casually pops half a dozen cloves into an apple pie or grates a little nutmeg over a junket is using spices which changed the course of history, For the clove grew nowhere else but in the five tiny islands of the Moluccas and it was the magnet which drew Columbus, Vasco da Gama and Magellan into unknown seas. The fabulous East might contain gold and jewels in quantity, but what these seamen were really hoping to discover for their royal patrons was the mysterious source of those spices which fetched such a large price in Europe. For centuries the spice trade had been the monopoly of Moslems, a state of affairs highly distasteful to Christian monarchs: Arab dhows and baggalas, using the monsoon winds of the Indian Ocean, brought the cinnamon of Java and Ceylon, the cloves and nutmegs from the distant Moluccas and the pepper from Southern India to the Red Sea and Persian Gulf for camel caravans to deliver the cargoes across the desert to Venetian merchants in the Levant. When Portuguese caravels brought these cargoes to Europe round the Cape, by-passing the Mediterranean, the days of Venice as a great maritime power were over. And now the first Englishman had come nosing his way into this centuries-old preserve.

After the tedium and discomfort of that long Pacific crossing, the beauty of Ternate must have made an impression even on such a hard-boiled lot as the crew of the *Golden Hind*. Tropical fish more fantastically coloured than any court gallant darted about in the crystal clear water, while the island itself seemed to consist chiefly of a towering, cone-shaped mountain which continually smoked. Dark green foliage covered its lower slopes and the level ground round its base. These were the groves of clove trees each some thirty feet high which flourished in the rich volcanic soil, for the smoking mountain was an ever-active volcano. A soft fragrance drifted out from the shore, compounded of the pungency of cloves, the cloying sweetness of

107

frangipane and the scent of nutmeg. It was an offshore breeze that told of riches far above the silver of Peru. Drake stayed four days during which he and the local sultan exchanged presents and, during a visit to the ship, the Sultan 'seemed to be much delighted with the sound of our music'. Drake and the Sultan came to a rather sketchy verbal agreement whereby the Sultan promised to sell his produce only to the English in return for their protection against the Portuguese. Drake always referred to this as a 'treaty', but both parties must have known that it had about as much substance as any other customary oriental civilities. However, Drake sailed with a store of fresh victuals and six tons of cloves—and at that time cloves were fetching more than five shillings a pound on the London market.

Drake careened the *Golden Hind* at an island populated only by 'bats as large as hens and crayfish of exceeding bigness'. Then he sailed on through one of the most treacherously beautiful seas in the world, full of islands hardly distinguishable from the purple clouds of dawn where the smooth surface of the water hid rocks and shoals, and sudden currents swirled the ship about. While making his way cautiously to the southward at eight o'clock on the evening of January 9th the *Golden Hind* was brought up all standing on a submerged rock. The wind was keeping the ship on the rock, the water astern was too deep for her to kedge off and for a time it looked as if this were the end—a ship full of treasure stuck fast in an unknown sea. In a crisis of this sort Drake was always at his best: 'our General', wrote one of his officers, 'as he had always hitherto shewed himself courageous, and of good confidence in the mercy and protection of God, so now he continued in the same'. The hands were mustered for prayers and the chaplain administered the sacrament to every man (most probably using the Communion Plate which had been picked up at Valparaiso so long ago). After that Drake and his men got busy helping themselves. Eight guns and three tons of cloves were jettisoned, and after twenty hours hard and fast, 'the wind, as it were in a moment by the special grace of God changing from the starboard to the larboard of the ship, we hoisted our sails and the happy gale drove our ship off the rock into the sea again, to the no little comfort of all our hearts'. Again Drake had Providence or luck with him—call it what you will—for the rock was shelving and smooth so that the ship's bottom had not been pierced or stove in, and instead of settling when she floated off the *Golden Hind* sailed on as seaworthy as ever.

Drake careened and victualled again before the long voyage home, then at last in March, 1580, he was clear of that dangerous part of the world and the *Golden Hind* was plunging her nose into a long ocean swell, glad again to be in her true element. There now followed a most astonishing feat. Drake took his departure from Java on March 26th; he made his first landfall, the Cape of Good Hope—'a most stately thing and the fairest Cape we saw in the whole circumference of the earth'—on June 18th, but sailed on into the Atlantic, not touching land until he arrived at Sierra Leone on July 22nd. After watering he made the long leg out into the Atlantic to cross the trades until he picked up the westerlies to waft him up the Channel.

When he spoke a fishing boat off Cawsand on September 26th the fisherman answered his hail that Her Grace the Queen was alive and well, but added that there was the plague in Plymouth. Then the *Golden Hind* was sailing swiftly across the smooth water of Plymouth Sound and they were home. But because of the plague and because he was not too certain what his reception by the Queen might be, instead of proceeding up the Cattewater, Drake anchored to seaward of St. Nicholas Island. His homecoming after one of the most astonishing feats of navigation and the most successful privateering voyage ever accomplished was quiet, almost furtive. The Mayor of Plymouth came off to the ship bringing with him Drake's wife, and the first Englishman to sail round the world probably got as great a thrill from displaying the presents, the porcelain, silks and taffetas, he had brought all the way from Guatemala, as from the feeling of achievement given by the navigation itself. For, more than the presence on board of his cousin the Mayor, more than the old familiar green fields and red earth of Devon seen through the stern port of his cabin, the delivery of these gifts made him appreciate the extraordinary fact that he was home at last.

CHAPTER VII

Northwards to Cathay

*

The Queen might be in good health, but much had been happening while Drake was away. Elizabeth had lost her privileged position in Europe: no longer could she play off Philip of Spain against the House of Guise. After the massacre of St. Bartholomew's Eve, in which Drake and his men had been so little interested when Captain Le Testu told them about it on the coast of Darien, the cleavage in France became more a matter of religion than of politics, with the Guises the champions of Catholicism in France. It was only natural that they should reach an understanding with Philip, champion of Catholicism the world over, and suddenly Elizabeth the Protestant found herself alone opposed to Philip the Catholic, who now had no need to keep Elizabeth on the throne of England.

To add to her anxieties, Philip had strengthened his position in the world when the old King of Portugal died leaving no children. There were a number of claimants to his throne and very desirable overseas possessions. Among these claimants was Philip of Spain, and it is not surprising that he turned out to be the successful one. He was on the spot and could back his claim with the finest army in Europe. At one swoop he had gained all Portugal's colonial empire and trading posts. East or west of the famous line Philip now had no competitor in world trade, excepting always those trespassers the English. Not that they were much concerned over his gains in Africa or the Indian Ocean, the acquisitions which disturbed English statesmen more than any others were the Portuguese fleet of twelve fighting galleons in good condition and a reserve of seamen, and, even more important, the fine strategic base of the Azores half-way across the Atlantic.

In the last couple of years Elizabeth's position had been weakened and Drake's sudden reappearance, his hold bulging with Spanish silver, did nothing to improve matters. The Spanish Ambassador in London, de Mendoza, made indignant protests demanding the return of the treasure, and the head of Drake— not that de Mendoza can have expected to get much satisfaction from the Queen. He got none. Elizabeth had her answer ready and when it came she made it appear as if England and not Spain were the aggrieved party. By ill treating her subjects, the Queen informed him, the Spaniards had brought all this on themselves; Spain owed her a large amount for the money she had been forced to spend in putting down rebellions fomented by Spain in Ireland and England; and womanlike, Elizabeth kept her most telling point till the last. Spain, she maintained, had no right to the whole of America, nor to try and prevent the free navigation of the oceans, 'seeing that the use of sea and air is common to all and neither nature, nor public use, nor custom can permit any possession thereof'. So much for the Spanish Ambassador, but there remained her own people. Burghley and some of the Council disapproved of the venture so strongly that they refused handsome presents which Drake offered them; but there was little mistaking what the nation as a whole felt on the subject.

The people of England looked upon Drake as a hero, while the Spanish Ambassador called him 'The Master Thief of the Unknown Sea'. The colossal cheek of the exploit appealed to them. But the man in the street had missed the real significance of the voyage: he was entranced by the glittering plunder, the gold, the silver, the rustling silks—whereas a few tons of unromantic cloves were far more important. The first Englishman had carried on trade of a sort in the Far East; that was the greatest achievement of the voyage. Elizabeth interpreted her people's mood with her customary insight: Drake was the people's darling, therefore he should be hers also. She sent for this man whom Burghley considered a pirate, and on his arrival gave him an audience lasting six hours; and every day after that singled him out of the crowd, 'often walking with him in the garden', as the Spanish Ambassador wrote in one of his vivid letters to King Philip. After depositions had been taken from the whole of the ship's company, from which it was clear that there had been no unnecessary violence or bloodshed, Elizabeth gave orders that when an inventory was made of the cargo before sending it to the Tower, only those items should be included which Drake chose to declare. Added to his previous takings this made Drake a very rich man, but the Queen could afford to be generous, for the cargo was worth a million and a half and she herself was a large shareholder in the venture. Elizabeth ordered the *Golden Hind* round to Deptford and on a spring morning, in her gilded barge with its liveried watermen, she visited Drake in state. Did the Spaniard want his head, she laughed, and ordered one of the Court with a golden sword to make him knight on his own quarterdeck, and afterwards, in the great cabin sat down with the new knight to a banquet, 'finer than has ever been seen in England since King Henry', as de Mendoza, who had not been invited, reported to his King.

The gay ceremony that April morning at Deptford, was something more than the conferring of a knighthood; it was calculated defiance of Spain, and from what more appropriate place could a Sovereign of England throw down the gage than from the quarterdeck of a ship? The Queen had at last come out into the open and approved officially of what her seamen had been doing. It was by the use she made of the sea that England had so often injured Spain during the last decade: the countless piracies and trespasses of English seamen in the Spanish dominions; the confiscation of the ships carrying money to Alva for his army in the Netherlands; and, though Philip thought Elizabeth had engineered it when she had not, the capture of Brill and Flushing by De la Marcq and his 'Beggars of the Sea' which had touched off the revolt in the Netherlands; the appearance of English soldiers, 'smart men in red coats' in the Low Countries; and now this latest wholesale plunder by Drake. All this was provocation enough, but Philip II, as one of those discerning Venetian ambassadors summed him up, 'was a prince who fought with gold rather than with steel, by his brain rather than with his arms. He acquired more by sitting still, by negotiation and diplomacy than his father did by armies and war'. So Philip sat still, hoping that the English problem might be solved by a Catholic revolt in England or by the assassination of Elizabeth. Letters from his ambassador in England showed that more and more England was becoming a power to be reckoned with: in January of this year de Mendoza had warned him that the English were building ships without cessation and were thus making themselves masters of the sea, that English ships were trading with the Levant, that an expedition was fitting out to discover a short cut to China north-westwards round America, after their latest attempt had failed to open a way eastward along the top of Europe.

The underlying cause of all this activity was the need to find new markets for English woollen cloth. For centuries England's true wealth had been her superb wool which all Europe demanded, and since the English had taken to weaving it themselves they had captured the cloth market of the Continent. But the convenient markets near home had now been closed to English merchants. When, early in Elizabeth's reign, Cardinal Granvelle, the Spanish Governor of the Netherlands had forbidden the import of English cloth in an early example of what today is called 'economic sanctions', the merchants had moved to Hamburg. Their success was too much for the Hansa towns, who soon squeezed the thrusting English out of the Baltic. If nearby markets were to be closed to them, then English merchants would seek new ones across the oceans of the world.

> Our well rigged ships will stretch their swelling wings
> And drag their anchors through the sandy foam,
> About the world in every clime to roam.

So the poet Drayton voiced the feeling of his day. This urge in Englishmen to sail away from their pleasant land was not caused by any itch for conquest—the English did not covet Spanish overseas possessions—or by a thirst for knowledge, but by the need to trade. It was this quest for markets that sent

English ships into unknown seas, that led them to the frozen coasts of Muscovy in the far north, to the Baltic and the Levant, even to the fogbound coasts of Greenland, for men were firm in their belief that there was a short cut to Cathay, imagined to be the most lucrative market of all. 'Our chiefe desire', wrote Hakluyt, 'is to find out ample vent of our wollen cloth, the naturall commodite of this our Realme, and the fittest place I find for that purpose are the manifold islands of Japan and the Northern parts of China and the regions of Tartary next adjoining'.

Englishmen were obsessed by this mirage of Cathay, although the most learned had only a vague idea of its whereabouts and none at all of what the place would turn out to be like if anyone ever reached there. But they were convinced that a short cut existed at the top of the world by which Cathay could be reached without the long voyage round the Cape. In May, 1580, when Drake was somewhere in the middle of the Indian Ocean on his way home, the Muscovy Company made its last attempt to reach 'the Northern parts of China' by a north-east passage. The Company chose Arthur Pet, who was one of its most experienced captains, and Charles Jackman, who made a name for himself as a pilot in two Arctic voyages under Frobisher, to command respectively the *George* of forty tons, and the *William* of only twenty—tiny cockleshells to attempt the most hazardous passage in the world. But if the ships were small and neither of them much larger than Drake's pinnace, the captains had the benefit of reams of instructions and advice from the leading geographers in England. Advice which optimistically laid down the conduct to be observed on arrival in Cathay and instructions to push on through the Kara Sea and then, 'In God's Name to proceed eastwards with the land on the starboard hand until Cathay is reached'. No doubt it all looked possible on an inaccurate chart in the security of a cosy study, but things look different up in the Barents Sea, even at midsummer. Incredible as it may seem to anyone who has sailed those waters, the two ships sailed round the North Cape of Norway beyond the White Sea, and passing to the southward of Nova Zembla they actually pushed on into the Kara Sea. After a couple of months of the most intense cold in fog and ice, and of trying to make headway against the screaming squalls which followed one another out of the east, the two captains saw that it was hopeless and turned for home. Pet managed to reach England, but Jackman who wintered in Northern Norway was never heard of again.

Many years before Charles Jackman died up in the Barents Sea, no one knows exactly how or where, another servant of the Russia Company, 'Anthonie Jenkinson, gentleman' had reached a point by land considerably nearer to Cathay than ever the seamen were to reach on their Arctic voyages east or west. On the day that Elizabeth was crowned, and while the young Queen was enjoying the tableaux in the City, the Rose pageant in Gracechurch Street, the singing children at Temple Bar, this Jenkinson and two companions were in Central Asia beyond the Caspian Sea and across the Oxus investigating the possibilities of trade in the great caravan junction of Bokhara. Dust, flies, dirt and the hubbub of a jostling crowd talking a babel of unknown tongues did not prevent these Englishmen from making a careful survey: looking over the silks of excitable Persians, fingering the cotton goods of the patient cross-legged merchants just arrived from India, or examining the hides and sheepskins of uncouth Russians. But because of wars on the caravan route across the Central Asian plateau they met no merchants from China, though they did learn that from Bokhara to Cathay took nine months by caravan. As Jenkinson had taken eight months to reach Bokhara from Moscow, he realized that trade with China overland could never be a paying proposition, and he also discovered that none of the foreign merchants in the bazaars of Bokhara would trade in the broadcloth and kerseys he had brought from England.

Jenkinson had sailed to Russia in command of the convoy which took back to his own country the Russian Ambassador, who had come over to England when Chancellor had been drowned in Pitsligo Bay. From Moscow Jenkinson had made his way overland to the Volga and down that river to the port of Astrakhan, where he bought a boat and so was the first Englishman to fly the red Cross of St. George on the Caspian Sea. By the time he and his companions reached Bokhara they had qualified for the record as Elizabethans, because the young Queen had ascended the throne in November. Jenkinson returned to London in 1560, after a journey which he described as 'so miserable, dangerous and chargeable as my penne is not able to describe the same', with much useful information, an interesting but inaccurate map of his travels and a yak's tail. He was not exaggerating: he had crossed the Arctic Sea and waterless deserts; he had lived on strange foods and roughed it across half a continent; he had fought off robbers and had been forced to pay heavy tolls to Turkoman chieftains, and at the end of it all his journey had been for nothing.

But Jenkinson was not the sort of man to be put off by hardship, danger or disappointment, and the following year he was back in Moscow on his way this time to the Court of the 'Grand Sophie' or Shah of Persia with letters from Queen Elizabeth. After sailing down the Volga and through the Caspian to the port of Darbend in the province of Shirvan he reached Kasvin in November, 1562. Thousands of miles away in the Atlantic another Elizabethan in search of trade, John Hawkins, was victualling his ships at the Canaries outward bound on the first of his voyages. Towards the end of November Jenkinson was admitted to audience of the Shah and the Englishman got off to a bad start. When he produced the 'Queenes Majesties letters' which were written in Latin, Hebrew and Italian, the Shah caustically pointed out that not a soul in his dominions could read a word of those languages. That was a poor enough beginning and the end came quickly when the Shah, after closely questioning Jenkinson, discovered that he was a Christian. The Englishman was dismissed from the presence, while to make matters worse, a Persian with a bucketful of sand followed Jenkinson all the way to the palace gate sprinkling sand in his footsteps, for, being an infidel, the ground he trod was defiled. For some time, Jenkinson was in danger of his life and was only saved by Abdullah Khan, the governor of the Persian province of Shirvan, of whom he had made a great friend on his way down to Kasvin. After some weeks, during which the Shah was considering sending Jenkinson as a 'present' to the 'Grand

Turke', he was finally allowed to depart unharmed. On the way back he met his friend Abdullah Khan, who seems to have been an independent sort of governor with a mind of his own because he signed an agreement allowing the Russia Company to trade free of customs dues with his province of Shirvan. Jenkinson reached London towards the end of 1564 after being away for over three years. He had opened up trade relations between England and Persia, and he was the first of a long succession of Englishmen who by sheer force of character have gained the trust and friendship of the most unlikely Asiatic chieftains.

Although Jenkinson had shown that trade to China overland by way of Moscow, with that difficult sea passage to start with, could never be feasible, and that the prospects of dealings with Persia were no better, the Russia Company would not be discouraged. Others of its servants made a succession of hazardous journeys, for with English obstinacy they were determined to trade with the East and they would not give in. So they were attacked by savage Tartar tribesmen, frozen in on the Volga, sunk by pirates on the Caspian, and even besieged for a whole winter in Astrakhan during a local war. Some of these men died violent deaths, others of fever, lying uncared for in alien cities. For twenty years they kept on trying, always with the hope that somehow they would be able to open a route through Persia to the spice port of Ormuz on the Persian Gulf, to India, or even beyond. The Russia Company only gave up when William Harborne obtained trading concessions from the Sultan of Turkey and the Queen granted a charter to the Levant Company to reopen trade through the Mediterranean—a much easier way of getting a share in Eastern trade than by the roundabout and expensive overland route. None of this journeying through Russia affected Spain, but it was the use of the Mediterranean and the renewed trading by sea which caused de Mendoza to write with concern to his King. This acute Spanish Ambassador saw clearly enough that Spain, with her possessions sprawling across the world, could not exist without dominion of the seas, and at the rate England was going she would soon be able to challenge his country for that dominion. For the same reason he thought it his duty to report English attempts to discover a north-west passage to Cathay, not that he feared they would ever find one, but because in the process of trying the English were becoming so expert at sea.

The existence of a north-west passage was accepted on the flimsiest of evidence; it was even argued that because there was a passage through to the Pacific (the Straits of Magellan) at the southern extremity of the American Continent there must be something very like it up in the north. The maps of European cartographers, though attractively embellished, were grotesquely inaccurate, and hardly any theory was too fantastic to appear as fact. Islands, seas, and even continents which owed their existence only to myth, hearsay or a disordered imagination were neatly engraved on the blank spaces of their charts as having substance. So King Solomon's fabled land of Ophir appeared in the Southern Pacific; and a passage into that ocean was shown on the sole evidence of a Florentine sea captain who, on a hurried voyage up the eastern seaboard of North America, had mistaken Chesapeake Bay for a clear water passage from the Atlantic to the Pacific. Cast-iron or even plausible evidence, however, is seldom necessary to convince a man of the truth of what he wants to believe; and there was a school of thought in England which held that a navigable north-west passage was there for anyone who had the initiative to go to find it. There were backers in the City of London and in the west country prepared to stake their fortunes on their opinion and sailors to risk their lives in the attempt. The search for this non-existent passage produced a generation of seamen who were to play their part in the war with Spain at sea, the chief among them being a tough, hot-tempered Yorkshireman named Martin Frobisher.

At the age of twenty Frobisher had arrived in London from Yorkshire to make his fortune, and because the best way for a young man of spirit to get on in the world was by going to sea, he embarked almost at once on a Guinea voyage. The Guinea trade was a hard school where the mortality was high, but Frobisher survived, and after a time tried the Levant trade in which he was lucky enough to make a friend of the son of a City Alderman, Michael

Lok, who was one of those who believed that there was a north-west passage. After some ten years of trading voyages Frobisher seems to have decided that he was not getting on fast enough, because he was had up before the authorities, 'on suspicion of having fitted out a vessel as a pirate'. So far Frobisher had not made a great success of his life and had to take employment where he could find it, so, deciding against piracy as a career, he served for a time on the Irish coast before turning up in London in 1574, where his friend Michael Lok was by now a man of standing in the City. He was also in the confidence of the select coterie of geographers and mathematicians who met in Dr. Dee's cosy library at Mortlake to hold endless discussions on the north-west passage. In contrast to these respectable theorists Martin Frobisher was a rather seedy master mariner with a none too respectable past. But though he had little time for abstruse mathematics and theoretical speculation, he was known to be a first-class practical seaman of immense physical courage, the sort of man ready to take on anything with a chance of profit in it. He was, in fact, whatever his past, the very man they were looking for to prove their theories. He and Lok decided to try for the north-west passage, though Lok found it difficult to find backers for a voyage with Frobisher in command. However, the money was found somehow, and the Queen even was induced to give her blessing to the venture, but that was all—she refused to take any shares. Nor would the City merchants subscribe towards it, and in the end Michael Lok had to put up most of the money himself. This was only enough to provide two small vessels of twenty-five tons and a ten-ton pinnace, carrying in all thirty-four men. A puny little fleet for what it was expected to do, because the experts had no idea that the mainland of Asia was so far away; they believed that Asia narrowed up north into a sort of finger stretching out towards North America.

On June 8th, 1576, Martin Frobisher in the *Gabriel* with the *Michael* dropped down from Deptford to Blackwall, saluting the Queen with a volley of their ordnance as they passed Greenwich and being rewarded with a wave of her hand out of a Palace window. About a month later Frobisher's navigator saw the jutting crags of the Greenland coast 'rising like pinnacles of steeples' in the afternoon sun. But soon after the hazards of the Arctic and the unknown proved too much for his companion. When a storm came howling down upon them and the pinnace foundered with all hands, the *Michael* 'mistrusting the matter conveyed themselves privily away and returned home with great report that Frobisher was cast away'.

But not a bit of it. Frobisher, with his main-mast sprung and his topmast gone, was still afloat and undismayed. He sailed on alone through that silent, mysterious sea until he entered a stretch of water with land on either hand. He at once jumped to the conclusion that he was in the passage described for him by the London geographers—that was America to port and Asia over there to starboard—so he named the place 'Frobisher's Straits' to match Magellan's at the other end of the Continent. It was not long before the name was altered to Frobisher Bay, because instead of entering a strait he had only sailed into a gulf formed by two promontories jutting out from the eastern end of what is now called Baffin Land.

On going ashore, Frobisher found that the local Eskimoes were eager to trade sealskins and furs for the looking-glasses, bells and other trifles that the English had brought with them. They came on board the *Gabriel* and seemed so friendly and peaceable that five of the *Gabriel's* men, with that feckless lack of discipline so common in Elizabethan seamen, took the ship's only boat without the captain's permission, in the hope of doing a little private trading of their own. They were captured by the Eskimoes and that was the end of them. It was also the end of the voyage, for the *Gabriel* now had no boat and only thirteen of her crew left, barely enough to work the ship home. So Frobisher failed to discover that he was not in a strait at all, but in a cul-de-sac; not that he appears to have been over-concerned where he was; he had quite enough to impress his backers on his return, except for one thing. Boat or no boat he was determined to take an Eskimo back to England as ocular proof that he had actually reached Asia. So he leaned out over the ship's side ringing a bell and pretending to offer it to the Eskimoes swarming off the ship in their kayaks.

At last one left the others and, paddling close in to the side, reached up for the fascinating toy. Frobisher promptly dropped the bell and with one hand hauled the man, kayak and all, out of the sea on to the *Gabriel's* deck. Then he sailed away and arrived at Harwich in October, 1576, with a 'strange infidel' and a piece of stone that one of his men had brought on board in the Arctic. The poor Eskimo soon died and people forgot all about him and his Asiatic appearance in the excitement caused by that lump of black stone. It transformed the search for a north-west passage, which had something heroic about it, into a rather sordid mining speculation.

Shortly before entering his 'Straits' Frobisher had sent a boat ashore at a small island off Baffin Land with orders to bring off some object, it did not matter what it was, as evidence that the ship had found land. Some came off with armfuls of the local vegetation, moss, flowers and grass, but one man with a little more sense returned with something durable, 'a piece of black stone, much like to sea coal in colour, which by the weight seemed to be some kind of metal or mineral'. Frobisher kept it as a souvenir and thought no more about it until a friend in London asked him what he had brought back from the strange land; whereupon Frobisher handed him the piece of black stone. The friend had it assayed and, although English goldsmiths pronounced it worthless, an unscrupulous Italian reported that it contained gold. At that a rumour flew round that the expedition had found a rich deposit—gold. In those days a mere whisper of the magic word was enough to unbalance the judgement of normally sane, hard-headed individuals, and not only of Englishmen. Nobles and rulers on the Continent were for ever parting with large sums to quacks who professed to be able to manufacture gold out of base metals, and the quacks did well until they ended on the gallows. Philip II of Spain believed the advisers who told him that there were islands near the Moluccas formed entirely of gold. In the breathless excitement of living in an expanding world, where anything seemed to be possible, it is not altogether surprising that men who were obsessed by the thought of gold should conclude that any new land must contain quan-

tities of the metal. Those Elizabethans were by no means the last
to take shares in a non-existent goldmine. People tumbled over
themselves to subscribe towards a new expedition; and the City
which had been so lukewarm before the previous voyage, now
headed by the great Sir Thomas Gresham, gave its backing. The
Queen promised £1,000 and poor Lok managed to raise another
£300. The Cathay Company was formed, and a penniless sea
captain, with a wife and children starving in a single room out at
Hampstead, found himself appointed 'High Admiral of England
in Cathay'.

The fiction was preserved that the next voyage also was being
made in order to find the short cut into the Pacific; though everyone knew very well that the real purpose was to get a supply of
that gold-bearing ore. Frobisher was quite open about it: he
made no pretence at further exploration and as soon as he had
loaded the ore hurried back with it to England.

After an audience of the Queen he joined his fleet which was
swinging round its anchors at Blackwall and boarded his flagship
the *Aid* of 200 tons, a ship lent by the Queen. Lok's pair of small
merchant vessels were going out again with Edward Fenton now
commanding the *Gabriel* and Gilbert York the *Michael*. There
were waiting on board these ships 120 men, including mining
experts and, for a reason which is not clear, six condemned
criminals who were to be landed with a store of arms and provisions in Greenland. There happened also to be a number of
unauthorized passengers, 'proper men', George Best calls them.
On May 26th, 1577, Whit Sunday, the fleet weighed, to anchor
again that evening at Gravesend; and next day 'we all received
Communion by the minister of Gravesend aboard the *Aid*, and
prepared us as good Christians towards God, and resolute men
for all fortunes'. On putting into Harwich for water and victuals
Frobisher found orders from the Council strictly forbidding him
to sail with more than his authorized complement. Accordingly
he sent ashore the extra passengers and also the six condemned
men 'which he thought for some purpose very needful for the
voyage'. It would be interesting to know what Frobisher had in
mind for these poor wretches. After a call at the Orkneys he sent

a last mail back to England by some English fishing boats home-ward bound from Iceland, and sailed out towards the Arctic. Then came twenty-six days of boisterous weather in the course of which they sighted 'many monstrous fishes and strange fowls which seemed to live only by the sea, being there so far distant from any land'; until on July 4th the *Michael* which was guide of the fleet suddenly fired a gun thinking that she had sighted land through the fog. The visibility improved and at ten o'clock that night they were able to recognize the high rugged coast and snow-capped mountains of Greenland. Next morning the ship's company of the *Aid* enjoyed a change of diet when they caught a halibut on an unbaited hook, a fish which they found good eating, if a little rich for stomachs accustomed by now to a meagre ration of salt cod. Frobisher did not stay long among the towering ice-bergs, the sudden fogs and the perpetual noise of grinding pack-ice along this coast, but shaped a course for his 'Straits'.

The *Michael* lost her topmasts on the way and suffered other damage in a storm which dispersed the ships over a sea thickly dotted with icebergs; but by the middle of July they had regained contact and arrived safely at the locality where the first ore had been discovered. However, when Frobisher landed with his mining experts 'he could not get in all that island a piece so big as a walnut where the first was found'. They found a deposit some-where else which the experts pronounced to be of even better quality, and quarrying operations soon began with Frobisher turning the first sod. By July in these latitudes the soil has thawed to a depth of two or three inches, but below that the ground is iron hard. On still days it is pleasantly warm in the sun though the air temperature may be well below freezing, but the least wind cuts like a knife and Frobisher's men had no clothing suitable for Arctic conditions. For the next five weeks gentlemen as well as sailors worked in gangs, blunting picks and crowbars in the ground, hauling the full baskets down to the boats in the crackling ice then squelching back through the spongy mud for more. It was an eerie, barren land with forbidding white mountains inland and fantastically-shaped bergs forever sailing out at sea. The work on an inadequate diet was hard and monotonous but they kept at it, only breaking off to see to the safety of their ships which were often in danger from the sluicing tides, the sudden gales or drifting ice; and on one occasion from fire when they only just got on board in time after something had gone wrong with the galley funnel of the flagship.

Frobisher, who could not forget the loss of those five men on his first voyage, had a low opinion of all Eskimoes—being of a 'subtle and cruel disposition'—yet 400 years ago they seem to have been not so very different from the simple and merry people of today, judging from Best's description of their reaction on first hearing the sound of English trumpets when 'they seemed greatly to rejoice, skipping, laughing and dancing for joy'. They were not, however, quite as simple and childlike as they appeared on the surface, for when Frobisher, accompanied only by his navigator, tried to take one of them prisoner by a trick they set upon the Englishmen who narrowly escaped with their lives, Frobisher getting an arrow in his behind. They reached the boats and at the roar of a firearm the Eskimoes turned and fled, whereupon one Nicholas Conyer, who was a Cornishman and a good 'wrastler', caught and threw one, and so brought back a captive to his Admiral. As a change from quarrying some of the gentlemen asked permission to go exploring inland and thus 'to do some acceptable service for their country'. But Frobisher, who knew his Queen, told them shortly that the purpose of the expedition was to obtain ore, that they would be doing far more good for themselves and their country by getting on with the job and making the venture show a profit. The first Englishmen to explore the Arctic had plenty of opportunity of observing the native way of life down here by the sea without going up-country, and they strongly disapproved of the filth and gloom in which the Eskimo lived in their huts of whalebone and sealskin. There was another brush with the Eskimo who had no chance with their bows against firearms and a woman was captured. But the season was far advanced and there were ominous signs of the water freezing round the ships. On August 21st the order was given for the quarrying to stop. By this time many were lame, their shoes were worn out, and their clothes in rags, no bottoms to the baskets, their tools were broken, but they had loaded 200 tons of ore. These men had had none of the thrill of fighting Spaniards under blue skies, of capturing treasure; instead they had fought the weather and toiled manfully for weeks in a temperature below freezing-point. They deserved all that Frobisher's second-in-command, George Best, had to say about them in his somewhat involved style: 'It is not a little worth the memory, to the commendation of the gentlemen and sailors herein, who, leaving all reputation apart, with so great willingness and with courageous stomach, have themselves almost overcome in so short time the difficulty of this so great a labour'.

They struck their tents, lit bonfires on a nearby hilltop, marched bravely round with the ensign, fired a final volley in farewell, and after this flamboyant good-bye, the wind being in the west, on August 23rd they sailed for home. At the end of the month the *Michael* was in trouble again during a storm, parting company, eventually to turn up at Yarmouth. It was a cruel trip home, the *Gabriel* lost her boatswain and master washed overboard, the *Aid* nearly lost her rudder and in the end sailed away from the *Gabriel*, leaving them 'to God and their good fortune of the sea'. The *Aid* reached Padstow but had to put to sea again because of a gale and so came at last to Bristol where she found the *Gabriel* which having no navigator was lucky to have met at sea a vessel from that port to lead her home. The ore was placed in Bristol Castle under four locks to await transport to Dartford.

The Queen gave Frobisher a welcome she usually reserved for a favourite or someone like Drake who had actually brought home the booty. Frobisher had brought nothing concrete; perhaps a woman's intuition told her that upon such men as this the safety of her realm might one day depend, or she may have scented a bargain—unlimited gold with no international complications. Whatever the reason, she summoned him to the Court lying at Windsor and surrounded by a throng of courtiers in their slashed velvet and jewels she listened avidly to the report of this rough seaman. It was optimistic enough to induce her to appoint a commission of 'gentlemen of great judgement, art and skill', to examine the evidence for a north-west passage, and report on the quality of the ore which had been removed to Dartford. As Dr. Dee, the leading propagandist for a northern passage, happened to be one of these gentlemen, it was only natural that they should advise Her Majesty that the odds were in favour of such a passage existing; but it is surprising that upon the flimsiest of evidence such an august body of men should also have recommended that the ore was promising enough to warrant another voyage. For after months of work the assayers at Dartford had only been able to discover faint traces of silver and at the most about a pennyweight of gold. But this was promise enough, and the Queen gave her sanction for a much larger fleet to make another voyage.

Exploration was forgotten. The Cathay company fitted out fifteen ships for an expedition with the sole aim of obtaining ore which had not yet been proved to be gold-bearing. A wooden edifice was constructed to be carried out in sections and erected in Baffin Land for use as a fort by a party of 100 men who would be left behind to guard the existing diggings and produce further quantities of ore for a fleet which would come out a year later. The captains of the ships kneeled to kiss the Queen's hand at Greenwich before sailing; while Frobisher was invested with 'a fair chain of gold', a gift which contained far more of that precious metal than ever was extracted from the Arctic ore, obtained at so much trouble and expense. That pair of tiny veterans the *Gabriel* and the *Michael* were going out again. George Best had a command of his own, Fenton was to be second-in-command, and Christopher Hall, Frobisher's navigator, was sailing again with his Admiral in the flagship, the Queen's *Aid*. Cornish tin-miners, stone-masons, assayers and soldiers, in addition to 'many wellminded forward young gentlemen of England' gathered at Harwich. When all were embarked each captain read 'The Articles and Orders to be observed for the Fleet' to his assembled ship's company. On May 31st, 1578, the Admiral made the signal to weigh, the fleet sailed out of the Orwell and after proceeding down Channel and rounding Ireland arrived at the beginning of July in the vicinity of Frobisher Bay.

The story of this sorry expedition is soon told. Everything

had to be done in a hurry. Frobisher had arrived too late in the year to allow enough time before the ice formed, and he was unlucky in striking an unusually severe season with the conditions all against him. For a start, he missed the entrance to his Bay in thick weather, and without knowing in the least where he was sailed on for some two hundred miles into what is now known as Hudson's Strait between Baffin Land and the north coast of Labrador—a piece of involuntary exploration which lost him much precious time. Some thought that this at last must be the true passage leading to 'the rich Countreye of Cataya', but these optimists had no chance of confirming their theory because Frobisher turned back. His orders were to gather ore, not to go exploring. Losing one ship on the way in a storm which scattered the fleet, he brought his ships at last to 'Meta Incognita', as Baffin Land had been named. The ship lost had carried all the gear for the fort, so, much to the relief of Captain Fenton and the men who were to have stayed with him, the idea of leaving anyone behind was abandoned. The Admiral at once landed every available man to start digging. Chilled, miserable and always in a hurry, the working parties had to carry on through fog, snowstorms and blizzards, with never a let up or sight of the sun. Under these conditions the men did not care what they shovelled, whether it were good quality or even if it were ore at all, so long as a sufficient volume of the stuff was got on board. By the time ice was starting to form, about the middle of August, a good many captains were of the opinion that they had tempted Providence long enough and that it was high time to be off home. But none had the resolution to approach Frobisher on the subject, and though all his people were obviously getting restive he kept them hard at it until the end of the month. By that time 1,300 tons had been loaded, much of it stones and rubble. He cut things so fine by holding on that a few ships only just managed to get clear of the ice, but they all straggled home eventually to arrive at one port or another during the month of October.

Frobisher arrived home to find that the bubble had burst and that the Cathay company was in liquidation. Although the findings of the assayers on the previous lot of ore had been kept secret,

enough of the truth had leaked out to finish the credit of the
company. The people who had taken shares—and they included
members of the Council, the Court, the nobility and leading
merchants in the city—had put their names down for so many
but had not yet paid over the cash; in modern language the shares
had been issued but they were not fully 'paid up'. Perhaps the
shareholders had hoped to pay out of their profits, but now that
there was a 'call' on so much a share when all chance of profit had
vanished, no one was keen to pay up. But the poor seamen had to
be paid, the hire of ships to be settled and many other items
accounted for, because the third voyage had cost something in the
region of £20,000, a considerable amount in those days. In the
general disappointment everyone turned on poor Lok. He paid
all he could, beggaring himself in the process, in fact Lok is about
the only person who comes out of this affair as an honest man.
With creditors dunning him he could only appeal to the Council,
pointing out that for the past three years he had been in charge of
all the business of Frobisher's voyages, that 'he paid £7500
which is all the goodes he hath in the world without exception;
whereby now himself and wyfe and XV children are left in a
state to beg their bread henceforthe, except God turne the stones
at Dartford into his bread agayne'. Providence decided otherwise,
the Council reluctantly parted with a meagre £430 and for the
next two years Lok sampled first the Fleet and then every prison
in London except Newgate. But Michael Lok was a man of fibre
and, no doubt owing to his knowledge of that part of the world,
he was made factor of the Levant Company at Aleppo. He died
at the age of 83 in the next reign with a couple of lawsuits from
Cathay company days still hanging over him. Perhaps the hardest
trial that Lok had to undergo was when Frobisher turned on him
with the rest, outdoing most in the violence of his abuse. Now
when Frobisher had turned up in London with no prospects and
without a penny, Lok had taken him into his own crowded home,
and while the first expedition was preparing had supplied this
seedy adventurer who could hardly write his own name with
pocket money, and even paid for his casual drinks (Frobisher
generally drank brandy), had given him everything he wanted

for that first voyage and fitted out the ships regardless of cost. In fact Lok had taken Frobisher out of the gutter and had made him into a national figure.

Frobisher was not a pleasant character, his only redeeming features—and they counted for much in that unsqueamish age —were his great physical bravery and a knowledge of practical seamanship. He was not a great navigator, in fact he complained to Dr. Dee that he could not understand the nautical tables and books of navigation which that worthy chose for him before the first voyage. He was rough and uncouth in his ways with such a violent temper that many of his officers had said that nothing would induce them to sail with him again; he would draw his dagger on anyone who crossed him, even threatening his second-in-command Fenton when they met in London after the voyage. The Cathay company had had more than enough of him and forwarded a damning report to the Council in which they accused him of cheating over wages and falsifying accounts. They complained that he had never subscribed one groat of his own money and summed him up as 'a bankerote knave'. This Frobisher undoubtedly was, but he was also the sort of man who could be of use to England and the Council ignored the report. With the threat from Spain looming up the Queen had need of such tough resolute seamen, whatever their private characters might be, and she appointed Frobisher to the command of the *Foresight* for blockading duties off the Munster coast. For the rest of his life Frobisher served as an officer of the Queen. In 1585 he sailed as second-in-command to Drake on the expedition to the Caribbean, and three years later was knighted on the quarterdeck of the *Ark Royal* when Admiral of a squadron in the *Triumph* fighting the Armada. His death was in character: racing with his usual reckless bravery ahead of his men in an attack on a Spanish fort at Brest he was wounded in the foot and paying no attention to it died of gangrene a few days later at Plymouth. Sir Martin Frobisher was not in the same class as Hawkins or Drake; yet in his way he served his country well, dying for it in the end.

And the ore? It was used to fill the potholes in a road at Dartford.

A fiasco like this might well have ended all thought of voyages to the north-west had it not been for a strong body of opinion in England which refused to accept that the destiny of the New World had been unalterably fixed by the Papal Grant of the previous century. There was a party in the country which thought that North America should be settled by Englishmen. Richard Hakluyt and Dr. Dee had been using their pens to get their countrymen interested in colonizing America. Hakluyt argued that England was overflowing with poor who could with advantage be transplanted into 'the temperate and fertile parts of America'; that the prisons were crowded with men detained on trifling charges who could better serve their country as colonists than by being strung up as criminals. Dr. Dee, enthusiastic as always, wrote a paper in which he tried to prove by using the most far-fetched arguments that Elizabeth had a valid title to the New World. His arguments are forgotten, but two words in that paper are not. In it the term 'British Empire' was used for the first time. A Sir Humphrey Gilbert, Devonshire squire and half-brother to Sir Walter Ralegh, had long been interested in the north-west. Ten years earlier he had written a *Discourse of a discoverie for a new Passage to Cataia*, which he had circulated in manuscript, and had also obtained the Queen's permission to explore in those parts. But now he forgot exploration, being captivated by the idea of colonization. He had the large, strategic idea of colonizing Newfoundland to serve as an advanced base when the passage was discovered. The venture was a private one backed by Ralegh, Sir Philip Sidney and Walsingham; the Queen giving it her blessing but no public money. On June 11th, 1583, Sir Humphrey Gilbert sailed from Cawsand Bay with five ships and 260 men who included shipwrights, masons, carpenters and artisans likely to be needed in a new settlement, as well as 'mineral men and refiners' to search for the precious metals which everyone was convinced abounded in any new lands. So much for the practical side, but there was more. The chronicler of the voyages goes on, 'Besides for the solace of our people and the allurement of the savages we were provided with music in good variety, not omitting morris dancers, hobby horse and Maylike conceits to delight the savage people whom we intended to win by all fair means possible'. In such a spirit did the first colonizing expedition ever to leave Britain sail down Channel with a fair wind.

This exalted mood was not enjoyed by the whole expedition; Edward Hayes, a deeply religious man, was only describing what he felt that bright June morning, and his feelings were shared no doubt by his leader but by precious few of the others who sailed with them. Nearly every undertaking of those days was an incongruous mixture of the heroic, the tragic and the farcical; and this expedition was running true to form by the time they were out of soundings. In the middle of the second night at sea, the largest ship, one fitted out at the expense of Sir Walter Ralegh, suddenly deserted the fleet without so much as a by your leave or a plausible excuse. Hayes, master and owner of the *Golden Hind*, could see no reason for behaviour which was odd even for those days, but Gilbert was not discouraged. With the Queen's parting present, an anchor of gold inset with a pearl, pinned to his doublet, he sailed on with four ships into a belt of variable winds and poor visibility which slowed up the fleet. Then in thick fog on the Newfoundland Banks he lost another ship. This was the *Swallow* which sneaked off when the fog came down instead of heaving to astern of the flagship according to Gilbert's standing orders. Her crew were not the sort to pay much attention to orders, for every man except her captain was by profession a Channel pirate and they had been impressed for this voyage instead of being sent to prison. Once clear of the fleet the sight of a stray Newfoundland fishing vessel proved too much for their professional instincts. Forcing their own captain below they took and looted the stranger, then turned her adrift after torturing her crew who had no hidden riches to disclose, after which they shaped a course for Newfoundland. When Gilbert reached that coast after a passage from Plymouth of seven weeks he was delighted to fall in with his missing ship; though he was a little puzzled by the extravagant behaviour of her crew who on turning out to cheer him, 'spared not to cast up into the air and overboard their caps and hats in plenty'—and they were all wearing new clothes.

Gilbert sailed along the coast and at the beginning of August entered St. John's to the great interest of the three dozen fishing vessels of four different flags which were lying peacefully in the harbour. On August 5th, 1583, Sir Humphrey Gilbert landed in state, and having read his Commission to a polyglot crowd of fishermen most of whom did not understand a word of these strange proceedings, took formal possession of the land in the name of the Queen. Then he announced that the religion of the place would be that practised by the Church of England, that it would be governed according to the law of England, and for good measure he added the warning that 'if any person should utter words sounding to the dishonour of Her Majesty he should lose his ears'. He then proceeded to loose an undisciplined rabble—his own men, upon this peaceful and law-abiding community where the English, French, Spanish and Portuguese worked amicably alongside one another. As soon as the colonists were allowed ashore many deserted and took to the woods where they lived as outlaws; one gang stole a fishing vessel after setting her crew ashore, some demanded to be sent home at once and many reported sick.

With no discipline to hold it together, Gilbert's colonizing expedition all but disintegrated on its first contact with a new land, and this was largely the leader's fault. Although the men he had chosen or had been given would have been a handful for anybody, Gilbert had little or no power of command over men, and he lacked that rare quality of leadership which can induce men far from the restraints of civilization or the power of constituted authority to follow and accept discipline against their natural inclination. Gilbert was no Drake. Like his cousin, Sir Richard Grenville, he was headstrong, wayward and obstinate as a mule, yet across the centuries he appears as a likeable and unusual man. A soldier rather than a seaman, and a scholar and country gentleman before either, he had served as a soldier in France, the Low Countries and Ireland where he had been knighted. He had not had a distinguished career, being unemployed for long periods, but he was well connected, and the Queen liked him. He was the first to suggest a University for

London, even going so far as to draw up instructions for the organization of its library; while his famous *Discourse*, written when in retirement at Limehouse, was well reasoned and it concludes with that noble definition of the faith which inspired his life. 'He is not worthy to live at all that for fear or danger of death shunneth his Country's service and his own honour; seeing that death is inevitable and the fame of virtue immortal'. Men of all nations have lived and died in that code but none has defined it with Gilbert's Attic simplicity.

Gilbert's patent had not long to run and he wished to annex as large a territory as possible before it expired. Under it he was to be the Governor of any new colonies and to receive large grants of land for his heirs for ever. But he saw that it was no use taking a lot of disaffected and unwilling men to the mainland of North America. He therefore sent home the sick and dispirited in the *Swallow*, after first transferring the pirates to his own ship the *Delight* where he could keep an eye on them. Also in the *Delight* was a Hungarian scholar, Stephen Parmenius, who was to write an account of the voyage in Latin at the request of Hakluyt, who had intended to sail but had been prevented at the last moment. During a stay at St. John's of only three weeks Gilbert revictualled, then 'sailed with the *Delight* of 120 tons, the *Golden Hind* of 40 and the *Squirrel* 10 tons' to the southward towards Cape Breton. Gilbert himself sailed in the little *Squirrel* so that he could explore the creeks and estuaries of the land he intended to annex for his Queen.

A week later, somewhere in the vicinity of Cape Race they found a sandy bottom at thirty-five fathoms. The weather was uncertain and the seamen tried to persuade Gilbert to keep away from the land and get out to sea, but he refused and insisted upon sailing close in up an unknown coast. For some reason they seem to have made a night of it in the *Delight*, for according to Hayes 'The evening was fair and pleasant, yet not without token of storm to ensue, and most part of this Wednesday night, like the swan that singeth before her death, they in the *Admiral* or *Delight* continued in sounding of trumpets, with drums and fifes; also winding the cornets and hautboys'. Next day the *De-*

light drove ashore in a gale and broke up almost at once. The unfortunate Stephen Parmenius was lost and all the pirates, a clear example, Hayes was convinced, of God's judgement upon them for their wickedness. All the stores were gone and only two small ships were left. The season was far advanced, the spirit had gone from the remainder—so on August 31st Gilbert left the coast of America and sailed for England.

In fine weather two days later Gilbert went on board the *Golden Hind* to spend a day in more comfortable surroundings. He was in good spirits though he felt the loss of so many of his men, and especially his library of books which had gone down in the *Delight*. When the time came for Gilbert to go the sight of the *Squirrel* lying off was too much for the seaman's eye of Edward Hayes. She was grossly overloaded with tophamper and guns and obviously unsafe at this time of year. Hayes tried his best to persuade Gilbert to make the Atlantic crossing in the *Golden Hind* but 'nothing cou d avail to divert him of a wilful resolution of going through in the frigate' and the answer Hayes got was what one would expect from Humphrey Gilbert: 'I will not forsake my little company going home with whom I have passed so many storms and perils'. It was a fine gesture of which the sensible Hayes disapproved.

About a month later when they were a little to the northward of the Azores they struck a full gale and a roaring, angry sea. On the afternoon of September 9th those in the *Golden Hind* were anxiously watching the *Squirrel* as she disappeared into a trough, apparently engulfed, only to reappear on the crest a few moments later. Hayes took his ship as close as he dared and as he came surging past the *Squirrel*, there was Gilbert perched up in the stern reading a book (it was More's *Utopia*) and as they went by they caught his cheerful shout above the tumult of the wind and sea: 'we are as near to Heaven by sea as by land'.

But a top-heavy little vessel like the *Squirrel* could not live for long in that sea, and 'the same Monday night', writes Hayes, 'about twelve of the clock or not long after, the frigate being ahead of us in the *Golden Hind*, suddenly her lights went out, whereof as it were in a moment we lost the sight, and withal our watch cried "The general is cast away" which was too true. For in a moment the frigate was devoured and swallowed up in the sea'.

Yet Sir Humphrey Gilbert did not live in vain, even if he got no farther than Newfoundland. His *Discourse* had fired the imagination of the least romanticized, but one of the greatest of English sea captains. Nor was all connection between the Gilbert family and the search for a north-west passage ended when the *Squirrel's* lights went out: his younger brother Adrian at once set about organizing a voyage of northern discovery. The Devonshire home of the Gilberts was near Dartmouth which had been a nursery of seamen since Chaucer's time and Adrian had made a voyage or two with a young neighbour from Sandridge whose qualities had greatly impressed him. Through the influence of his half-brother, Sir Walter Ralegh, and of that great patron of all sea affairs, Sir Francis Walsingham, Adrian Gilbert and his associates were granted letters patent by the Queen authorizing the search for a passage to China and the Moluccas by sailing to the northward. A rich member of the Fishmongers' Company, William Sanderson, together with a number of west country merchants provided, the financial backing and Adrian's neighbour John Davis was given command of the expedition.

Neither John Davis nor his voyages has ever been the subject of a Boys' Book of Adventure, yet his voyages were as varied, dangerous and daring as any of those undertaken by his better-known contemporaries; and Davis himself was one of the greatest seamen produced by England. He has been little noticed, perhaps because there was nothing spectacular about him: he did not challenge Spain single handed, he never returned loaded down with treasure, or even with the report of any, and his great Arctic voyages failed in their object, the discovery of a quick passage to Asia. The finding of a north-west passage was the ambition of his life, but with Davis this urge, common enough in his day, was different because for him the short cut was not only a quick way to the spices and wealth of the East, it was also a chance to bring the Gospel to the Heathen. 'Sith it is so appointed', he wrote, 'that there shall be one shepherd and one flock, what hindereth us of England not to attempt that which God himself hath appointed to be performed'.

This was hardly a point of view to recommend itself to the ordinary Elizabethan mariner who was not an ardent Evangelist. In that flamboyant and piratical age, John Davis was a worthy man, honest, brave, unassuming, and worthy men do not as a rule attract notice from the crowd. He was the true seaman for whom good navigation is its own reward, and he alone of the sailors who had been there came back from the Arctic with a coherent account of where he had been. His positions were accurately fixed; not wild approximations, more the result of imagination than of observation. A scientific navigator, he invented the Double Quadrant by which for centuries after his death seamen were to determine their latitude, and he wrote *The Seaman's Secrets*, a technical handbook for mariners far in advance of anything on the subject that had appeared in English. Honest and steadfast in all he undertook, fearless as an explorer, humane and considerate as a captain, John Davis was the forerunner of Cook and the great school of English seamen who charted the seas of the world.

On June 7th, 1585, Davis sailed from the peaceful haven of his native Dartmouth on the first of his three voyages to the desolate north-west. Before the end of July he had made his landfall in southern Greenland and was duly noting in his log how, 'the lothsome view of the shore and the irksome noyse of the ice was such that it bred strange conceits in us'. With his two diminutive vessels, the *Sunshine* of fifty tons and the *Moonshine* of thirty-five, he worked his way slowly up the west coast of Greenland until he reached a fiord he named Gilbert Sound, which is the site of the present Godthaab. From here he stood away to the north-west until early in August he sighted land in 66° 40′ N. This was Baffin Land and coasting south he discovered Cumberland Sound, but as contrary winds prevented his exploring it he turned for home where he arrived in September, convinced that a navigable passage existed in the north-west.

Although he started his second voyage in the following year

a month earlier he accomplished little, for owing to the need to make the voyage pay for itself two of his ships had to be detached to get fish and furs. On his arrival home in October still convinced but with no tangible results, many of the merchants who had originally backed him lost confidence in him and no more money was forthcoming. But Davis would not give in: 'Surely it shall cost my hope of welfare', he wrote to Sanderson, 'and my portion of Sandridge (his Dartmouth property) but, I will, by God's mercy, see an end of this business'. Sanderson stood by him, and with the backing of Walsingham and the Lord Treasurer more funds were provided, a striking commentary on Davis's character that two men who had burned their fingers once in Arctic specu-lation should be prepared to back an explorer who had only failure to report.

In May, 1587, a time when Spanish fleets were busily fitting out for the attack upon England, Davis sailed on his third voyage, the last attempt of the reign to discover a north-west passage. The expedition consisted of three vessels, two which had to fish to make the venture pay for itself, and a pinnace 'for the discoverie'. Davis, of course, was in the pinnace, and though she was leaking like a sieve they reached a latitude of 73° N., the highest yet reached by man. Between Greenland and Baffin Land he observed water free of ice stretching away to the north-west. But northerly gales drove him back, and after exploring Cumber-land Sound only to find it land-locked, he reached England in September without having discovered his passage. However, the sight of that clear water up in Seventy-three North had made him more convinced than ever that the passage existed; and he wrote to Sanderson telling him that he thought two ways led to it, those waters which are now known as Davis Strait and Hudson Strait. This was guessing, but Davis was correct. In recent years it has been shown that by way of them the Pacific can eventually be reached from the Atlantic, although the route is too difficult and uncertain ever to become a commercial highway. Davis did at last reach the Spice Islands, but via the Cape and the Indian Ocean as a pilot for the East India Company. He ended his life, ironically for an Arctic explorer, only a degree or two north of the Equator, being murdered by Japanese pirates at Patani on the east coast of the Malay Peninsula.

John Davis did not achieve his life's ambition, and on his Arctic results he might be considered a failure. However, he was the first scientific Arctic explorer. His accurate and methodical observations brought some order to the chart of the north-west, clearing away the welter of myth and misconception which had so far confused the cartographers; and his work prepared the way for Hudson and the many other explorers who have since penetrated into those barren wastes. When Davis reached home in the autumn of 1587 the threat from Spain was imminent. Every sailor was required in Home Waters, and the following summer he was in command of the *Black Dog*, a small vessel attending on the Admiral as a Channel pilot during the Armada campaign.

Arctic exploration may have brought no tangible profit to England, but in the long run it produced something more important for a small but thrusting maritime power. It advanced England's knowledge of the science of navigation. When Frobisher set out on his first voyage he had taken with him half a dozen navigational books, each written by an Englishman, among them was *Mandeville's Travels* (price one shilling) and a set of navigational instruments made in London by Humphrey Cole. All these had been paid for by Michael Lok and chosen by Dr. Dee, who for many years was the brains behind Arctic exploration. Dee was a man with a brilliant mind and a baffling character. Those who knew him personally could never be quite certain whether he was a genius or a humbug, and he was most probably something of both. After a dazzling classical career at Chelmsford Grammar School and St. John's College, Cambridge, he turned to mathematics and studied at the University of Louvain, where his talents soon brought him into touch with all the leading mathematicians and geographers of the day. Mercator was so taken with him that he presented him with a pair of globes. But what earned Dee a European reputation was a course of lectures on Euclid delivered at the University of Paris. After this, Pedro de Nunez, the brilliant Portuguese cosmographer and mathematician, the man who first described the method of great circle sailing, corresponded with Dee. Eventually Dr. Dee returned to England and settled at Mortlake, where the local people were quite sure that he was a wizard. He certainly looked it, being a tall, gaunt man with a flowing beard who wore a long black gown; and anyone who peeped through his library window could see shelves of thick volumes and mysterious pieces of apparatus. The conclusion of the people of Mortlake was only natural in that credulous age. Books and pamphlets on every conceivable aspect of navigation and geography poured out in a continual stream from Mortlake and though many of his theories about the Arctic turned out to be hopelessly wrong, his knowledge of mathematics and astronomy was unrivalled in England. He was an opinionated recluse, but he was always ready, and only too eager, to put his knowledge at the disposal of practical seamen. At one time or another he had instructed in the theory and practice of navigation an illustrious succession of English sailors and explorers; Richard Chancellor, Stephen and William Borough, Pett and Hackman, Martin Frobisher and his navigator Christopher Hall, Humphrey and Adrian Gilbert, their cousin, Walter Ralegh, and Adrian's friend, John Davis. All these men had known that study at Mortlake, its shelves of leather-bound volumes, its two Mercator globes, the only globes in England, its quadrants and navigational instruments, the untidy desk littered with closely-written sheets of paper, for Dee was never too busy to push aside his latest work in order to give advice. In fact, some of his pupils, Frobisher among them, thought that for one who had never himself made a voyage he was a little too free with it. Dee had constituted himself a one-man Navigation School for Arctic Exploration, and whether he were likeable or not, his dynamic energy, combined with a good mathematical brain, undoubtedly furthered in England the knowledge of navigation and geography.

It may have been his skill at this last which gave him his entrée at Court, because by this time geography had become a popular branch of learning. Beautifully engraved maps of the world, of England, or of the local county now hung among the pictures on the panelled walls of Elizabethan houses, and, for a gentleman who could only travel in the imagination within the four walls of his study, there was a wide choice of books. Did he think of emigrating, he could study a *Report of the True State and Comodities of Newfoundland* or a *Pleasant description of the Fortunate Isles*. He could range in distant oceans with *a Discourse of the Navigations which the Portugales do make*, or, if he preferred his travel nearer home, *A Perambulation of Kent*, and if he liked his horrors neat there was always *A short and Pithy Discourse concerning Earthquakes*. The mental horizon of the average Englishman had widened; he looked beyond the borders of his country, beyond the shores of his island to distant seas and strange lands, and this mental development was reflected in the poetry, drama, and literature of his time.

For the first half of the sixteenth century Portugal and Spain, oceanic countries both, had been the leaders in technical knowledge of navigation and geography, but now England was fast catching them up and before the end of Elizabeth's reign she would be supreme. In 1581, William Borough, one of Dee's pupils, published his *Discourse on the Variation of the Compass or Magneticall Needle*, and almost as a companion volume in the same year an instrument maker, Robert Norman, announced his discovery of dip in *The Newe Attractive*, and by means of his dip circle accurately measured the dip for London. What a seaman and craftsman had started an Archdeacon of Salisbury Cathedral carried on. William Barlow, the inventor of the compass box, explained Dip and Variation in less scientific language in *The Navigator's Supply*. These descriptions of erratic and inexplicable behaviour of a compass needle finally led to one of the greatest geniuses of the reign, William Gilbert, propounding the theory that the earth was itself a great magnet which explained everything. On the continent Mercator had for years been producing charts on his projection. They were beautifully engraved, but of not much use to practical navigators because no one knew how to use them, until an Englishman, Edward Wright, by explaining the construction of Mercator's projection, revolutionized the making of charts and gave the seaman something he could use and understand.

Before the end of Elizabeth's reign, English seamen were sail-

ing on the great circle, triangulation was understood, and Englishmen were carrying out accurate land surveys and making charts.
Wright and Molineux, to the order of Sanderson, Davis's backer,
had constructed the first globes made in England. The problems
of latitude, dip, and variations had been solved—only that of longitude remained and it was left to another Englishman, John Har-
rison, a village carpenter, to solve it over a century later with his
Chronometer. In becoming an oceanic power England took the
lead in technical and practical maritime knowledge, a lead which
she has never lost.

CHAPTER VIII

The Walls of the Realm

*

While some in England were trying to perfect the methods by which a ship could find her way about the ocean, others were designing the ships to use those methods, and the man who made himself responsible for this was John Hawkins. Since his return from San Juan de Ulua, he had made no more voyages to the West himself, although he had sent out his trading vessels. He had to remain at home because he held the dormant appointment of Commander-at-Sea designate in the event of war, a position which enabled him to carry on the family business at Plymouth. During sudden alarms, such as that caused by the discovery of the Ridolfi plot, he hoisted his flag in command of a squadron to cover the Western Approaches. He was thus in a position to know the state of England's Fleet, and the more he learned the more anxious he became. His experience in Mexico led him to consider Spain as the arch-enemy of his country, and whatever the shifts and changes in the international situation, he remained convinced that in the end England would have to fight Spain. When she did England would need an efficient up-to-date fleet; and almost single-handed, John Hawkins set about providing his country with that fleet.

Queen Elizabeth had inherited a navy which was a going concern, thanks to her father's genius for administration in matters to do with the sea. When he died Henry VIII left behind him the most powerful fleet in Europe, composed of three-masted vessels armed on the broadside, vessels whose lines had assumed finer proportions as his reign progressed. This was due to his shipwrights, who included two men of genius, James

142

Baker and Peter Pett, and to the fact that his craftsmen were no longer hired by the job, but were a permanent body of men employed on a fixed salary. They were England's first dockyardmen and were allowed a break in the middle of the forenoon for cheese and beer, which they probably needed as their working day started at five in the morning and lasted until night. In Henry's day they worked mostly by eye and rule of thumb, and the senior shipwright would go off into the woods with his mates where he would pick trees of suitable size and shape and mark them to be felled, making arrangements for them to be hauled or floated to his yard. Although they used no drawings or intricate calculations, they solved the problem of building ships which could withstand the stresses set up by the discharge of cannon and they designed them with lines which conformed to a 'cod's head and mackerel tail' or with a full form forward and tapering away aft, proportions which were in favour until only the other day. Soon they were building some of the finest ships in Europe, keeping the technique of design a secret which they passed on from father to son. A hundred years after James Baker and Peter Pett, an English historian writing of the Craft or Mystery of Shipwrights prayed, 'may this mystery of shipmaking in England never be lost till this floating world be arrived at its own haven, the end and dissolution thereof'.

But of far greater importance for posterity than the fleet he built was the organization Henry VIII set up for administering it. Before his day the King's ships had ferried an occasional army over to France, sailed home and paid off, their job done; or they had sailed out, fought a battle, returned home and again paid off. The work of the fleet was confined to isolated incidents and one man, The Clerk of the Ships, was capable of dealing with it. But then things changed, voyages were prolonged into campaigns and there was the Channel guard to maintain during the winter months. The King realized that if he wanted his fleet in readiness for instant service all the year round, there must be behind it an organization of dockyards, storehouses and magazines. This was clearly beyond the power of one man to run, and in 1546 he instituted the Navy Board to administer his Navy. The Board was responsible to the Lord Admiral, one of the great Ministers of State, and it consisted of the Treasurer, the Comptroller, the Surveyor, and the Master of the Ordnance for the Ships. The model of the Board was completely English, nothing like it had been seen before in any country, and its most valuable quality was its permanence. A skilled and experienced administration kept the shore installations running so that in peace or war there was continuity and in an emergency the English Fleet could be got to sea with speed and efficiency.

On her accession Queen Elizabeth had inherited what no other Sovereign in the world possessed, a fleet with a permanent organization to maintain and administer it. But for the first twenty years of her reign she had such a struggle to get the country on its feet again financially after the chaos of the preceding reigns that she could spare little for the Navy. She could not afford to bring the fleet up to strength by new construction and there was hardly enough money for the necessary replacements. Alarmed at the state of the fleet, in 1560 her Ambassador in Paris wrote to her chief minister, Cecil, exhorting, 'Bend your force, credit and device to maintain and increase your Navy, for in this time, considering all the circumstances, it is the flower of England's garland'. It was all very well for Sir Nicholas Throckmorton to send poetic exhortations from Paris, but there was little that the Queen or Cecil could do about it. The real culprits for this lack of money for the Navy were the House of Commons, who would not vote sufficient supplies to the Queen and the Navy Board itself.

The Queen gave the Navy its fair share of what she had, but almost as much stuck to the fingers of the Board as was ever spent on the fleet. Although the administration was hopelessly corrupt, it somehow managed to get the fleet to sea when required which shows that the chain of command was intact. The fleet, however, was growing out of date and at inordinate cost to the Crown. It was all too easy for the Board; the Queen was grossly overcharged for all stores and repairs in her yards, ships were built of timber already paid for by her and a bill rendered for a brand-new ship. In fact, the tricks used in their swindling were those which had been in use ever since a monarch first had to employ a steward. It was quite beyond the layman of Elizabeth's time to supervise the naval experts or to penetrate the fog of technicalities in which they hid the irregularities, but it was not beyond the powers of one who was himself an expert, John Hawkins. Not only was he vitally interested in the state and composition of the fleet which he might have to command at any time, he had also a pretty shrewd idea of all that was going on. He had had dealings with the Board in the past, had been forced to sail that condemned old hulk the *Jesus of Lubeck* to the Indies and back, and a year or two later had taken her out again, an old relic that should never have been on the list of the Queen's Ships at all. Also, he had married the Treasurer's daughter and through this family connection had learned many of the Board's secrets. It was most probably due to his influence and indirect pressure that in 1570 the Board started to build some vessels after his own heart, long in proportion to their beam, fast, handy and heavily gunned; of these, the *Revenge*, launched in 1575, won immortality. By this time Benjamin Gonson, the Treasurer, son of that Gonson who had been King Henry's Clerk of the Ships for twenty years, had grown old and tired. Most probably he was honest, but he was too weak to stand up to the naval members of the Board, the chief of whom was Sir William Wynter, a masterful and choleric sea officer. But more serious even than the robbery was the mental attitude of the naval members, who refused to acknowledge the fact that the nature of sea warfare had changed during their eighteen years of office. It was no longer what it had been when they were young, a matter of blundering about the North Sea or the Channel in high-charged ships carrying crowds of soldiers, it had become an affair of the wide oceans where a totally different fleet was required.

At last, towards the end of 1577, Hawkins could no longer bear the sight of money which should have gone into the building of an adequate fleet being poured down the drain instead. In order to show exactly how the Queen was being cheated and the country endangered, he marshalled all his facts and arguments, with great care and clarity, and embodying them in a paper entitled 'Abuses in the Admiralty touching Her Majesty's Navy. Exhibited by Mr. Hawkins', he forwarded it to Burghley. Instead of suffering the fate usual to papers stating unpalatable facts, this one produced action. On January 1st, 1578, Hawkins was appointed to replace his father-in-law as Treasurer of the Navy, and the man who more than any other was responsible for the defeat of the Armada, started on the most difficult task of his life. Old Gonson was only too pleased to retire, but he felt some qualms for his son-in-law, remarking sadly as he went, 'I shall pluck a thorn from my foot and thrust it in yours', words which must often have recurred to Hawkins as he fought to overcome the incessant and malicious opposition to his policies.

John Hawkins was that rare combination in any age, a seaman who was also a good businessman. He had a tidy mind and he took office with a policy cut and dried. He had long realized that he could never hope for the funds to build a large navy, but he was confident that he could provide an adequate fleet with what money he was allowed if it were wisely spent. The Navy had only eighteen ships of over one hundred tons when he became Treasurer; and many of these were obsolete, short in the keel with towering superstructures and quite unsuited for the new type of ocean warfare which he advocated. Hawkins had had experience of long voyages, three times he had sailed beyond the line, and he knew what was needed to keep a fighting fleet at sea for months if need be, something his colleagues on the Board had never contemplated. In 1570 he had recommended an attack upon the treasure fleet off the Azores, for he appreciated that the frontiers of a maritime country are the range of her fleet and that the best way of dealing with Spain was in her waters and not near the shores of England. His strategy did not differ in principle from that which England had always employed, all he wanted was to apply it over a wider area. He set out therefore to transform the existing fleet into an oceanic navy.

The organization was there to hand for Hawkins to build a navy of this modern type, but the money was not. The only way he could get the new ships he considered essential was to pay for them out of the money saved from the ordinary day-to-day expenditure upon the Navy. This was a large amount. The ships had to be overhauled periodically, their masts, spars and rigging needed frequent renewal, and the shore installations, the workshops, docks and permanent moorings, cost almost as much to maintain. The whole business was too complicated and technical for laymen to supervise its costs efficiently, and this is where, under Gonson, too much money had been disappearing without showing adequate results. The first thing Hawkins did was to take all this upkeep and maintenance out of the control of the Board and put it out to contract—a bold procedure. He cannot have been too surprised at the howl which came from the Board at being suddenly cut off from a pleasant source of income which had been regular for so long as almost to have become a perquisite, but he could hardly have expected Sir William Wynter to create such a fuss that Burghley had to send him to cool off on the coast of Ireland in command of a patrolling squadron. Hawkins's own colleagues were only a hindrance to his plans, but to make up for their obstruction, he found all the help he needed in the Royal Dockyards.

A new generation of shipwrights was coming to maturity, men who had improved upon the methods confided to them by the fathers, and the chief among them was Matthew, son of King Henry's James Baker. Matthew Baker had served as apprentice to his father, he had grown up in a shipyard with its smell of boiling pitch and the rhythmic buzzing of two-man saws, and in 1572 at the age of forty-two he had been appointed Master Shipwright, the first English craftsman to hold that honourable title. His pay was one shilling a day. As the father had been responsible for the design and construction of the ships of King Henry's fleet, so the son was the chief designer of Elizabeth's. But where old James Baker had worked by eye and flair, Matthew brought this ancient craft to rule and he worked from his own drawings. These were no simple matter for the total surface of the hull of a ship is made up of a great number of curved surfaces, all different, which have to be so constructed that they merge into a smooth and symmetrical whole. Matthew Baker had devised a method of calculating and drawing these curves so that he was the first English shipwright ever to set down the 'lines' of a ship on paper.

One valuable result of this achievement was that instead of the form of a new ship existing only in the inscrutable mind of the shipwright so that no one could have any idea of what it would look like until it began to take shape on the slip, it was now possible to see from his plans on the drawing board what the builder intended. His ideas could be discussed and modified. Fortunately for us, Samuel Pepys, an acquisitive but discriminating collector, preserved a number of Matthew Baker's drawings which he came upon in the archives of the Navy when he was Secretary. He bound them in a collection which he called 'Fragments of Ancient Shipwrightry' and bequeathed them with the rest of his library to Magdalene College, Cambridge. It is possible, therefore, to make a fascinating journey in time: to pass from a study of the mechanically-produced blue-prints for the modern *Vanguard*, the ninth of her name in the Royal Navy, to savouring the delicate artistry of Matthew Baker's drawings, done with a quill pen for the first *Vanguard*, a ship which fought against the Spanish Armada. The comparison shows that although methods of construction and material have changed, the fundamentals of the shipwright's art have remained the same.

A Master Shipwright of those days was responsible for more than the design and construction of the ships, he was in charge of the dockyard, its shore installations and workmen. Drydocks, wharves and storehouses all came under him, he fed and paid the shipwrights and even ran the Dockyard Police. He was half a dozen modern Admiralty departments rolled into one, yet shipwrights were unusually long lived. During this busy period of transition and expansion, Matthew Baker's principal colleague was the Peter Pett who had accompanied Matthew's father on a tour of inspection of the King's Ships in Portsmouth Dockyard over thirty years before. Yet here he was at Deptford yard, with which the name Pett was to be associated for generations, still hard at it. In 1573 he had built the *Foresight* of 300 tons and the *Achates* of 100 tons, both ships which fought against the Armada.

But the most important ship to be turned out by Deptford Yard was the *Revenge* launched in 1575, the first to appear of the new oceanic type of warship.

The *Revenge* was a departure from anything that had been launched before, and from her there developed the 'Sailing Ship of the Line' which was to give Britain the mastery of the seas in the centuries to come, a type which reached its flowering at Trafalgar. The true significance of the *Revenge* lies not in her blazing, heroic end at the Azores but in what she stood for—a new kind of sea warfare. During Elizabeth's reign the future direction of England's policy was decided and it was to be effected by ships like the *Revenge* and her successors out in the open sea. The *Revenge* was of medium size, 500 tons, fast, handy and heavily gunned, a ship which could keep the sea for long periods and was also easy to manœuvre in close action. Her upperworks were painted green and white, and lying 'low and snug' in the water, she delighted the eye of an Elizabethan seaman whose memoirs have come down to us. She was not overcrowded and her complement of 250 men, made up of 150 sailors, 24 gunners and 76 soldiers, reflected the new trend—towards the movable battery and away from the floating fortress. She was commanded by a seaman, the larger part of her company were seamen who also worked the guns, and she was intended not for hand to hand fighting but for free manœuvre and the rapid discharge of her broadsides. Her main armament, carried on a single gundeck, consisted of twenty-two muzzle-loading guns, and surprisingly, the range of her broadsides was not so very far short of that of Nelson's *Victory*. Who should be given the credit for the *Revenge*: Hawkins who had recommended her type, Baker and Pett who built her? Not all of it to them, for many had been concerned in her evolution: Henry VII who built the first King's ship, his *Regent*, solely for fighting, Henry VIII who thought of mounting heavy guns in ships, and James Baker who worked out how to do it, and those Elizabethan seamen who had made long ocean voyages. All these had had a hand in her inception, Hawkins, Baker and Pett were merely the men on the spot when her time came. For, like any new departure in naval construction and design, the *Revenge* was the result of accumulated experience properly applied to meet changed conditions.

As the money Hawkins was allowed would not run to building a fleet of *Revenges* he did the next best thing by converting the older ships one by one as they came in for overhaul. When a ship was built of wood it was possible to carry out drastic reconstruction without great expense by using her original timbers. When the entry occurs in the Pipe Office accounts of so much spent on such and such a ship being 'rebuilt' it often means that she went into dockyard hands as a clumsy old tub, broad of beam with an old-fashioned high superstructure, to emerge some time later almost as a new ship. Most of her towering upperworks had gone, new gunports gaped in her side, while an addition to her length had given her a measure of slender grace—the only thing about her that had not changed was her name. All this was due to Hawkins who as Treasurer was responsible for everything to do with the ships, their hulls and fittings, construction and design, the materials and workmanship that went into them, and for the whole administration of the dockyards which built and served the ships. As much from inclination as from duty Hawkins often left the musty air of a London office, with its unending accounts and nagging from his colleagues, for the purer atmosphere of a shipyard, so full of healthy purpose and activity.

A ship in those days was entirely hand fashioned; there were no ingenious machines to help the builder or supplant the hand and eye of the craftsman. The building of ships or boats has always been an esoteric craft where the workman uses special tools adapted to his purpose. The Tudor shipwright used an adze to level off a plank of wood, just as his kind had done since its blade was a sharpened stone; yet one of Hawkins's shipwrights could produce as level and smooth a surface with his adze as could the carpenter with a plane. Planks and timbers were secured with trenails, wooden pegs up to thirty-six inches long, which were always cut from the top part of the tree so as to be free of knots and sap. The holes for them were driven with an auger, after the adze the shipwright's most essential tool—so valuable that one shipwright went so far as to declare that the inventor of the auger should have been deified. The caulkers, who were responsible for the watertightness of the ship, used a wooden mallet and a wide, flat-edged blunt chisel called an 'iron'; to this day each mallet has its own individual ring, and the owner can always tell at once which is his own mallet. The caulkers were also responsible for smearing a ship's bottom with 'graves', a fearsome mixture of tallow and resin which they kept bubbling in large cauldrons on the dockside. This treatment was known as 'graving', and the dock in which it was given came to be known as a graving dock, a term in common use today. They had also another duty, one which they must have been very careful to do well at this time, for it was an invention of Hawkins's own. This was sheathing the bottom of a ship by nailing a skin of elm planks over a mixture of hair and pitch smeared over the bottom timbers, as a protection against the worm which attacked a ship in tropical waters. The fleet which was slowly taking shape was modern in design, built from the best materials obtainable, by craftsmen who took a pride in their workmanship. Hawkins was a fastidious man who would stand for nothing shoddy, and if he could not have quantity he was determined, if need be, to beat the Spaniards with quality.

In spite of calculated obstruction and virulent accusations of fraud from his colleagues on the Board, Hawkins went serenely on with his self-imposed task of transforming an old and out-of-date fleet into one that was modern and ocean-going. He seemed impervious to criticism and it was this bland indifference to the opinions of those who considered themselves his elders and betters that finally proved too much for poor old Sir William Wynter and made him explode about Hawkins in a letter to Burghley: 'He careth not to whom he speaketh, nor what he sayeth, blushe he will not'. By 1583 the opposition had created a situation whereby the Council were forced to act, and a Royal Commission directed a number of experienced sea captains, among them Drake, Frobisher and Ralegh, to inquire into the allegations. After a full inquiry Hawkins was vindicated, but under that calm exterior he had been suffering and in the course of the campaign of vilification he had been deeply hurt. Public men can never afford to be unduly sensitive, and although Hawkins could disdainfully brush aside charges of fraud as 'trifling slanders' he was touched on the raw when, as he put it, 'the very walls of the realm were brought in question'. It was more than he could stomach that old fogies like Wynter, who had supplied him with that leaking coffin, the *Jesus of Lubeck*, for a voyage to the other side of the world, could freely make statements that the ships under Hawkins's care were rotten and unseaworthy. He wrote a dignified letter to Burghley complaining of the way his colleagues were behaving, 'their slander hath gone very far and general', he ended, 'only to be avenged of me and this service, which doth discover the corruption and ignorance of time past'. There was not long to go now before the test came, and, by the time it did, Hawkins had so repaired the damage caused by the 'corruption and ignorance' that his ships gave their own resounding answer.

In *Considerations touching a war with Spain* Francis Bacon picked on the essential character of the English fighting ship: 'not of so great bulk indeed, but of a more nimble motion and more serviceable'. From four to six hundred tons was considered the ideal size; the four ships of one thousand tons that were in the Navy fought against the Armada, a desperate campaign in Home waters where anything that could float was needed, but they were not used again for the rest of the war as being too large for foreign service. The Elizabethan warship would not appear as much of a beauty to eyes accustomed to the majestic sweeping line of modern ships—picturesque rather than seamanlike—though she was a great improvement on the old high-charged ship from which she had been developed. She still had too high a poop for symmetry, and she preserved the beakhead beyond the stem, an unsightly legacy from the old-fashioned ships which pitched like rocking horses in a head sea and needed this breakwater to lessen the impact of the oncoming seas.

The picture facing this page is a contemporary drawing of the latest ship in the English fleet to fight against the Armada. She is the *Ark*, launched at Deptford on June 12th, 1587, a ship built to the order of Sir Walter Ralegh, but bought from him by the Queen while still on the stocks for £5,000. Although slightly on

Contemporary drawing of the *Ark Royal*

16th Century shipwrights. A fanciful picture of the building of Noah's
Ark

the large size, 800 tons, her appearance and sail plan are that of the average Elizabethan fighting ship. She does not look as if she can have been much of a flier but she was the fastest ship in either fleet. Her largest boat she tows astern, the others are stowed in the open space between the poop and the forecastle known as the waist, a space also used by the seamen who trimmed the sails. She carries no jibs or staysails to help in working to windward. In heavy weather her topmasts could be housed, an improvement introduced by John Hawkins. Her two after-masts, the mizzen and Bonaventure-mizzen are lateen rigged. Whatever we may think of their appearance she and her kind were the finest warships afloat, fast and easy to handle in moderate winds, yet staunch enough to weather almost any storm. There was no wheel, steering was done by a primitive arrangement called a whipstaff which was difficult to manipulate and made accurate steering as we know it today impossible. But the ships got there and back again, which is what matters at sea. The high poop housed the whipstaff and binnacle, the officers' quarters and the 'great cabin'. When she was launched the *Ark* had damask curtains to the glazed square ports of her great cabin, with chintz and velvet hangings on the bulkheads—the whole carried out in a rather startling colour scheme of green and white, the Tudor colours. These were the standard soft furnishings for a captain's cabin: but when Lord Charles Howard came to hoist his flag in the *Ark* he most probably brought furnishings more in keeping with his taste and position.

Most of the crew lived on the gun-deck in messes which could be separated from one another by canvas screens let down from the beams overhead; at night they rolled themselves up in blankets or coats and slept on the bare cold deck. The sailors wore a distinctive dress, which was not a uniform but so general as almost to be one: a sort of tam-o'-shanter cap, a small and probably dirty ruff round their necks, a rough canvas jacket and long, bell-mouthed trousers—a cheap and sensible working rig. Their rations would have been generous if they had been eatable which generally they were not: a pound of biscuits a day for each man, a pound of meat on four days a week and of fish on the other three.

They were also issued with olive oil, cheese and butter and one gallon of beer a day per man. This last was an illusion because after a few days at sea it used to turn acid and gave everyone a mild form of dysentery—the whole fleet was down with this undignified complaint by the time the Armada was driven off. If a man was ill or wounded he had to bear it on the mess-deck without any special care or comfort. The deck below the gun-deck contained the bread-room, various stores and a few dark, airless cubby-holes for subordinate officers. This deck was immediately over the hold, where the powder was kept in magazines, the beer, water and provision casks were stowed and the gravel ballast carried. The ship's galley was perched on a brick platform on top of the ballast and an Elizabethan cook certainly earned his pay. In summer or the Tropics, being so far below, his galley was infernally hot, while in any latitude he had to work in a powerful stench exuding from the gravel (the stench came from bilge water seeping into ballast which was seldom changed for clean). Down below, the ships, so gay aloft with banners and streamers, were dark, damp and badly ventilated, but the Elizabethan seaman did not live in conditions so very much worse than those endured by his successors in the next two centuries.

Service in the Navy was not continuous because the Queen could not afford a fleet permanently in commission. Ships were manned only when they were required for a voyage, a campaign or as the result of a sudden alarm. All seamen in the country were liable for service in the Navy and the word included merchant sailors, adventurers who had done a privateering voyage or two to the West, pirates and fishermen. When the fleet had to be manned, there were some volunteers and the rest were given 'coat and conduct' money of a penny a mile for their journey and ordered to report at a rendezvous whence they were drafted to ships. As they had been given money for a coat in order to join, they only got conduct money of a halfpenny a mile for the return journey after their service. Needless to say in either direction most of the conduct money went upon ale. There was no great rush of volunteers to join the fleet in defence of their country against the Armada which was expected almost any day. The reasons for this apparent lack of patriotism at such a time were that the fleet had been too often mobilized as one scare succeeded another, pay in the Navy was bad and there was no chance of prize money. This last was the deciding factor; conditions afloat had nothing to do with a reluctance to serve. A successful captain could get all the volunteers he wanted for a privateering voyage on which the men would cheerfully put up with far worse conditions and food than they were likely to get on a campaign in one of the Queen's ships. If the English fleet was not manned with the almost religious fervour with which Spaniards of all classes flocked to join the Armada, the men who did come grumbling and joking to man the Queen's ships were a tough lot who knew their jobs. Their fervour, after the manner of Englishmen, was not so much for the 'cause' as for the personal pride they took in the way they worked their ships and fought their guns.

Seamanship and gunnery used in a combination entirely new to sea warfare was the ultimate reason for the victory of the English fleet over the Spanish Armada. A more determined leadership, better ships, sounder material, all these contributed to the result, but it was mainly brought about by the quality of the men who worked the sails and manned the guns of the Queen's ships. This is not to say that the English sailor was personally any braver than his Spanish opposite number, but he had been better trained. The English were bred to the job and in their element, the Spaniards were not. Only three months before the battle, the representative of a great maritime power, the Venetian Ambassador in Paris, was informing his Government of this difference: 'The English are men of another mettle from the Spaniards, and above all the Western nations enjoy the reputation of being active and expert in naval operations and great sea dogs'. In his opinion a contest at sea between a nation which produced the best sailors in Europe and one which had the finest infantry in the world could have only one result.

The English tactical plan, conceived by John Hawkins and for which he had built and adapted the fleet, was to fight at a distance, relying on the sailing qualities of the ships and superior gunnery. It was simple, but at that date revolutionary—a com-

THE WALLS OF THE REALM

plete break from the traditional conception of sea warfare. It
changed the nature of the naval battle because it depended for
its success on outranging the enemy. Ever since San Juan de Ulua,
the only occasion to date on which warships of the two countries
had been in action, John Hawkins had been quietly insisting that
the English fleet should be armed, in the main, with guns of the
culverin type. The culverin was a long-range gun. Compared to
the squat battering-pieces, which had the proportions of a toad,
the culverin was long in proportion to its bore. It was a muzzle
loader, about fourteen feet in length, and roughly thirty calibres,
or thirty times as long as the bore. The culverin fired an iron shot
weighing only seventeen pounds and its extreme range was about
two miles. Its disadvantage was the lightness of the projectile;
the weight of the average English broadside was only 300 lb.,
and as this was discharged at a distance, it is hardly surprising
that no enemy ship was sunk directly by gunfire in the Armada
fighting, although the English gunnery may also have been to
blame. At no time in history has marine gunnery been a science of
precision—from the conditions it has to work under it cannot
hope to be—yet Elizabethan gunnery against the Armada must
have been almost haphazard.

This was less the fault of the men at the guns than of those who
made them. The gunfounders were staunch individualists working on their own, deep in the woods of Kent, Sussex and Surrey.
No gunfounder would share the secrets of his craft with another,
and none of them believed in standardization. Each gun, cast of
iron or bronze, was an achievement on its own, cast without much
thought for accurate duplication. The result was that no two
guns dragged away on sleds for their journey to the Tower of
London, although they were of the same type, were of identical
weight, length, or even bore. It was largely a matter of luck
whether the shot exactly fitted any particular gun; if it were too
large it could not be used, whilst if too small for the bore, the re-
sultant ballistic problems were ignored by the Elizabethan gunner. The Gunnery handbook for 1588 laid it down that a gunner should be 'a sober, wakeful, lusty, hardy, patient and quick-
spirited man'—he needed to be all that. But in spite of their im-

perfections, English guns were the best in Europe and fetched a good price on the Continent. So many were finding their way down to secluded creeks on the south coast instead of to the Tower, that even as late as 1587, the Queen found it necessary to reissue an order forbidding the export of English cannon.

Now that boarding in order to fight it out hand to hand had been superseded by the new tactics, there was no need to cram into a ship every man she could carry. Hawkins had always maintained that one of the deadliest dangers at sea was overcrowding, because it led to dirtiness of ship and crew and therefore to epidemics, and a ship could not carry the victuals to feed a large crew properly. Overcrowding was unnecessary; he believed— and had proved it at sea—that the ideal for a ship was to have a crew just large enough to sail and fight her efficiently, with a few spares to replace casualties: she could then easily be kept clean, the men fed better, and she was not continually having to return to harbour to revictual. At the back of Hawkins's mind there was always the question of 'endurance'; how long a ship could remain at sea. In 1585 he persuaded the Council to revise the mobilization plan of 1582, which allowed for a proportion of one man to every one-and-a-half tons, and to allow instead a proportion of one man to every two tons—the manning scale on which the Navy fought the Armada.

Not only was Hawkins determined to have ships of the highest quality, he wanted the best men to sail and fight them, and being a businessman, he knew very well that if he wanted quality he would have to pay for it. In the same year, therefore, he managed to introduce another reform, long overdue: he had the sailor's pay raised. It has never been easy to persuade any government of the necessity for this, and while Hawkins's arguments, as ever, were sound, it was his manner of presenting them that won the day. In recommending the rise in pay, he wrote to the Council: 'By this means Her Majesty will be furnished with able men, such as can shift for themselves and keep themselves clean without vermin or noisomeness. Small wages cause the best men to run away, to make mean to be clear of the service' (or as we should say 'work their tickets'). All that is good sense, but, as he realized, it was not really enough to move a reluctant Treasury, so he concluded: 'There is no captain or master exercised in service but would undertake with more courage any enterprise with 250 able men than with three hundred of tag and rag'; and he went on to prove that a rise in pay would save money, because a small number of well-paid men would cost the Queen less than a larger number of badly-paid misfits. That did the trick, the Council agreed and the pay of the sailor was raised from six shillings and eightpence to ten shillings per month.

In addition to improving the quality of the men, Hawkins also hoped that this rise in pay would have some effect on desertion. It had little or none. During the reign of Elizabeth I it was nearly impossible to get men to serve in the Navy; they could be impressed but they deserted as soon as they saw a chance—and they can hardly be blamed. Whatever his rate of pay, the sailor was paid quarterly and was lucky if he saw his money at all, because there was no proper system of ledgers and accounting. In addition to that he was half starved, although the ration laid down for a man was more than he could eat; but he never had the chance of eating it. Thieving victuallers ashore and dishonest pursers on board had both had their cut before a little rancid butter and weevily biscuit reached the poor sailor. The whole system of pay and victualling was rotten with dishonesty and inefficiency; the only solution was a total reform of the whole system, which was quite beyond the power or ingenuity of Hawkins, or indeed, of anyone to effect, until nearly three hundred years later. The Navy as a Service was in its infancy, but in spite of its blemishes it was somehow a lusty infant. M. Oppenheim, an historian who never allowed his enthusiasm to affect his meticulous accuracy, had this to say: 'It speaks sufficiently for the courage of the Elizabethan sailor that during the whole reign, only two English men-of-war were captured by Spain, and then only after desperate fighting against overwhelming superiority of force. The one was the *Jesus of Lubeck*, the other the famous *Revenge*. It speaks equally well for his seamanship afloat and the skill and good workmanship of shipwrights ashore, that with the exception of the small *Lions' Whelp* no dockyard built ship was lost by stress of weather, by

fire, or by running aground. During the same years, and sometimes during the same gales that English ships weather success-
fully, whole Spanish fleets foundered at sea.'

By the year 1585 the careful and skilled administration of John
Hawkins had saved the Queen enough money to start some in-
tensive new construction. During the next three years, two more
of the *Revenge* class, the *Vanguard* and the *Rainbow* were completed, as well as a ship of 150 tons, and eight ocean-going pinnaces. In addition, the Queen was able to buy, when it was nearly
finished, the *Ark* belonging to Sir Walter Ralegh.

The fleet which Hawkins had set out to build was beginning to
take form and to be of a useful size, though not yet large enough
for comfort. It was none too soon, for the war with Spain which
he had so long foreseen was upon John Hawkins and his countrymen.

CHAPTER IX

War 1585. The Caribbean

*

The antagonism of two countries as opposed in outlook and interest as Spain and England could not indefinitely be tucked away out of sight in tropical seas beyond the line. Sooner or later the fundamental issue between them had to come into the open. Spain claimed the sole right to trade with her possessions overseas; England, on the ground that the seas were free, insisted on her right to trade wherever there was water to float her ships. Spain was old, the height of her summer was past, she was out of date and not strong enough at sea to protect the rights she claimed; England was young, in her springtime, brash, thrusting and capable of trading where she pleased. That the one was Catholic and the other Protestant exacerbated the quarrel, but was only incidental and not the cause. A decision on the point in dispute could never be reached through the skirmishes of unofficial adventurers and colonists in distant waters. It would only be settled in Europe by the two nations opposed in arms.

Matters had not come to a head until now, because neither Elizabeth of England, nor Philip of Spain believed in war. They both hated it. The Queen deplored its bloodshed and extravagance, its waste and the misery it caused. She thought it foolish because the victor was no better off after he had won; and she believed that everything could be settled by arbitration. King Philip hated the waste of war and he had been warned by his father, the Emperor Charles V, never to become involved in a war against England. Both longed for peace and security, and each pursued a course of diplomacy to achieve them. Beyond the shifts and stratagems, the plots and assassinations, the sudden changes in allegiance or favour, the goal of each was the same, the ultimate advantage of the people and realm. Provocation from either side, plots, incidents, insults, the open hostility of their subjects overseas; none of these during the past years had caused war, because the two Sovereigns thought that they could get all they wanted through diplomacy. But there comes a time when the aspirations of sovereigns or peoples, however estimable, are powerless to affect events or stop the surge of history. Such a time had now arrived; it had become obvious, and not only to the English, that the decisions of the savants at Tordesillas, who partitioned the world nearly a hundred years before, were outmoded and intolerable. The sea was there for anyone who cared to use it. So Queen Elizabeth and King Philip, in spite of themselves, were impelled inexorably towards war like iron filings under the invisible influence of a magnet. And when the break finally did come, it was caused, not by some flagrant act of piracy, by religious intolerance, or by the discovery of a plot, but by the situation in the Netherlands.

The Low Countries were a part of the inheritance which Philip had received from his father, the Emperor Charles V; they were a Spanish European colony, and his subjects in the Netherlands revolted against the harsh intolerance of Spanish rule. It was to England's interest to encourage this revolt, one of her best markets was Antwerp and she did not relish a rival power with naval bases just across the Narrow Seas. From going fairly well the revolt had languished, the Dutch were beaten back until they had only a narrow strip of territory with the sea at their backs—and that fact kept the revolt alive, the Dutch being supplied through Brill and Flushing. In 1584 William the Silent, the inspiration and strength of the revolt, was assassinated at Philip's instigation and the rebellion should thereupon have collapsed. That it did not was due to his son Philip of Nassau, the native tenacity of the Dutch and Queen Elizabeth of England. When it looked as if the Dutch might be driven out of their last stronghold by the brilliant young Spanish Commander, Alexander Farnese, Duke of Parma, Elizabeth became seriously concerned.

For, said the Queen, 'if the nation of Spain should make a conquest of those countries, in that danger ourself, our countries and people might shortly be'. After the death of their great leader, William the Silent, the Dutch asked Elizabeth for help. She swayed to and fro, she sent over negotiators who could not agree, and she could not make up her mind to send over an army until she had it made up for her—by King Philip. He had learned through his spies of these negotiations, and while he had reluctantly endured the unofficial help England had been giving the Dutch because he did not want an open break, when Elizabeth leagued herself with the rebels—it was enough. The Queen, however, was still hesitating and nothing had really been decided when an apparently unrelated and trivial event brought matters to a head.

On the morning of Wednesday, May 26th, 1585, 'a tall ship of London', the *Primrose*, was lying off the port of Bilbao in Biscay, quietly discharging her cargo of wheat. She was one of a number of English grain ships similarly employed in Spanish ports on that day. And none of them would have been there at all because of the uncertain relations which then obtained between England and Spain if the King had not given them special safe conduct. This he had done because he urgently needed grain to deal with a famine caused by the failure of the Spanish harvest, and the quickest way of getting it was to have it brought in English bottoms. But once the ships were in his ports he gave orders for them to be seized, an impulsive act of treachery not at all in keeping with the usual caution of King Philip. This embargo was to have consequences which must have surprised him considerably, for such a proceeding in those days was looked upon only as a normal act in the course of diplomacy. He had not allowed, however, for the stupidity of one of his Governors, nor for the escape of an English ship, the *Primrose*, which happened to have a very wide-awake captain and a resolute crew.

For no apparent reason on this Wednesday morning the Governor of Biscay suddenly arrived on board, making polite speeches and offering freshly-picked baskets of cherries. During the two days she had been unloading the *Primrose* had noticed nothing unusual or suspicious, and this might well have been a courtesy call; but with the sixth sense of a seaman where the safety of his ship is concerned, Captain Foster began to wonder what was behind this unusual visit. As he ushered his guests into his cabin to entertain them in the English fashion on 'beere, beef and bisket' he managed secretly to pass the word to his crew to be on the look-out for trouble. After dinner in the cabin, the Governor went ashore, but reappeared some while later in a boat crowded with about seventy Spaniards dressed to look like merchants. The Governor was allowed on board, the others told to wait in the boat. Instead, they scrambled over the side producing hidden weapons and seized Captain Foster before his crew had fully realized what was happening. While two Spaniards held a dagger to the throat of the English Captain, the Governor called upon him to surrender his ship, brandishing a document which he said was his authority from King Philip. The English sailors had now pulled themselves together and, while some hidden below with firearms fired into the Spaniards through hatches from below, those on deck sailed in with their swords and daggers. After a sharp fight one Englishman and many Spaniards were killed on deck, and the remainder of the Spaniards were bundled over the side to be drowned. By six o'clock that evening the ship had been cleared of Spaniards and Captain Foster hurriedly made sail before anything else could happen. But as her sails were filling, his men heard the most piteous cries from over the side. They hauled four wounded and half-drowned Spaniards on board. Their humanity was rewarded, for one of these wretches turned out to be the Governor who made the trip to England with his orders hidden in his boot. On June 8th the *Primrose* anchored safely in the Thames. Her arrival had the effect of bringing the Queen to a decision on the question of Spain; for the orders in the Governor's boot, which he had produced to prove his own innocence, revealed the disturbing fact that the English ships had been seized upon the personal order of the King so as to provide shipping for an invasion of England.

There was a howl of indignation from a country united and angry, and, responding to the mood of her people, Queen Elizabeth acted with unusual speed and decision. Within days of the return of the *Primrose* she had commissioned Drake to organize an expedition to rescue the embargoed ships, Sir Walter Ralegh was sent off with a small squadron to attack the tunny fishery off the Spanish coast, and her envoys in the Netherlands were instructed to inform the Dutch that she would send over an army —and that meant war.

Being committed to formal war after many years of unofficial hostilities, the question for the Queen was how best to wage it. Should the principal effort be made on land by giving direct help to the Dutch armies, or at sea by striking at the Spanish communications? She answered this question by evading it, she tried to do both. She could never make up her mind to one course or the other, she switched her effort from sea to land, and back again, and in the end, as Ralegh said, 'She did all by halves'. She made the great mistake of trying to do too much and dispersing her strength.

She cannot altogether be blamed—it is easy to see what should have been done after the event—but at the time things are never so clear. It is unlikely that at the start she could see the picture of the war as a whole, or the connection between the resistance of the Dutch and sea power which sustained that resistance; or between Spanish sea communications and the maintenance of Spanish armies in the Low Countries. But the Queen had advisers who knew very well and did not tire of telling her that the one certain way of subduing Spain was by destroying her fleet and cutting off her supplies. The Queen ignored their advice. She never fully grasped the meaning of sea power, it was too intangible, and the idea of using it as a weapon was new. She had never seen it at work—or if she had, had not recognized it—nor could she appreciate the dominance of sea power when properly used. And who can blame her, when so many of the great captains in history have failed to understand its significance. But what Elizabeth could appreciate was the actual presence of a Spanish army a few hundred miles from her capital, an army which every month was nearer to the coastline opposite her own shores. So she proceeded to attack Spain where it was strongest, on land.

Mistakes in strategy are frequently made because the course which afterwards proved to have been wrong, seemed at the time to be the most effective, if not the only one possible. The military venture in the Netherlands was a waste of effort, of lives and equipment, and the army could never have produced a definite result in the Low Countries. The only place where it was possible to bring that about was at sea where Spain was extremely vulnerable.

Spain owed her position as a leading power in Europe, if not her existence, and her ability to wage war in the distant Netherlands, to the use she made of sea communications. The Western treasure pouring into Seville from the Americas provided one-fifth of her total revenue. Cut that line and her credit, never very good, would disappear and she would go hopelessly bankrupt. Spain's ventures were kept going by loans from European financiers, and these loans depended upon the punctual arrival of the treasure fleets. She supplied Parma in the Netherlands with stores, reinforcements, arms and new equipment from her Biscay ports across the Bay and up Channel. Cut that line and the Spanish armies in the Netherlands would eventually wither away. Then she obtained all her naval stores, masts, planking, cordage and tar from the Baltic, either direct down Channel or northabout round the Orkneys. Without that source of supply she could neither supply Parma in the Low Countries, nor maintain the shipping to operate her treasure fleets.

In the excitement immediately on the return of the *Primrose* the first idea had been merely to retrieve the embargoed ships, but after second thoughts the expedition was given a more important objective. In the Council, Walsingham and Burghley urged that it should be used to cripple the King of Spain before his invading fleet was ready, and on July 1st the Queen duly signed a fresh commission for Sir Francis Drake, who was now to take the offensive on the grand scale. The quickest and most obvious way of hurting Spain was to cut off the Western treasure by a strong attack on the Caribbean, but the operation was expected to pay for itself. First of all, therefore, the three provincial capitals in the West Indies, San Domingo, Carthagena, and

Panama were to be taken for what they might yield in the way of loot. After that, Havana was to be occupied to serve as a base for an English fleet operating in the Caribbean. This was sound strategy: here was a coherent campaign planned to strike a decisive blow at a vital point, and if it had fully succeeded it might well have put an end to the Spanish war before it had properly begun.

The way in which the most grandiose plan yet conceived in England was put into effect, seems curious today, but it was typical of the age and eminently sensible when the Crown had little money to spare. The venture was turned into a Joint Stock Company. In other words, anyone could take shares in a vital operation of war, and hoped at least to get his money back if not a handsome profit. Hawkins's second and third voyages had been financed in this way, so that there was nothing strange about it for Elizabethans. The Queen, the Court, the City, members of the expedition itself, as well as many private citizens, all took shares. In addition to subscribing £10,000, the Queen sent two ships, the *Aid* and the *Bonaventure*. These ships had been built in 1561 and modernized twenty years later under Hawkins's first building programme. They are proof of the soundness of his methods for both ships lasted into the next reign, while no ship of the time had such continuous and distinguished service as the *Bonaventure*. Most of the ships on this expedition belonged to private citizens and the City of London fitted out many of their finest vessels, one of them being the *Primrose* which was the innocent cause of all this activity. Rather surprisingly in view of his past record, the City nominated Martin Frobisher as leader of their contingent, and in the middle of July the citizens of London flocked down their great highway the Thames to hold a sort of water carnival as Frobisher, with his flag in the *Primrose*, sailed down-river to join Drake's flag at Plymouth.

Twenty-nine ships, large and small, were soon assembled in Sutton pool and the Cattewater at Plymouth, ranging from Drake's flagship the *Bonaventure* of 600 tons to the galliot *Duck* of less than sixty. They included the *Galleon Leicester* built as flagship for an abortive expedition to the Moluccas, well-found

merchantmen of London equipped to fight their way in convoy
through the Mediterranean to the Levant, a few from the west
country belonging to Drake himself and, as might have been expected, at least one owned by John Hawkins. But more important
than the ships were the men who were to sail them; and the
trouble on such a popular expedition must have been to decide
whom to leave out. Drake as Admiral and General had Thomas
Fenner as his flag-captain, Martin Frobisher was Vice-Admiral
in the *Primrose*, the Queen's cousin, Francis Knollys, was Rear-
Admiral in his brother-in-law's *Galleon Leicester*, Edward Wynter, son of the old Sir William of the Navy Board, commanded
Her Majesty's other ship the *Aid*, and an experienced soldier,
Christopher Carleill, Walsingham's son-in-law, combined the
duties of Lieutenant-General of the land forces embarked and
command of the London ship *Tiger*. Drake's youngest brother
Thomas was there and some old *Golden Hinds* who now held
commands of their own; Tom Moon, who had already twice
sailed as carpenter with Drake, George Fortescue, John Martyn,
Edward Carless, and young Richard, son of John Hawkins, with
his first command in the *Duck*. It was a distinguished company—
a judicious mixture of experienced seamen, Court gallants and
old shipmates. The whole force, sailors and soldiers, numbered
2,300 men, hardly excessive for the job in hand.

Its importance can be measured from the fact that the force
was ready to sail by the end of July, having only been thought of
in June, which was fast moving for those days. Walsingham, a
great believer in the offensive, wrote to Leicester what he thought
of it: 'Upon Drake's voyage dependeth the life and death of the
cause according to man's judgment'. He wanted to get Drake
away as quickly as possible and he hoped that the favourite would
be able to get the Queen's permission; Elizabeth, however, was
in one of those moods of indecision which drove her advisers
nearly mad, but for which she generally had her own good reasons.
Even at this late hour she thought she might avoid war if she did
not go too far, so she was having second thoughts about fighting
by the side of the Dutch and feared to let Drake loose in the
West Indies. The weeks went by, the ships consumed their

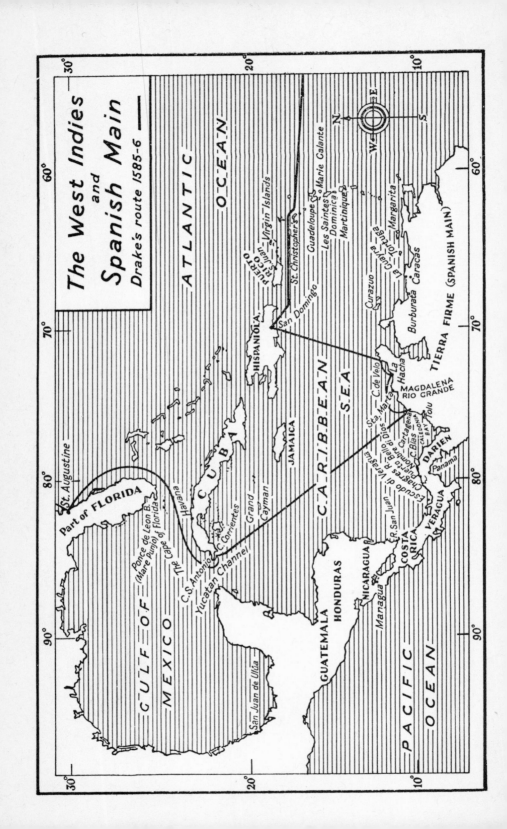

The West Indies and Spanish Main

Drake's route 1585-6

ATLANTIC OCEAN

GULF OF MEXICO

MEXICO

St. Augustine

Part of FLORIDA

Ponce de Leon B. (Mare Punto) of Florida

The Cape

Havana

C.S. Antonio

C. Corrientes

Yucatan Channel

Grand Cayman

CUBA

JAMAICA

CARIBBEAN SEA

HISPANIOLA

San Domingo

PUERTO RICO

S. Juan — Virgin Islands

St. Christophers

Guadeloupe

Marie Galante

Les Saintes

Dominica

Martinique

Margarita

Tortuga

Curazuo

Cunazuo

Buxurata

Caracas

TIERRA FIRME (SPANISH MAIN)

C. de Velo

La Hacha

Sta. Marta

MAGDALENA
RIO GRANDE

Cartagena

C. Blas

CALEDONIA BAY

Tolu

DARIEN

Nombre di Dios

Chagres R.

Panama

Escudo di Veragua

R. San Juan

VERAGUA

COSTA RICA

NICARAGUA

Managua

Managua

HONDURAS

GUATEMALA

San Juan de Ulúa

PACIFIC OCEAN

stores; out in the countryside the crops ripened and were gathered in; it was mid-September before the word came. Then on September 12th Drake hurried in from his country estate, Buckland Abbey, in a frenzy to be away before the Queen could change her mind. On the 14th, the wind being fair, he sailed without sufficient water, and leaving piles of stores on the quayside.

Drake's first need was fresh water so he made for the Spanish coast and anchored his squadron in Vigo Bay, where he learned that the embargoed ships—whose rescue was the ostensible purpose of the expedition—had long since either escaped or had been released. In spite of this news he made a point of threatening and insulting the local Governor, who could do very little about it. The Governor may have been powerless but he was no fool: he quickly removed all valuables from the town of Vigo to the mountains inland; when the English squadron moved up to the harbour of Vigo he at once offered Drake fresh provisions in the hope that he would consume them elsewhere; and he forwarded a slightly exaggerated report of the size and armament of the squadron to the King—procedure reminiscent of that normally adopted by his colleagues in the Indies. After a stay of about a week, during which Spain had not been able even to threaten him with a naval force, Drake took advantage of a northerly wind and sailed 'none knew whither', as the King wrote plaintively to de Mendoza in Paris. But King Philip had a shrewd idea, for he cancelled the sailing of the outward-bound Plate Fleet and instructed his Admiral Santa Cruz to be ready with a squadron to go after Drake should he make for the Indies. The King of Spain had been insulted and defied often enough in his colonies far away, but never before in his own home waters, and as Drake sailed down the coast of the Spanish peninsula, the couriers were spurring across Europe with news of this blow to Spanish prestige.

The homeward-bound Plate Fleets had reached San Lucar with their treasure earlier that month and there was nothing to prevent Drake from going straight to his objective. He dropped down to the Canaries to water and provision before the Atlantic crossing, which was normal practice. Apart from having spent rather too long at Vigo, his movements so far had been consistent with a campaign in the Indies; but when a heavy swell prevented his landing at Palma he sheered away to the Cape Verde Islands which were off his course and had nothing to do with his objective, the Spanish colonies in the Caribbean. An attack on these islands was a diversion which could neither harm the enemy nor contribute anything to the campaign. As things turned out this sideshow nearly wrecked it. Even Drake could find no better excuse than that the attack was to avenge treatment given William Hawkins five years before at Santiago. It is more likely that he went there to give his force a little practice in landing operations, and at the same time to cheer up his men with some booty early in the voyage. Whatever the reason, the Cape Verdes put up no sort of resistance and provided no booty.

This was because some French privateers had paid a visit three years before Drake. They had massacred the inhabitants of Santiago and cleared off with a good haul of loot. When Drake's fleet appeared in the offing, therefore, the islanders were taking no chances, they removed their valuables and made for the interior leaving their towns deserted. Drake spent ten ineffectual days in the Cape Verde Islands. There was no fighting to blood the soldiers, he failed to extract a ransom from the Governor and there was no booty for anyone. But he did fill up with water and fresh provisions and after burning the three main towns in the island sailed on November 26th with his force in good health and spirits and altogether very pleased with themselves.

This happy frame of mind lasted until they were in mid-Atlantic, seven days out from Santiago, when a mysterious epidemic swept through the fleet. 'The Sickness', so a captain of musketeers recorded, 'seized our people with extreme hot burning and continual agues whereof few escaped with life'. And those who caught it yet survived were left helpless invalids for the rest of the voyage. No ship escaped. In the flagship alone a hundred men fell sick, while each day as they bowled along before the northeast trades every ship in the fleet reported more deaths. Within a few days 300 men had died, to be dropped overboard in the wide Atlantic while the fleet sailed on. The expedition had been infected with an acute form of that fever for which the Cape Verde Islands were notorious; and Drake had been at Santiago, the unhealthiest island of them all, just after the rains, the dangerous time of year. The crossing was a quick one of eighteen days to the Antilles, which they reached in the middle of December. After watering at Dominica, Drake sailed on for four days to St. Christopher island, where everyone went into camp ashore while the ships were cleaned and disinfected. On this remote and lonely island the force spent Christmas and gave twenty of their comrades who died there a decent burial. But they also had a stroke of luck; they took two Spanish ships from which they got provisions and a Greek pilot who knew the Caribbean. This man had appeared at an opportune moment; for at a Council of War held on the island Drake had announced his intention of proceeding direct from there to the attack of San Domingo, capital of Hispaniola.

The oldest town in all the Spanish Indies and for a long time the capital, San Domingo was a city which for dignity, size and grandeur could rival almost any city in Spain itself. Above its wide avenues and stately buildings brooded the great cathedral where Christopher Columbus lay buried. San Domingo had a European reputation, and at a time when any place distant and unknown was automatically credited with fabulous wealth, it was reputed to rival the mythical cities of the East. But this rumour, too, was a myth, for no treasure was shipped from San Domingo now that the mines of Hispaniola had been worked out, only hides and sugar. The place was the administrative centre for the Spanish Indies and inhabited mostly by civil servants. It was about the only place in the Caribbean which had never been attacked and laid waste by marauding French or English corsairs because of its fortifications and strong natural position. Few but Spaniards had ever been there, and as rumour feeds on ignorance, Drake can hardly be blamed for thinking that it was a very rich prize. This was the place he had selected for the opening attack of his campaign, and he soon learned from the Greek pilot that it was a very different proposition from anything he had yet attempted in these waters. A strongly-fortified castle commanded the entrance to the harbour which was naturally protected by a difficult bar. A direct assault would be no good and Drake's only hope was to land some miles along the coast through the surf and try to take the place by a flank attack.

A detachment of ships sent on ahead lay off the city for three days firing guns and by feints making the garrison believe that the attack was to be a frontal assault. While this was going on, the main fleet assembled well off shore, opposite a place where the pilot pointed out a way in through the line of surf. Drake himself landed to reconnoitre and get the help of the local Cimaroons whose job it was to deal with the Spanish picket which guarded the shore opposite the entrance. On the afternoon of December 31st the soldiers embarked in the boats of the fleet and, very uncomfortable in the swell, were taken in to lie rolling and heaving off the entrance listening to the roar of the surf. The tropic night came suddenly and now that they could not see it the surf sounded more deadly than ever. Word came that the picket had been killed to a man and in the darkness Drake led the way in. One by one the boats came up to that threatening grey line, the roar of the surf became deafening, certain death seemed to grope at them from either side, then suddenly they were gliding through still water, and almost before they knew it had grated on the sand and were jumping clumsily out of the boat. By the time the sun rose on the other side of the bay and they could see what they were doing, the entire force had been landed without a casualty and unknown to the garrison at San Domingo. It was a fine exhibition of seamanship and discipline. 'Our general having seen us landed in all safety returned to his fleet bequeathing us to God and the good conduct of Master Carleill our Lieutenant General; at which time, being about eight of the clock, we began our march'. Such was the laconic entry in the journal of Captain Walter Biggs of the Musketeers summing up this difficult but successful operation.

While the army was marching along a well-made road which took them through pleasantly-wooded country Drake moved the fleet up towards the city and came to an anchor opposite the castle. As they approached, the ships ran out their guns and opened fire, while their boats were hoisted out as if Drake intended a landing under the guns of the fort. A frontal attack would have been suicidal, but because of what he had heard about them, the Spanish Commander put nothing beyond these English, so horse, foot and guns hurried out of the city to line up along the foreshore as if Drake's were the real attack. They were hardly in position when from their right flank came the sound of drums and trumpets. To their surprise they saw two columns advancing on the gates of their city. Carleill and his men after their ten-mile march had arrived with drums beating and colours flying. The Spanish Commander reacted quickly and for a while there was a brisk action. His horse changed front at the gallop to hold off the enemy until he could bring up his guns. The Spanish horse tried the old colonial trick of driving a herd of cattle at the enemy and then working round to his rear. But Carleill's men kept their heads and when the Spanish guns eventually got off a round, it was their last, for Carleill in person led a charge on the guns before they could reload. For a time there was wild confusion until in the end a mixture of Spanish horse and foot, terrified cattle and Englishmen with their blood up surged through the gates together. At 1 p.m. the two columns met in the market square and a huge St. George's Ensign floating out in the breeze from the top of a building told the fleet that the soldiers were in the centre of San Domingo.

The attack on San Domingo was that military exploit, so rare in the annals of war, the textbook combined operation, neat, tidy and successful where everything went according to plan. Surprise was complete, timing perfect and the feint deceived. If the opposition was weak the defenders can hardly have been expected to do better. The garrison contained only eighty regulars, horse and foot, the remainder being composed of armed civilians who are never a match for disciplined troops. It is small wonder that they broke under the determined onslaught of Carleill and his men. They were issued with quilted jackets instead of armour and the attack took place at a time of day when the Spaniard in the colonies would be taking his siesta. They cannot have been inspired to do great things by the example of the Governor, a civilian like themselves, who left the city to its fate and struck out for the interior as soon as he saw the fleet in the offing.

At one o'clock in the afternoon of New Year's Day the English were established in the heart of the city; that night the last of its defenders evacuated the castle which commanded the harbour; next morning Drake took his ships in and San Domingo was his. So far all had gone well, now came disillusionment. There was no treasure. Copper coin there was by the ton but no stacks of gold and silver, and even in their homes the townsfolk used china or pottery instead of plate. These were not the homes of rich merchants but of civil servants who lived comfortably and no more. Their houses were superbly-built mansions, their furniture beautiful, all worthless because it was not transportable. The only 'official' booty that fell at once to the English was the ships in harbour and the guns of the defences, for neither of which would the shareholders in England give a thank you. Drake had to have hard cash and the only way of getting it was by way of a ransom.

From all that he had heard about the city and the impression of solid wealth its streets and buildings gave him when he got there, Drake was led to name an impossible figure as ransom. When the Spaniards said, quite truthfully, that they could not pay it, he thought to apply pressure by burning their town piecemeal, calculating that before he had gone very far the Governor would disgorge. Every morning a working party of 200 sailors was landed for this duty. But the houses had been so well built that they found to their surprise they could not start a general conflagration which would have been only too easy in the towns and villages they came from in England. So while the sailors kept on trying to burn the city house by house, the haggling over the ransom went amicably on with the Governor holding out. The soldiers, all this time, were quite enjoying themselves living in this 'famous and goodly builded city' which was well stocked with provisions. They came across a few pieces of plate but on the whole amused themselves by living well and decking themselves out in fine suits of new clothes which they found in the houses. Those expert plunderers, the sailors, did much better for themselves, 'We had in this town much plate, money and pearls hidden in wells and other places', says the log of the *Primrose*, which looks as if they had not devoted all their time to fire-raising. After a month the damage they had caused was not great but Drake could waste no more time. He had to accept the Governor's figure of 25,000 ducats, equivalent to about £7,000 of his money. He provisioned the fleet, stowed the cannon in his holds, re-embarked the soldiers and on February 1st, six weeks behind time-table, shaped a course to the southward for the capital of the Spanish Main.

The rich island of Margarita was next on the list and Drake had intended to deal with it on the way, but he found the wind unsuitable for an attack and as he could not waste any more time he coasted along the mainland to Carthagena. This was a different problem from San Domingo and far tougher because there was practically no way of getting at the place by sea or land without every movement being observed. Carthagena was a strongly-fortified walled city with a garrison about equal to the number of men Carleill had remaining; it was fully alert and expecting Drake. The town was built right on the sea with impassable marshes protecting it one side and a lagoon the other, while attack from seaward was impossible. This lagoon was formed by a narrow peninsula which ran from the city walls like a natural breakwater to broaden out into a sort of promontory three miles from the city where there was an entrance from the sea. A spit of land running at right-angles and reaching almost to the opposite shore formed a snug, inner harbour. Drake knew it well from the old days. In his pinnace he had once ridden out a storm in the outer harbour; he had not been strong enough to attack on that occasion, but chilled, wet and hungry though he was, with his men beginning to murmur, he had spent his time studying the lie of the place and its approaches with an eye, no doubt, to capturing it one fine day. Even in his dreams Drake never admitted the impossible which is why he so often achieved it. He now had before him a walled city impregnably situated with an alerted garrison. The only possible approach to the city along the natural break-water had been barred at its narrowest point by a formidable trench. Two galleys had been stationed in the inner harbour so as to enfilade anyone storming the trench. On the face of it an attack looked to be out of the question and some of the men thought it impossible. And so it would have been for anyone without Drake's facility for quick improvisation. He might be the Queen's Officer in command of an important expedition, but he still saw things with the eye of a privateer, not for him the slow ritual of conventional warfare. This insouciance really only worked well when his forces were small and under his personal control, where his was the last word. Then Drake was at his best, and he was never more brilliant than at Carthagena.

In the early afternoon of February 9th Drake led the fleet past the city within cannon shot. This was quite close enough as he sailed by to observe detail and he must have noted the state of readiness ashore, the general air of being prepared to give him a hot welcome: the crowded battlements with the gunners at the ready, the trench bristling with obstacles, the galleys moored in close support, a glint from the lance of a patrolling Spanish horseman. There is no record of when or how Drake first hit upon a plan for capturing the city. He was already acquainted with the main features of the place, but it is unlikely that as he sailed up to Carthagena he had any coherent scheme in his mind—certainly he had issued no detailed orders. Very probably the solution came to him in the few seconds that his ship, plunging in the swell, was abreast the seaward end of the entrenchment across the neck of the peninsula. He had left it until very late and even to him it must have looked a desperate affair, but it was the only one offering. Luckily he got on very well with Carleill who was the ideal partner for Drake, he did what was asked of him without question or raising objections. Much of the success of the expedition was due to the teamwork of these two men and if the plans were Drake's the execution of them was left to Christopher Carleill.

At about four o'clock in the afternoon Drake took the fleet in to the Outer Harbour and anchored, while the Spaniards watched and wondered. As she let go her anchor the largest English ship shifted her standard from the masthead to the main shrouds. The Spaniards knew what that meant because they used the same signal themselves for a council of war. At once a great traffic of small boats converged upon the flagship. Drake now outlined his plan to the senior officers and gave his orders. The essence of the plan was much the same as for the capture of San Domingo: a convincing demonstration to divert attention from the main attack which would be mounted elsewhere, with the disadvantage that here at Carthagena the feint could never be mistaken for the real thing for long enough to make the enemy deploy in the wrong direction. At dusk Carleill would land with all available soldiers on the promontory near the harbour mouth, then advance along the beach of the peninsula until they came to the entrenchment, then if they kept almost in the surf they could outflank the defences and be in dead ground where the fire of the enfilading galleys could not reach them.

That was to be the main attack; Frobisher, it was hoped, would provide the diversion. As soon as Carleill ran into trouble Frobisher was to attract attention with the pinnaces and ship's boats by making as if to force the entrance from the outer to the inner harbour. The Spaniards knew that forcing it was impossible: the narrow gap was shoal water, it was barred by a chain and covered by a fort mounting sixteen cannon of various sizes.

After dark, Carleill got his men ashore on the wooded promontory unopposed and not long after the various columns were hopelessly lost in thick brushwood. But by midnight—and it must have been a hectic few hours—he had collected his force and formed it up on the seaward side of the peninsula. All they had to do, he tersely informed them, was to 'march forward as easily as foot might fall, keeping close by the seawash of the shore', and they could not possibly lose their way again. As they stealthily advanced both the city and the fleet seemed to be sleeping under a blazing canopy of stars. It was tough going, the inner rank struggled along through soft sand, while the outer rank got their feet wet whenever a wave larger than its fellows came hissing up the beach to ripple round their ankles. But they kept steadily on and when they were only a couple of miles from their objective ran into a strong cavalry patrol. This scrubby terrain was no sort of country for horsemen and at the first volley from English musketeers the patrol retired to give the alarm, their job done.

At this moment, far away on Carleill's right, all hell broke

loose. Lurid flashes lit up the sky and the noise of a violent can-
nonade came booming over the scrub. The sound and fury continued for a while only to die away again as suddenly as it had
begun. After that there was silence. The English volley at the
patrol had been taken by Frobisher for his signal and he had made
straight for the gap without reckoning the cost. In that starlight
there was no hope of taking the fort unawares, it spotted the
attackers at once and opened fire. The pinnaces and boats pressed
on while men's hats were blown off, masts were shot away and
cannon balls sheered boats' oars off at the gunwale. It was too
hot a reception to stand for long and the flotilla hauled off. To
judge from the determination with which this forlorn attempt was
pressed home and from remarks in the log of the *Primrose*, it
would seem that there had been some misunderstanding over
which was the diversion and which the main attack; though
Drake and Carleill would both know that no feint can be successful
which can easily be distinguished from the real thing. As things
turned out, this gallant demonstration by the small craft had little,
if any, effect on the operation as a whole: it drew no men off from
the close defence of the city, but it may have had a moral effect
on the taut nerves of defenders wondering, as they had been for
hours, where, when and how the great pirate Drake was going to
attack them.

They had not long to wait now for the answer. The stars
were beginning to lose some of their brilliance, but it was not
yet dawn when a narrowing of the peninsula along which they
were marching told the English that they were getting close to
their objective. The tide was out and Carleill now took them
right down the beach to wade until they were within striking
distance. Leaving them halted in the water he went on himself
to have a closer look at the Spanish position. The land here was
only fifty yards across running down to the sea on one side and
to the harbour on the other, and these two beaches had given
the land a pronounced camber. A solid-looking stone wall protected by a ditch ran across the neck, the right flank was protected
by the sea, the left by two moored galleys, and six cannon were
mounted along the wall to deal with a frontal attack. The Spaniards

thought they had made the position impregnable, and so at first glance it seemed to be. Carleill, however, in that uncertain morning light had spotted its one weakness. The wall and trench stopped a little way short of the sea in order to allow for a retiring picket to pass round that flank to regain the shelter of the wall. To remedy this the Spaniards had built an extension in the form of a line of wine butts filled with earth. By attacking on this seaward flank, Carleill saw, the guns on the wall would not be able to bear, while those in the galleys and their small-arms would be blanked by the slope of the ground. Carleill had seen his chance, all now depended upon his men. These had been on the move without food or rest for twelve hours; they had floundered through heavy sand, tripped over tussocks in the dark, waded through the sea and were now standing knee deep in the water waiting to attack. Even a tropic dawn strikes chill, they were cold, hungry, tired and wet, but in the next few minutes these foot soldiers were to show what Englishmen could do, when given the lead. How those officers and men conducted themselves in that dawn action was modestly described in his journal by a soldier who went forward with the first wave to attack, Captain Biggs of the Musketeers.

It is clear from the account of this fair-minded soldier that although English equipment was superior—the pikes were larger and the body armour better—what really gave them the day was the speed and dash of the attack following the lead of their officers. Ordering the musketeers to hold their fire until they were right up to the enemy, Carleill drew his sword and charged with them. The pikes were on their heels and without stopping to reload, musketeers and pikemen surged forward in a body. 'Down went the butts of earth, and pell mell came our swords and pikes together, after our shot had first given their volley, even at the enemy's nose. In this furious entry the Lieutenant-General (Carleill) slew with his own hand the chief ensign-bearer of the Spaniards who fought very manfully to his life's end'. At this moment too, Captain Sampson commanding the pikes was wounded by a sword thrust, while another English officer after a hand to hand combat took prisoner the Spanish officer in command of the position. Once they were into the entrenchment the enemy broke, and without a pause Carleill's men drove forward and through the city gate. Sweeping on over barricades and brushing aside any opposition, their momentum took them to the Plaza in the centre of the town. 'Every man', says Biggs the Musketeer, 'as well of one part as another, came so willingly to the service, as the enemy was not able to endure the fury of such hot assault'.

The main body of the enemy soon lost interest in the defence of their city. Once the English had reached the Plaza in the centre of the town they were troubled no more by their recent adversaries who had kept on going, through the city and out of it until they had reached the hills inland to which their wives and families had been evacuated. As at San Domingo most of these men were armed civilians. Next day the fleet moved from its anchorage towards the fort which promptly surrendered. It all sounds as if the taking of Carthagena was very easy, but the collapse of morale and resistance only occurred after Drake had displayed a masterly combination of planning, speed, audacity— and a certain amount of luck; after such a feat of arms the captors certainly deserved more than they got out of it. Now at last the capital of the Spanish Main was his, the Atlantic depot for the Indian trade, home of the richest merchants in the Caribbean. Before leaving England he had estimated the sack of Carthagena at over three hundred thousand English pounds; and it might well have been worth all of that had not the merchants wisely spent their three weeks' grace while he was at San Domingo in carting off their valuables to the safety of the hills. As soon as Drake had settled in he demanded a ransom for the city of 300,000 ducats, or in his money, £100,000. The Spanish Governor said he could not pay anything like that and offered about a quarter of what had been asked. After this opening gambit the negotiations began in earnest, and it now became a question of which side could hold out the longer.

'We stayed here six weeks', Biggs wrote in his journal, 'and the sickness still continued with us, though not with the same fury as at first'. The epidemic was the deciding factor of the negotiations, for though deaths were fewer, those who recovered were left with their wits affected and the number of men reporting fit for duty was fewer every day. Drake soon realized that he could not allow the negotiations to drag on indefinitely so he gave the city over to the sack and began to burn the outskirts to see if this would bring the Spaniards to their senses. The Governor's defence was time, something which Drake could not afford, and after studying reports on the health of the English garrison, he refused to budge from his original offer. He may not have been aware of it, but the Governor's position was the stronger in that the sack had produced very little; and English soldiers who could treat a serious epidemic as something to be joked about, saw nothing to laugh at in a sack which produced no treasure. It was a serious matter for these men who were all volunteers—not pressed men—serving for a share in the profits instead of regular pay. They had now seen three cities in a row, each apparently bulging with riches, yield no loot worth considering, and it was more than they could bear. They lost their good spirits and there were signs that their discipline too might go. The prodigies they had performed so far had been made possible by their fine temper and morale as a body. By now not so many were left. One hundred had died during the stay at Carthagena, another 150 were sick, only 700 men were fit for duty. Many objects of the expedition still remained to be carried out, among them the capture of Panama on the far side of Darien. In the circumstances what was Drake to do? For the first time in his life he sought the answer to a problem from a Council of his officers.

As any decision on the future course of the expedition depended on the soldiers, Drake addressed two questions to a committee of his Land-Captains; and the answer they gave him is a measure of the quality of Christopher Carleill and his team. To his first they replied that although they had only 700 fit men remaining they were prepared to hold Carthagena against all comers, provided the Sea-Captains could look after their ships without help from the soldiers if a Spanish fleet arrived. To his second question also they returned a clear and unequivocal answer. They did not think it wise to attempt the capture of any other place, and gave their reasons. For one thing there was no knowing when they might not have another outbreak of fever; for another, their men had now captured three cities to find no loot, and they feared that as their presence in the Caribbean was known, Panama, Nombre de Dios or Havana would have been cleared of valuables before their arrival. They thought, therefore, that Drake should accept the ransom and sail for home; but in spite of all this they declared that they were ready to undertake any service which their General might require of them. Having dealt with the operational side they added a rider of their own. They wanted their share of the ransom from Carthagena to be given to the men. Or, as their resolution stated: 'We do freely give and bestow the same wholly upon the poor men who have remained with us in the voyage (meaning as well the sailor as the soldier), wishing it were so much as might see a sufficient reward for their painful endeavour.' The 'Resolutions' were signed by Christopher Carleill and all his officers.

These conclusions must have been very much what Drake had reached in his own mind, and it was now for him alone to make the decision. As a responsible officer of the Queen, against the failure to achieve his objective in the Caribbean he balanced the fact that the Queen would not look at all favourably upon requests for supplies and reinforcements coming from Carthagena. A naval undertaking in those days was supposed to be self-supporting, to make money not to spend it. If he had still been a privateer on his own he might have had a go at Panama, but he was not. He decided to sail for England.

He and his men had been settled in at Carthagena for some time, and such was the English discipline that there had been no incidents. With their innate friendliness, the English soldiers and sailors seem to have got on very well with the local residents, while Drake and his senior officers wined and dined the Governor and officials and even the local Bishop sat down at table with the heretics. The Spaniards returned the hospitality. It was an odd situation in which both sides showed good sense, leaving the abuse and hatred to those who were not on the spot and enjoying themselves like civilized people.

Though the atmosphere was pleasant and friendly the English kept on their toes and had a sentry posted in daylight hours up the church steeple. One morning this man reported two small inter-colony trading vessels in sight making for the harbour, and scenting a chance of some booty at last Captain Thomas Moon of the *Francis* and Captain Varney of the *George* raced off to intercept in a couple of pinnaces. The Spaniards could see their sails over the low spit of land and to avoid a fight beached themselves at the harbour mouth, about the place where Carleill had landed: their crews jumped ashore and hid in the thick bush just off the beach. As the two captains with casual disregard of any precautions were standing on the deck of one deserted vessel a sudden volley came from the bushes a few yards away. Varney was killed instantly. Thomas Moon was taken back to the city seriously wounded; and a few days later the man who had scuttled the *Swan* for Drake long ago, who had announced the arrival of the English in the Pacific that evening at Valparaiso, died far from home and was buried among his enemies.

The Governor paid over the sum he had offered all along and Drake prepared for sea. The English loaded the sixty guns of the place, some furniture and silks from the homes of the richer merchants, embarked a mixed bag of galley slaves which included 100 Turks, and, what must have upset the Spaniards more than anything else, removed every church bell in the place. Then on March 31st the Spaniards heaved a sigh of relief at seeing their uninvited guests wind out through the narrow entrance, but were horrified to see the whole lot back again two days later. A prize Drake had taken at San Domingo was unseaworthy and he had to distribute her cargo of guns and church bells and slaves among the rest of his fleet. While this was being done the cooks of the fleet were sent ashore to bake biscuit in the ovens of the town, and had the time of their lives being entertained by the friendly citizens. Then at last the English sailed again and this time stood away to the northward, shaping a course for the Yucatan Channel.

Almost the last item Captain Biggs the Musketeer recorded in his journal was the 'Resolution of the Land-Captains' at Carthagena, for he died of the effects of fever on the passage up to Cuba and a brother officer named Cates took over the journal. On April 16th Drake was sailing north across the Caribbean with a well-found squadron and a force of battle-trained soldiers ready for anything—the Caribbean and all its isolated settlements were at his mercy. That same day on the other side of the Atlantic a Spanish squadron at last put to sea in order to prevent what had already been done. After watering and giving the invalids a run ashore at Cape San Antonio, Drake was held up along the north coast of Cuba by adverse currents and winds until on May 23rd he stood away for Florida and five days later was off the Spanish settlement of St. Augustine where Hawkins on his second voyage had been so generous to the Frenchman, de Laudonnière. Soon after that the Spaniards had wiped out the French settlement and now their garrison manned the forts up the river.

The soldiers showed that there was nothing wrong with their spirit when they took St. Augustine by a brilliant night operation in ships' boats. They returned with the garrison pay chest and a dozen brass guns, but without Carleill's second-in-command, Captain Anthony Powell, who was killed.

On June 9th the fleet arrived off Roanoke in Virginia to find Ralegh's colony in the doldrums because the mistake had been made of sending out a body of soldiers as colonists instead of a community. One hundred and three disillusioned persons were embarked. Drake picked up the westerlies and on July 28th arrived at Portsmouth, 'to the great glory of God, and to no small honour to our Prince, our country and ourselves'.

No one did well out of the expeditions, the shareholders got back fifteen shillings for every pound invested and should have counted themselves lucky, the poor soldiers and sailors each got six pounds as their share for ten months' service, but the Turkish galley slaves most probably got the worst deal of all. Through the Turkey Company these unfortunates were returned to the Sultan who most probably sent them straight to his own galleys.

The effect on Europe was electric. Down came King Philip's credit. 'The Bank of Seville is broke', Burghley noted, 'the Bank of Valencia also very likely. It will be such a cooling to King

Philip as never happened to him since he was King of Spain.'
Parma had not the money to continue his victorious advance in
the Netherlands; it was halted not by Leicester's army or by the
Dutch, but by Carleill's soldiers wading along a spit of land 4,000
miles away in the Caribbean. The Flemish bankers, Parma reported, 'ponder much over this success of Drake'. So did the
Venetians and one or two of the Council, but not the Queen.
The pervasive dominance of sea power was beyond her understanding and she did not follow up the blow. Having won the
initiative she threw it away to continue her own brand of diplomacy.

CHAPTER X

1587 — On the Coast of Spain

*

Lord Treasurer Burghley, experienced, cautious and controlled, the Officer of State chiefly responsible under the Queen for the safety of the realm could never wholly approve of Drake or what he did, and with the rest of the Council he was disappointed in the results of this latest exploit. It had not paid its way and now peace with Spain was out of the question; his mistress needed money and longed for peace. But as the old statesman pondered in the quiet of his study at Theobald's over the results of this raid, the immense damage it had done to Spanish trade and prestige, the chaos into which it had thrown the King's finances, he could not resist noting with a certain dry relish, 'Truly Sir Francis Drake is a fearful man to the King of Spain'. This only echoed what all Europe was thinking, and Burghley might have added to its results the new confidence it had given the nation. With sure instinct the ordinary people of the land saw that Spain, this great colossus, was vulnerable, and though they knew in their hearts that war was inevitable, after this campaign, they no longer dreaded it. The strategists in the village alehouses, with clearer insight than their rulers, saw where Spain should be attacked and that their safety lay at sea. But the Queen had lost the initiative and for the next three years the activities of the fleet were regulated by King Philip's preparations for his Armada, the English squadrons being tied to the coast of Spain or their own home waters.

At about the time Drake was picking up the westerlies to bring him home across the Atlantic, couriers from Spain were on their way to Rome with instructions for the Spanish Ambassador.

King Philip had come to a decision on the English question. Before reaching it he must have spent much time in anxious thought and even longer upon his knees praying for guidance, because the step he proposed to take went against all the advice given him by his father the Emperor. He had decided to invade that Kingdom. The 'insult' at Vigo, the raid into the Caribbean and the arrival of Leicester with 7,000 men in the Low Countries all helped to form this resolve. Now, three years after the victory at Terceira in the Azores, his Admiral Santa Cruz had presented him with a detailed plan for subjugating the English, but it had been too expensive and the King had put that plan aside. The time had now come when something had to be done, so the file was reopened.

Even if the plan were modified it would still need more money than he could afford, and the instructions to his Ambassador were to see what he could get out of the Pope towards the expenses. Olivarez, the Ambassador, was to put the thing across as a religious enterprise, he was to skate over King Philip's political motives or what he stood to gain by it and stress its aims as the Conversion of England, the restoration of Mary Queen of Scots, the avenging of martyrs. Olivarez did his best and no doubt made it all sound most edifying, but the Pope did not rise to the bait. As one studies his portrait one is not surprised. Pope Sixtus V is shown as a large, hearty man with a very knowing look in his eye. He had no great opinion of Spanish promises and through the smokescreen he saw that the whole business was for Philip's benefit. Added to that he had a sneaking regard for Drake and the Queen and did not mind saying so in public. All that Olivarez could get after working on him for eighteen months was the promise of a million crowns, but not a penny would Philip get until his army had landed in England, and privately the Pope thought his money fairly safe.

With an Ambassador furthering his interests at the Vatican, King Philip made a start on the preparations for his vast undertaking. His cell in the Escorial was littered with charts of the English coastline, he called for a more detailed plan of attack from his Admiral Santa Cruz, set Parma to widening canals in the Low

Countries, began scouring Europe for tonnage from the Baltic to the Mediterranean and placed orders for cannon with the Italian gunfounders. Philip had regained the initiative because he had decided on war, while Elizabeth still dreamed of peace and for fear of endangering it would do nothing decisive. The first reports of Spanish preparations started to come in during December, 1585, but they were so vague and unsatisfactory that no notice was taken of them. Anyhow, the Government were far too preoccupied with the case of Mary Queen of Scots to think of anything else, for the Babington Conspiracy had just been discovered, and Sir Francis Walsingham was engaged in collecting the evidence which would condemn the Queen of Scots, and settle that question with a blow of the headsman's axe. During the whole of 1586 nothing was attempted at sea, except that John Hawkins was given the chance of testing for himself the result of his shipbuilding policy.

Very few details of this expedition have been preserved, not even the reason for it or his orders, but the details we do know are illuminating. He was ordered to sea in August with five of the Queen's ships. Three of these, the *Nonpareil*, the *Lion* and the *Hope*, were old ships which had been cut down and rebuilt, the fourth was the *Revenge* and the last of 150 tons, the *Tramontana*, just out of the builder's yard at Deptford. Hawkins flew his flag in the *Nonpareil* and took as his second-in-command, William Borough, the Clerk of the Ships on the Navy Board, who had been Hawkins's inveterate critic and enemy, who disagreed with Hawkins's policy of design and had violently opposed the cutting down of the old high-charged ships. Now he was to sail in one of these converted ships, and as he is not recorded as having made any criticism of the sea-going qualities of the *Lion*, he may have been pleasurably surprised to find her a good seaboat. He and Hawkins got on very well together. For a long time Hawkins had advocated intercepting the Plate Fleets by keeping a squadron cruising off the Azores and the composition of this one makes it look as if that may have been its object. If so, it soon became confused with another, that of Channel Guard, for in August the Babington Plot was made public, and England was flooded with rumours, all of them false, but the Queen and her Council were nervous lest the Guises should attempt a raid from France. Instead of proceeding at once to his station, Hawkins was ordered to 'ply up and down the Channel'. He was kept at this for three weeks, and when at last he was released, he arrived in the area too late. The Plate Fleet and the East Indian carracks were safely home, but he did pick up one straggler with no treasure on board.

From the Captain of this ship we have a first-hand account of the sort of navy John Hawkins had produced. He treated this Spanish seaman well, showed him over the *Nonpareil* and the *Lion*, and the Captain was most impressed by all he saw. The report he made on his return to Spain is a vindication of Hawkins's time on the Navy Board. In both ships the sails were new, the ships clean and everything well-found. The *Nonpareil* carried live sheep and pigs on board and her men were issued with fresh fruit—a typical Hawkins touch this last, for he believed in keeping his crew healthy and paid for these delicacies from his own pocket. He released the Spaniard to tell what he had seen and after this testing cruise, which might have been something much more, reached home at the end of October.

'God be praised', a Madrid correspondent wrote in November to his principals at Augsburg, 'the fleet from New Spain has arrived'. The news coursed through Europe like sap up a tree, bringing new life and hope to the international bankers, most of whom held too many of Philip's promissory notes for comfort of mind. As the King's credit revived, so his preparations gained momentum; stores, ships and troops which had been held up for lack of funds started to move, all converging upon Lisbon and Cadiz. Now a country cannot buy up vast quantities of naval stores in the Baltic, set shipwrights to building in Lisbon, Barcelona and Naples and requisition shipping from Hamburg to Sicily without the rest of Europe knowing all about it. The English spies on the Continent had only to keep their ears open and their stream of circumstantial reports seriously alarmed the Council. Although the Queen's advisers knew and accepted the fact that Philip was set on conquest by invasion, the year ended with

England nominally at peace and the Queen exchanging expensive presents with Parma, a proceeding which greatly puzzled the European bankers when they learned of it. Before the year was out, however, the Council managed to bring Elizabeth out of her daydreams of a negotiated peace for long enough to listen to their urgent warnings. They persuaded her to try and stop the Spanish concentration by getting her blow in first. During Christmas week she gave orders that a squadron should be ready for sea in March, but its purpose, its destination and that Drake was to sail in command were all kept a profound secret.

While most of King Philip's activities were as open as the day, because they could not be hidden, very little was known on the Continent of what was happening in England. This was not for want of trying on Philip's part; he had to know what England intended and how far she had got with any preparations because his assembling ships were at the mercy of a raiding squadron. There had been a time when de Mendoza in England had supplied Philip with all the information he needed, but de Mendoza was now Spanish Ambassador in Paris. The King in his desperation turned to de Mendoza again and ordered him at all costs to find out what was afoot across the Channel. But even that master of intelligence work could produce very little. What is known today as 'security' in England was surprisingly good. During the scare in the previous summer the regulations had been overhauled, but more important and effective than any official measures was the temper of the people. While by order new arrivals at the inns of London had to register and were at once reported to the authorities, people reported a strange face in a seaport to the authorities of their own accord. The general effect of all this was that even if a spy did manage to set foot in England, he found it very hard to get any information at all, and what he did get he found almost impossible to send out of the country. King Philip was certain that a squadron was fitting out but even de Mendoza could not get an inkling of its destination. This is not surprising, for the Queen had not yet made up her mind, and very few in England knew where it was to go, though Drake had his own ideas of how the squadron should be employed once he was out to sea.

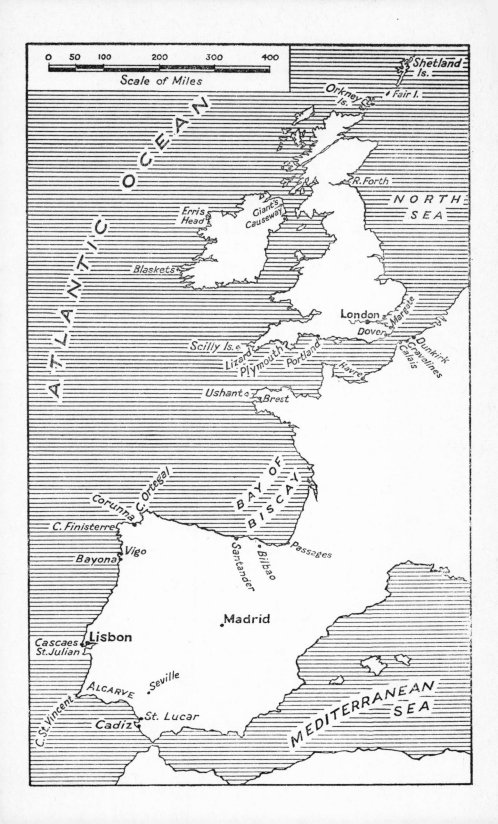

Scale of Miles

0   50   100   200   300   400

ATLANTIC OCEAN

Shetland Is.

Orkney Is.

Fair I.

NORTH SEA

R. Forth

Erris Head

Giant's Causeway

Blaskets

London

Dover

Margate

Scilly Is.

Dunkirk

Gravelines

Calais

Lizard

Plymouth

Portland

Havre

Ushant

Brest

BAY OF BISCAY

C. Ortegal

Corunna

Passages

C. Finisterre

Santander

Bilbao

Vigo

Bayona

Madrid

Cascaes

St. Julian

Lisbon

Seville

ALCARVE

St. Lucar

C. St. Vincent

Cadiz

MEDITERRANEAN SEA

The primary object of the expedition was to prevent the concentration of Spanish forces which were collecting at various assembly points round the long coastline of the Iberian peninsula. Santa Cruz, the commander-in-chief, with the Portuguese fighting galleons was already at Lisbon. Here in March, 1587, he was awaiting the Guipuscoan Squadron from Passages on the Biscay coast, galleys and supply ships from Cadiz, troops and more ships from Carthagena inside the Mediterranean, and even galleasses from Naples. Stores and provisions had to be at the right place at the right time for these forces, and the co-ordination of all movements was an intricate operation which could be paralysed by the sudden appearance of an enemy squadron on the Spanish coast.

The force selected for this national responsibility was a mixed one, financed, like the Caribbean expedition, on the joint stock method and this, too, was expected, not only to fulfil its mission, but to make enough to pay for itself while doing so. The Queen, the Lord Admiral, Drake himself and the London merchant companies were the principal shareholders, and of the ships engaged, the greater number were privately owned. The Queen provided four ships, the *Bonaventure*, Drake's flagship, the *Golden Lion*, with William Borough as his second-in-command, the *Dreadnought*, Captain Fenner, and the *Rainbow*, built by Peter Pett at Deptford, the latest off the stocks in Hawkins's new construction programme. Drake provided three ships, the Lord Admiral one, while the Levant Company sent a fine contingent of seven ships. These 'Levanters' were almost as good as warships, because they were specially built and armed for the Mediterranean trade, where as often as not they had to fight their way through against Spanish detachments or Barbary pirates out of Algiers. Three of the ships now on their way round from London to Plymouth had formed part of a convoy which, only the summer before, had beaten off a superior Spanish force when attacked in the Narrows as they came up to Pantellaria homeward-bound. In all, Drake had twenty-three ships and pinnaces with ten companies of soldiers embarked as a landing force.

The first orders he received were confusing as they named two distinct and separate objectives. He was to prevent a junction of the Spanish contingents and stop the passage of their supplies round the coast—all part of the same operation—and, as a hopeful afterthought, he was to capture the homeward- or outward-bound treasure fleets. It was, presumably, to be left to luck or to Drake which he went for first. There was never any doubt in Drake's mind which was the main objective; and when he was directed to 'distress the ships within the havens themselves', he thought it too good to be true. Those were still his orders on April 1st when the 'Levanters' which had been delayed by contrary winds at last sailed into Plymouth. They must have thought then that a hurricane had struck them. Drake was so sure that the Queen would change her mind that he gave them only twenty-four hours to water and take in what provisions they could and sailed next morning before any revised orders could reach him, whether they were ready or not. 'The wind commands me away', he wrote to Walsingham when he was safely at sea, 'our ship is under sail. Haste! from Her Majesty's good ship *Bonaventure*', he ended. The letter was dated April 2nd at which time his ship was not only under sail, but out of sight of land.

He was just in time, for while the Levanter crews had been feverishly throwing stores on board anyhow, hoping to strike them down later, a messenger from the Council had been riding post from London with revised orders which would have altered the whole nature of the Expedition. Hearing rumours that Philip had slackened his preparations the Queen had been doing some wishful thinking. Perhaps she could avoid this war after all, and Drake's orders were going too far. 'You shall forbear', read the paper in the messenger's pouch, 'to enter forcibly into any of the King's havens; or to offer any violence to any of his towns or shipping within harbouring, or to do any act of hostility upon the land'. All that Drake was to be allowed to do was capture any treasure ships he came upon, though even then he was to 'avoid the effusion of any Christian blood'. In other words, Drake's original orders were cancelled; and as the courier rode off the Queen felt a little more comfortable and went on with her futile negotiations with Parma. But luckily for the Queen and her country, when the messenger clattered into Plymouth there was no one to whom he could deliver the Royal command. The Sound was empty, all that remained were untidy piles of stores on the quays of Sutton Pool.

Meanwhile a fair wind was carrying Drake, in execution of his original orders, swiftly across the Bay to Finisterre, which he raised three days out from Plymouth. Beyond this Cape, as so often happens, the weather suddenly altered and the fleet was scattered by a south-westerly gale which took five days to blow itself out. However, the general standard of seamanship in that mixed fleet was so high that ten days after being dispersed, every ship had turned up at the rendezvous just to the northward of the mouth of the Tagus. Here Drake spoke two homeward-bound Flemish merchantmen who informed him that at Cadiz there was a mass of Spanish shipping getting ready to sail for Lisbon, the port of concentration. This was the chance he had been hoping for; and with his smaller ships sweeping inshore to pick up coasting craft he pressed on for Cadiz until on April 19th he was within striking distance. He had not worried about stragglers and without waiting for them to catch up, the *Bonaventure* shortened sail, while still out of sight of Cadiz, and put out the flag of Council which was at once obeyed by all ships still in company.

Drake was conforming to a regulation dating from the time of Henry VIII, which by tradition had the effect of making the Council of War give the orders and the Admiral only the instrument for carrying them out—a state of affairs not at all to Drake's liking. He never minded listening to the ideas of other men, so long as no one objected to his carrying out his own. When Borough arrived on board the flagship he was disturbed at what he found. From the general activity and the snatches of conversation he caught as he passed knots of excited officers on his way aft to the great cabin, he got the impression that Drake had decided on his course of action before even the Council had been held. Borough's guess was right, there was no discussion. Drake curtly informed his senior officers that as the wind was fair he was going in to attack at once, and so dismissed them. Borough was profoundly shocked. He was a sailor of the old school, he had sailed with

Chancellor as far back at 1553, he was an expert on the Arctic and theoretical navigation, and for the last seven years he had been ashore as Clerk of the Ships on the Navy Board. He could not stand these new men or their ways. This whole affair was highly irregular. All the fleet was not present, this was a desperate venture, before which, it was expressly laid down by regulation, there should be a properly conducted Council of War, and no orders of any kind had been issued. Greatly daring, Borough protested and said what he thought of it all. But Drake had done his campaigning in the Caribbean where regulations had never existed, while as for Councils, had he not managed to sail round the world without them. He was as much of the new idea as the ships Hawkins built; poor Borough was out of date, he belonged to the old era of high-charged ships, and there were none of them off Cadiz that afternoon. At four o'clock the wind being favourable, Drake stood in for the harbour of Cadiz, and all Borough could do was to follow.

Drake had the talent, possessed by all the great captains, of knowing when to take a chance. This flair combined with a genius for quick improvisation often made it appear after the event as if the obstacles had been fewer than they were, just as a class batsman can make any bowling look easy. The dangers ahead of him now were formidable and varied, but after learning what he could about the place from neutral vessels encountered on the passage down he judged them to be a fair risk. A dozen twelve-oared galleys were stationed in the port, and these, because they were an unfamiliar enemy, were regarded by many in the Queen's ships with dread and foreboding, particularly by Borough who was convinced that ships armed on the broadside would be helpless against them. The harbour had a difficult entrance obstructed by shoals and reefs, the only deep-water channel leading past the guns of Cadiz and batteries on shore.

Drake led in, followed by the other Royal ships in no proper order or formation, and as he opened the harbour mouth he could see a forest of masts clustered in the outer harbour, and beyond them in the distance of an inner harbour, more ships, large and small, including one great fighting galleon belonging to the Marquis of Santa Cruz. Once in, as he knew from his neutral informants, he had all these at his mercy because most of them had no crews, many were impressed merchantmen whose sails had been removed to prevent them deserting, and hardly any ships had as yet received their guns. The twelve galleys came racing out to meet him as a fair wind carried him smoothly towards his objective. Crossing the bows of the galleys the Queen's ships in succession poured in raking broadsides. Crushed and mangled by this concentrated fire, they faltered, stopped and broke. One was beached to save her from sinking, two made off for the inner harbour, the remainder retired close under the shore batteries. At the noise of the first English salvo there was panic among the anchored ships, which cut their cables and tried to get away to the inner harbour, but by this time their crews were jumping overboard as the 'Levanters' got in amongst them. Those ships which had sails were kept, the others plundered of their stores, and in the general excitement a large Ragusan merchantman mounting forty brass guns was sunk by mistake. The destruction went on unhindered, the plundered ships were fired and as night fell the harbour was lit by the glare of burning ships. After a while Drake withdrew his force from this inferno and the danger of drifting hulks on fire to anchor at the entrance out of range of the guns of the town. The glare from the inner harbour died down till all was dark, and in their anchored ships the English dropped off to sleep.

Some distance inland at Aranjuez, the King of Spain was having a restless night. At about the time Drake was entering Cadiz a courier with urgent dispatches had intercepted King Philip as he was on his way back to the Escorial from conveying the newly-acquired relics of St. Leocadia to Toledo Cathedral. The dispatch was from Mendoza in Paris to inform him that Drake's destination was Cadiz, and the King received the news with the calm to which he had disciplined himself, but there was little that he could do until the report was confirmed. Perhaps in his waking moments he was comforted by the nightingales, which sang that night, as always in the spring, from the leafy avenues of his summer palace.

1587—ON THE COAST OF SPAIN

The next day turned out to be a long one for the English and full of confused incident. This began with the dawn when Drake in person took a flotilla of light craft on the flood tide into the inner harbour to destroy the galleon of Santa Cruz, which Drake enjoyed with a sort of impish glee. Borough saw nothing funny in this exploit; he disapproved of the whole proceeding and thought that hanging about an enemy harbour like this was an unnecessary and criminal risk. He warped his ship the *Lion* to the mouth of the harbour where galleys came out to attack this isolated target and Drake had to send the *Rainbow* to get his second-in-command out of trouble. Inside the harbour, Drake's men were still hard at it striking down into English holds a wonderful variety of provisions intended for the Armada—no Queen's ships had ever been victualled on such a scale. By noon, the men being exhausted, Drake gave the order to proceed out of harbour —whereupon the wind died away to a flat calm. Drake anchored. By this time the Spaniards ashore had reacted with speed and vigour. Troops were pouring into Cadiz, guns were mounted on the foreshore where they could bear on the anchored fleet, fireships were loosed with the tide and time after time the galleys came into the attack. Now the man behind all this activity, the local authority who had set it in motion, was a countrified nobleman who lived on his estates just across the way from Cadiz. The ships present were to meet him again under different circumstances. He was the Duke of Medina-Sidonia.

The harbour was covered with a dense haze of powder smoke, and in the middle of it the English endured for fourteen long hours. The conditions were perfect for galleys, a flat calm and the enemy in an enclosed harbour, but all their attacks were beaten off, for the galleys carried one long-range gun while the *Bonaventure* on the broadside carried sixteen, and the calm also favoured accurate gunnery. The bogy of the galley was laid that day. English boats diverted the fireships on to sand banks where they burned themselves out and their smoke billowed across to join the cloud over the harbour, into which the shore batteries were firing hopefully. The sun went down but no breeze came. At two in the morning Drake and his officers saw the cloud

197

around them thinning out and felt a puff or so of wind upon their cheeks. The land breeze was getting up; their Admiral made sail and brushing the galleys aside the English ships swept out of harbour in a ghostly procession.

This is the exploit which above all others has caught and held the popular imagination through the centuries, but Drake himself knew very well that it was not the main object of the expedition. It was, in fact, an incident in a campaign and one which did not contribute nearly as much towards the ultimate purpose as some far less spectacular patrol work carried out a month later. From what Drake learned in Cadiz of the strength and disposition of the Spanish forces he saw that he had not yet inflicted any great damage on the Armada as a whole. But if the material damage was slight, the moral effect was tremendous. The rest of Europe was stupefied by the news, the odds altered in England's favour and Philip's credit came down with a run. No one had seen anything like it before: the capture of a remote colonial settlement was only to be expected, but to sail into one of the main ports of Spain itself was waging war in an entirely new way. Drake now proceeded to give a demonstration of the proper use of sea power and the advantage held by a fleet operating on exterior lines. When he sailed away from Cadiz his course was reported as being due west. In an hour or two he had vanished. But where had he gone, to Lisbon, the Straits or to the Azores to intercept the homecoming treasure fleets? No one could say. King Philip decided correctly to try and save his most vulnerable and valuable, possession, the treasure fleets, and couriers were sent galloping off with orders to Santa Cruz at Lisbon to sail for the Azores at once. It was as well that Santa Cruz had no ships ready for sea because Drake was only chasing a Spanish squadron reported to be patrolling off Cape St. Vincent. When this squadron hurried into safety at Lisbon, Drake took over the station it had just vacated.

Cape St. Vincent is the corner of land which juts out into the Atlantic like a pointing finger between Lisbon and the Straits of Gibraltar; and as the greater part of the Armada, troops supplies and armament, had still to come round from the Mediterranean, this was the obvious station from which to prevent their reaching Lisbon. But if he wanted to remain on this station for any time Drake would require watering places and an anchorage, and as the Cape offered both he made up his mind to occupy it. Poor Borough, a sound professional officer but opinionated, chose this moment to make a dignified protest in writing. Most of his objections were justified, though he seemed to be haunted by the fear of enemy galleys. Drake had had enough of Borough and his protests; accusing him of insubordination and treachery he placed the old gentleman under arrest in his own flagship the *Lion* and appointed a new captain. William Borough was enough to madden a saint, as he had proved while a member of the Navy Board, but he was neither insubordinate nor treacherous—almost worse, he was without tact. Drake was in something of a fix: he could not remain on this coast without a base on the Cape, but if he landed on it he would be far exceeding his instructions. No one who has made up his mind to do what he knows he should not, likes to be reminded of the fact; and if Drake feared neither Spaniard nor Devil he had a healthy respect for his Queen who would strongly disapprove of his landing force.

Now Drake's daemon took charge, and not even the risk of the Queen's anger could deter him, so the operations of the next few days were conducted under somewhat unusual conditions. In the *Bonaventure* was the Admiral intent on carrying out not the Queen's policy but his own, with his conscience in the shape of his second-in-command safely tucked away in the *Lion* and taking no part in the proceedings. At dawn on May 5th Drake landed his assault force of 1,000 men near the small port of Lagos at the base of the peninsula, but when the soldiers got within musket shot they found that the Spaniards also had seen the strategic value of the place. A strong garrison was manning newly-built fortifications; the troops were re-embarked and the fleet moved down to Cape Sagres, a projection near the tip of the finger. It was a wild and lonely place. On three sides the cliffs fell sheer to the sea and on their summit, seemingly impregnable, stood Sagres Castle. Drake led the landing party in person, and covered by the fire of his musketeers, with his own hands helped to place faggots against the gate of the castle, because he had no artillery

199

to batter it down. The Commander of the Castle was mortally wounded early in the fight, and the garrison surrendered when Drake had lost only two of his men killed. It sounds easy but it was a brilliant feat of arms only made possible by luck and audacity.

The English were now on historic ground, brooded over by the spirit of a man greater than their Admiral, a tall fair man with English blood in his veins, Prince Henry the Navigator, grandson of John of Gaunt. Here at Sagres, with the Atlantic rollers ever pounding at the cliffs while the seabirds dipped and circled overhead, Henry dreamed his dreams but did not live to see his finest come true. Nearly a hundred and forty years before he had built at Sagres a palace, a church, an observatory and quarters for the mathematicians and cosmographers who formed his Court. His captains and pilots came here for instruction or to receive their orders, and here the Prince brought his charts up to date as they returned to report each new discovery. From this barren windswept headland, which Drake only needed as a temporary base, had come the faith and inspiration to discover half the unknown world.

The soldiers who had captured the place were far too busy dismantling the guns of the Castle and rolling them over the cliff to wonder why there was a settlement there at all. Now that water and an anchorage were secure Drake made off to Lisbon hoping to bring Santa Cruz to action, but he had no luck. The Spanish Admiral could not come out to fight as his ships had no crews and Drake could not go in after him because the entrance to Lisbon harbour was too heavily fortified. But if Drake achieved nothing of importance at Lisbon, at least his appearance upset the King, who sent out a whole series of orders which were at once countermanded and altered for an attack on the Azores when Drake suddenly vanished. But he had only been blown away by a northerly gale and on May 12th he was back again, snugly anchored under the lee of Cape St. Vincent, the report of which set the couriers galloping off once more with a new set of orders.

'Meantime', so the Venetian Ambassador reported to his Government, 'the English are masters of the sea and hold it at their discretion, Lisbon and the whole coast are blockaded'. While the larger ships were making the headlines, the light craft were getting on with their job undisturbed and the total effect of their unpublicized efforts was to cause far more harm to the Armada itself than the spectacular raid on Cadiz. A fleet in those days depended largely on salt fish for rations, while all salt provisions, wine and water were carried in wooden casks; and in addition to a fishing fleet after tunny off the Algarve coast, a busy coastal traffic was carrying hoops and staves of seasoned wood for making casks to Lisbon. But patrolling day and night the light craft saw to it that nothing along that coast could move. In about three weeks of hard work they ruined the fishery by destroying sixty fishing boats with their nets, and they also destroyed seventeen hundred tons of hoops and staves. In the following year the Armada sailed short of provisions and ran short of water because of leaky casks of unseasoned wood. Through its general unreadiness and bad organization the Spanish Navy could do nothing to stop this destruction of its essential supplies. But if the Spaniards could do nothing there was one enemy at sea which not Drake nor any Admiral had yet learned how to beat off, and that was disease.

By the spring, after seven long months with no fresh vegetables, most people in Europe were in a low state of health and suffering from a mild form of scurvy. At sea where conditions were harder a fleet which sailed in the spring soon had men developing the symptoms. After only two months at sea the English at St. Vincent were going down like flies, and as there was no place in the Squadron for invalids, Drake loaded them into a couple of the prizes taken at Cadiz with the idea of sending them home. He gave the remainder the chance to get ashore and changed the foul ballast in his ships for clean. While this was going on he wrote a report of his proceedings after Cadiz for Sir Francis Walsingham. He says that he could hold on here indefinitely and asks for more of the Queen's ships, 'six of Her Majesty's good ships of the second sort', for with them, now that he was established on this coast, he could go on to greater things. He continued with the sentence which was widely quoted out of its context as 'Drake's

Prayer' in the Second World War. 'There must be a beginning of any great matter but the continuing on to the end until it be thoroughly finished yields the true glory'. To Drake that was no prayer, it was an elegant sentiment thrown in to impress a cultured reader. He is back in character, however, for his ending: 'Haste, from Her Majesty's good ship the *Elizabeth Bonaventure*, now riding at Cape Sagres this May 17th 1587'. There is the seaman talking, very proud of his address. Having just written to say that he was prepared to stay on the coast indefinitely, Drake had second thoughts, as a result of which he came to one of his sudden decisions. He had a great many sick, his victuals were getting low and the men themselves were none too happy. They had sailed into Cadiz, and covered themselves with glory, they had defied Santa Cruz off Lisbon, they had made bonfires of fishing nets and staves until they were sick and tired of it, but up to date they had taken not a scrap of booty. The Elizabethan seaman was always content to let the glory go, so long as he got the loot; but if there were none he soon got restive. Drake who knew his men was no doubt feeling the lack of it himself; he saw that it was high time to be after 'some little comfortable dew of Heaven, some crowns or some reasonable booties'. The place to find these was the Azores.

Drake had always used the Portuguese well; he put the crews of the captured fishing vessels ashore unharmed, even giving them presents of money. As a result of this policy he had some useful allies ashore and from these he had learned that a great carrack was expected now that the fine weather season had come. She had been wintering at Mozambique and after the usual practice of ships returning home round the Cape she was due at any time now to make the Azores. He felt justified in leaving the Spanish coast because he had seen to it that the Armada would not be able to concentrate for some time to come, and anyhow his orders were to attack treasure ships. With a clear conscience, therefore, he sent his sick home in a couple of prizes and on May 22nd shaped a course to the westward.

One day out from the Spanish coast they ran into a full southerly gale in which the *Bonaventure* nearly foundered. But three days later when the weather moderated all the Queen's ships were in company, even the *Spy* and *Makeshift*, pinnaces of fifty tons, were there riding easily over the long swell; but the London ships had lost touch and were nowhere to be seen. While the flagship was hove to repairing storm damage a strange sail was sighted down to leeward. The *Lion* in which Borough was still under arrest and the *Spy* went off to investigate. The stranger was one of the homeward-bound prizes off her course, and as she filled her sails and made off to the northward, those watching in the *Bonaventure* were astonished at the strange behaviour of the *Lion*; instead of rejoining, she too stood away for home and was soon hull down. Her temporary Captain returned in the *Spy* with the explanation. He had been transferred to the pinnace when the crew of the *Lion* had refused to rejoin the flag, saying that they were short of food and water and were off home. Drake, of course, decided that Borough was the instigator of the mutiny, and in the tumbling wastes of the Atlantic summoned a Council of War to try the mutineers in their absence. The only witness was an officer who had been bundled off his ship, but the Court duly found everyone guilty of mutiny and sentenced Borough and all the *Lion* officers to death. After this irregular proceeding the officers of the Court returned to their ships and the fleet sailed on.

There were no other excitements until they were sixteen days out from Cape St. Vincent, when on June 8th Drake raised St. Michael's, the most eastern island of the Azores, which lies by itself some distance from the main group. All day this lonely peak rose slowly from the sea until by evening the precipitous grey cliffs of rock rising sheer from the water's edge had taken on form and detail. But something else was there too, and not part of the island. After peering for some time at this object close under the cliffs, those in the *Bonaventure* decided that without doubt it was a large vessel. Night fell and the fleet lay to, but at daybreak the stranger came out to meet the *Bonaventure*, expecting friends and dipping her ensign repeatedly to get these strangers to show their colours. 'But we', says one who was watching all this, 'knowing what she was would put out no flag until we were in shot of her'. By an incredible piece of luck she was the very ship they were after, the great carrack from Mozambique and beyond. Once in range the *Bonaventure* opened fire and at the same time, 'We hanged out flags, streamers and pendants', the eye-witness goes on, 'that she might be out of doubt what we were'. The pinnaces closed in like dogs baiting a bear and the great towering ship could only fire over them, being unable to depress her guns. She lay there helpless with the English ships all around her, waiting for the kill; and when one of the larger ships ranged up alongside to board, she struck her colours. As she was carrying passengers which included women and children she had no choice.

She was the *San Felipe*, a floating treasure house from the East with a fantastically rich cargo of gems and spices, silks and calicoes, pepper, cinnamon and cloves, indigo and nutmeg—all nearly worth their weight in gold. Nothing like it had ever been taken before. But even more valuable than the spices in her hold were the sailing directions and charts in her great cabin giving away the secrets of how to find them. For centuries this knowledge had been closely-guarded by the Arab traders. Columbus and Magellan had hoped to find the source of the spice trade; Vasco da Gama had wrested the secret from the Arabs and now with the peak of St. Michael's in the distance Drake had learned it from the Portuguese.

That for the time being was that. More great ships were on their way home but Drake could not wait for them. He needed water and victuals so he made his best way home with his prize and on June 26th anchored in Plymouth Sound. Four days later, while the *San Felipe's* cargo was still being inventoried, Santa Cruz sailed from Lisbon to the Azores to escort her home. The cargo of the great carrack was worth more than twice the cost of the whole expedition. It fetched £114,000 of which the Queen got £40,000, Drake £17,000, and after some argument because their ships were not present, the London Merchants £40,000. Drake went on with his vendetta against Borough, but the Council decided that he had exceeded his authority and that the sentence was not legal. Borough was acquitted of mutiny and desertion, kept his office of Clerk of the Ships and two years later was promoted Controller of the Navy.

Instead of following up her advantage the Queen proceeded to throw it away by giving King Philip time to recover. Upon Drake's return she paid off most ships in commission to save money, and this when the coast of Spain lay unprotected, and a succession of rich carracks were streaming home to Lisbon past the Azores. They might relax in England, because the Armada had been delayed, but King Philip did not deviate from his purpose. If the Armada could not sail as intended, then it would sail later in the year or early in the next. England must be conquered. So, far away in the Escorial, King Philip took up his pen, wearily, for his gout was troubling him, and set to work on the huge task of repairing the damage and making new preparations.

CHAPTER XI

Philip II of Spain

★

From the earliest times it has always been the habit of monarchs to choose some pleasant part of their dominions in which to build their country retreats. The palace was hidden away amongst little woods and rolling parkland; lakes and rippling streams and gardens were there to enchant the eye, and the palace or lodge, if small, was designed for luxury and ease. The locality chosen was smiling and sheltered: for the average monarch always built his retreat solely as a place where he could enjoy himself, where the problems of State could be forgotten in the pleasures of the chase, the table, or the boudoir—where care was an unwelcome intruder. Not so Philip: all he wanted was a retreat where he could be alone—to work.

After a long search of his realm he had found a place to suit him near the little village of Escorial tucked away in the foothills of the Sierra Guadarrama. The road from Madrid to Escorial led across a tract of country which was no more than a desert. In summer, waves of heat shimmered over the dusty plain; in winter, icy blasts came whistling down from the mountains. It was more than a day's journey from Madrid—far from the bustle and distractions of a capital city with its scandals and intrigues, its ceremonies and perpetual audiences and appearances in public, when he had to dress up in a style befitting the most powerful monarch in Christendom.

At first sight the Escorial might have been a monastery of unusual size. It was that and more: it was a country palace, a royal burial place, a museum—but above all it was a church. The centre of the whole edifice, towering with its great dome over alll

Philip II of Spain as a young man. From a painting by Titian

the other buildings, a replica of St. Peter's, Rome, was the monu-
mental Church of San Lorenzo.

Philip had laid the first stone with his own hands some twenty-
five years before and now, in 1587, except for a few stray workmen adding some final touches, the Escorial was finished—if
ever such an undertaking could be considered complete, for the
King went on enriching, now its great church, now its library,
now its picture galleries, until he died in one of its rooms and
went down to join his father in the vault beneath the High Altar.
For a quarter of a century Philip had given a great deal of his
time and attention to the palace, for it was his *magnum opus*.
Years earlier he had been always sneaking away to Escorial where
he stayed quite happily in a house with a leaking roof, to study
and alter the plans, to watch the walls slowly rising and to keep
an eye on the workmen. These were selected as much for their
moral characters as for their skill. Philip would have no man employed on this almost sacred task who drank or swore, who fought
his neighbours or who did not often receive the Sacrament. As
some small reward for working under such rigorous conditions,
the craftsmen were regularly paid, which was more than could be
said for almost any other state servant in the Spain of those days.
Whatever else in his wide dominions might suffer for lack of
money, it would not be the Escorial.

It was in keeping with his character that Philip should have
built this vast palace, not in a spirit of rivalry with other kings,
or even his own grandees, but as the result of a vow made years
before to a Saint. In 1557 his troops had routed the French at the
Battle of St. Quentin on August 10th, which happens to be the
Feast Day of St. Lawrence, and Philip had vowed to build a
memorial to the Saint in commemoration of the victory. Now
St. Lawrence had attained his martyrdom by being grilled to
death over a fire, and the dedication of the Escorial to him accounts
for its unusual ground plan. It was built in the form of an enor-
mous gridiron. For a palace so original, Philip had employed the
best architects in Spain, but they were not to be allowed a free
hand—the King had decided views of his own. His instructions
to the architect, Herrera, a pupil of Michelangelo, were precise:

'Above all, do not forget what I have told you—simplicity of form, severity in the whole, nobility without arrogance, majesty without ostentation'. For its interior, however, he poured out money on decoration and embellishment. The leading painters of Italy, which is to say of the world, were enticed to Spain to decorate its walls and ceilings with their frescoes. He commissioned paintings from Titian and all the masters of the day for its galleries. He ransacked Europe for rare books and illuminated manuscripts to fill its library. He scoured his dominions for the marble and the porphyry, the precious woods and jewels to enrich the church, and the Low Countries for choirboys to sing in it, because their voices were less harsh than those of Spanish boys. He collected sacred relics wherever he could find them for its chapels. The marble crucifix over the High Altar had been carried on the backs of men on foot all the way from the workshop of Benvenuto Cellini in Rome.

Philip was a connoisseur and no detail was too small for his personal attention, no expense too great for his rapidly-emptying purse, if it had to do with 'El Real Monasterio de San Lorenzo del Escorial', to give that unique edifice its full name. The result was rather like a barracks of greyish-white stone, gloomy and forbidding. But even if those towering walls did look as if they could accommodate an entire army, the sweep of their rigid lines gave the palace an austere beauty of its own. It did not obtrude upon its surroundings, but seemed to grow naturally out of those wild, inaccessible hills. It was, in fact, a masterpiece—and Philip's own. Surrounded by all this magnificence of painted dome and frescoed gallery, of towering church and shady cloister, tucked away in a northern corner of this vast building with its twelve thousand doors and windows was a tiny cell, no more richly furnished than any occupied by one of the monks of St. Jerome who were installed in the Monastery. Within it at a table piled high with papers sat a shrunken, ascetic figure dressed in black. This was Philip the King, owner of it all.

Thirty years of overwork and responsibility had left their mark on Philip: his hair and beard had turned white, his shoulders were rounded, his cheeks deeply furrowed, so that at 61 he had all the appearance of an old, old man. In his youth, although he may not have earned it, he had been given the reputation of being a great lover, but now he had put all passion behind him. Gone were the days when Titian could send his royal patron those paintings of voluptuous nudes 'Danae' and 'Venus and Adonis', in which each naked goddess displayed her ample charms, one facing and one with her back turned, 'so that the room where they are put may be more pleasing to the eyes', as the painter explained in an accompanying letter. There was no place in the Escorial for such worldliness. Only religious pictures were now commissioned from the artists: 'The Ecstasy of St. Francis', 'The Descent from the Cross', 'Ecce Homo'. Even in the privacy of his monastic cell, Philip, a great lover of books, allowed himself none of the glories of his library. No, the Writings of Maria Teresa of Avila or *The Spiritual Exercises of Father Rodriguez* were the only books that lay on his bedside table. And should his eye stray for a moment from his work to wander idly round his cell, it would immediately be caught by a chart of the Seven Deadly Sins and their inevitable consequences painted on the walls.

Philip always used to say that if he had not been a king he would have chosen to be a simple country gentleman with an adequate rent roll. Here in the Escorial he could dress like one and be comfortable; instead of the stiff brocades and pinching shoes of Court dress he could wear plain black, relieved sometimes by the Collar and Chain of the Golden Fleece. Best of all, he could shuffle down the long corridors in carpet slippers because the only treatment for his gout which the Court physicians could think of was to bleed him in the foot and leg several times a day. While this had no effect on the gout it succeeded in giving the King a pronounced limp. Although he ate sparingly and drank little he lived in almost continuous pain—his servants sometimes wondered how he could stand it—yet he never complained, nor, at some sudden agonizing twinge was there ever the outburst that would have come from an ordinary mortal. But then, Philip was not an ordinary mortal, he was a king, and in fitting himself for that high office he had set out to obtain complete control over himself. How well he succeeded a Venetian who knew the King intimately bore witness: 'No one ever saw him in a rage, being always patient, phlegmatic, temperate and melancholy'.

The King had trained himself to rise early and work through till late at night. Now he drove himself without mercy—work, work, work with never a thought of rest: poring over dispatches, studying the maps of his geographer Ortelius, annotating reports on their special wide-margined paper, correcting the grammar, the spelling and even the style of the dispatches of his secretaries. No detail was too insignificant for his calm deliberate consideration. After reading a letter from his Ambassador in London, describing some small insects which that official had seen crawling across the windowpane, 'probably fleas', he noted in the margin. Apart from gossipy letters from his Ambassadors his only relaxations were an occasional game of chess with Ruy Lopez—the inventor of the famous gambit—services in the church—or more work. The trouble was that when his father had instructed him to depend on no one but himself, Philip took the advice literally. So the King insisted on seeing to everything himself, even to ordering the details of religious processions in remote parts of an Empire which ranged from China to Peru. He was a slow worker who went at his own pace, and he never seems to have been able to distinguish the trivial from the important, so that urgent decisions affecting the campaign in the Netherlands were put off while he considered the knotty question of the length of the gowns to be worn by the students of Salamanca University. Although he dictated until two or three in the morning without making much impression on the papers which piled ever higher on his desk, Philip refused to be hurried. 'Time and I', he would say, 'are a match for any other two'—to the exasperation of an Ambassador whom he kept waiting eight months for an answer.

The vast sprawling empire was governed and administered by Philip himself, assisted, in theory, by a couple of secretaries and a number of councils. In practice, the secretaries were only clerks who wrote at his dictation, while the councils could advise but nothing more. All decisions were made by the King. As he became older Philip hardly ever attended a meeting of the Grand

Council and slowly but inevitably he became the slave of his own paper work. Whether the question to be decided was the planting of vines in Peru or the height of a bridge over some tiny little Andalusian stream, the procedure was the same. The matter to be decided would first be placed before the King on sheets with specially wide margins. After making his remarks in the margin he would send the paper to the appropriate Council. After a while it would come back with the result of the deliberation of that Council. Philip would give these further study, fill more margins with remarks and send it to the Council of State who would eventually return it with their opinions. The King would then go over the whole mass of papers again and at last would make his decision. It was no wonder that they were saying in Italy: 'If death came from Spain, we should live to a very great age.' Slow and cumbrous as this system was, the marginal notes show that Philip had more sense and a firmer grasp of most subjects than any of his advisers. He was slow but he was generally right. He was trying to be a one-man civil service and it was too much for one as frail and old as he, but he would never give in—he would go on until he died.

There had been a time when this work had been a happy, family affair. While Philip's quill scratched across the paper signing documents, not with his own name, but simply with the words 'I, the King' after the proud fashion of Spanish monarchs, the Queen, his wife, sanded the letters and his daughters took them to the Groom of the Chamber to be folded and sent off. He was always happiest when he was with his family, and he was never too busy to write amusing details of his travels round the kingdom and to ask how many teeth the baby now had. Philip had been a dutiful son, he was a good husband and a devoted father. But now he was alone: his fourth and last wife had gone down to join the others in the Royal Mausoleum under the High Altar of the church; his beloved daughter Isabella was grown up with a home of her own.

Philip suffered from taking himself too seriously—he was a man with a mission. That it was far beyond the power of one frail mortal to carry out never crossed his mind. It was a task pleasing to God—it could not fail to be—and one that had been handed on to him by the man he considered perfect, the greatest man who had ever lived, his father the Emperor Charles. That was enough for Philip, he never questioned his destiny; he never doubted even when at the end of eighteen hours' work the pile of papers in front of him was as high as ever. He did not falter when his gout was excruciating, when the instruments of his policy were incompetent or corrupt, or both—when everything seemed to go wrong at once. The toiling figure in the Escorial was convinced that he had been chosen to sustain the Catholic faith throughout the world and to preserve intact the possessions handed on to him by his father. It was a pious ambition. But new thoughts were bubbling up, new trends were sweeping the world: the Reformation had come to stay, the Low Countries were in a state of seething unrest, England was prepared to fight him for the Freedom of the Seas.

As he worked Philip was tormented by a gnawing ache more insistent even than the shooting pains of his gout: if he could not allay it, he foresaw the collapse of his ambitions, the failure of his mission in life, the end of his dreams. Philip was short of money. On one of the few occasions that he let his feelings get the better of him he declared: 'I am now living from day to day without knowing how I shall live on the next or how I shall procure that of which I am so much in need'. This may seem an astounding admission for the most powerful monarch in the world, upon whose possessions the sun literally never set, who owned the mines of Mexico and Peru, whose argosies brought back the silks and spices, the gold and jewels of the East and West. But Philip was only speaking the bare truth.

This paradoxical state of affairs was not all the fault of the King. When his father handed on to him the greatest empire the world had ever known, there came with it a staggering load of debt. Then there was the value of money: the huge inflow of bullion from the New World into Spain had lowered the value of money and so sent prices up, causing a form of inflation. Philip can hardly be blamed for the operation of an economic law which neither he nor anybody else at that time understood; but he can be blamed for his fiscal policy. He restricted manufacture in Spain so as to buy more cheaply from abroad—not that this restriction needed much encouragement; for Spaniards were by nature disinclined to manufacture. Above all, Philip tried to operate a form of government which was too centralized, expensive and inefficient to be borne by the economy of the time.

Spain herself could not send her colonies what they needed; her only exports were priests, soldiers or young men in search of a quick fortune. Ever since the conquest of Granada, new horizons had lured the adventurous and the best elements out of Spain. The empire had expanded too quickly, so that her population had fallen and she had few manufacturers, and therefore no stable trade. Philip mistook silver for wealth and by forbidding any other nation to trade with the colonies, there was a flow of goods one way, into Spain. And at home the faulty system of taxation did not provide sufficient internal revenue to pay for Parma's army in the Netherlands and all the other expenses to do with running the empire.

In his embarrassment Philip resorted to quacks and foreign moneylenders. There were in Spain certain officials known as 'arbitristas' whose sole duty, in return for large rewards, was to invent get-rich-quick schemes. Their fertile imaginations produced any number of these but the one thing they did not produce was hard cash, whereas the moneylenders at least furnished that, though at the usual rates of interest. A large proportion of that treasure from the New World, brought over in convoy by the warships of the 'Indian Guard', was pledged before ever it arrived in Seville and the bullion from Mexico and Peru, far from going to swell the King's exchequer, was piled high instead in the strong-rooms of the bankers of Augsburg, Antwerp and Genoa. The bankers in the end took a heavier toll of the 'Indian' treasure than did the English.

When the burden of affairs became too heavy, there was always the consolation of religion. Philip could push aside his papers and take refuge in his own stall in the Upper Choir of the church. But if he were ill or there were no time he could look down into the church from a little window in his cell. For a few moments he would gaze down on the High Altar, far below, and on a Feast Day, while the acolytes swung their censers, the innumerable tapers and candles would twinkle mistily through the clouds of incense. And as the clear young voices of his Flemish choir-boys floated up into the vast dome, he could watch the priests in their gorgeous vestments during the moving ceremonial of Conventual Mass. Then, with the smell of incense still in his nostrils and the plain chant of the choir rising and falling in the distance, he would turn away comforted and go back to his desk.

It might seem that this devout, overworked recluse could hardly have been the 'mighty enemy' that Burghley called him. But the English were on the other side of the hill; they could not know all that was going on in Spain or Philip's empire, and even if they had known they would not have been much the wiser or have been able to read the signs aright. As for Spain's being hard-pressed for money, that was nothing new; there was hardly a ruler in Christendom who did not live in a perpetual state of waiting for something to turn up. The seeds of Spanish decay were there, but they were a long way underground; no vigorous shoots had as yet cracked the surface, so that their presence was hardly suspected, even in Spain. No, what the world saw was a Spain immensely strong and rich, every year the Flotas brought in new and untold wealth. When Elizabeth was trying to find the money to rearm England, there arrived in Spain twenty-five million pounds sterling of treasure. One has only to consider the map of Philip's world-wide dominions to see what Burghley must have felt about it. Few in Europe gave England a chance and a good many people looked forward with a certain amount of pleasurable anticipation to the discomfiture of these proud and insolent islanders. England was a small country all alone, except for some rather dubious allies in the Low Countries, while Philip could call on the resources of the world. In spite of inefficiency, corruption and a suicidal economic policy, Spain was richer by far than any other power. She was still the most formidable opponent in the world.

Consider her record. Spain was the champion of Christianity; she had thrown the Infidel out of her own borders and had smashed the Turks at Lepanto. A mere handful of determined men had conquered a whole new world in America and brought millions of souls to the fold of Mother Church. Ever since the conquest of Granada, nearly every Spanish undertaking had about it the fervour of a religious crusade. The Conquistadores might be cruel and ruthless in their conquests but they were convinced that whatever they did was for the greater glory of God. Cortez was quite genuine in his efforts to convert the Aztecs in Mexico and insisted on explaining the mysteries of the Faith at every opportunity, even when his audience could not understand a word of what he was saying. When Mendana set out from Peru in 1567 to look for the Isles of Solomon, reputed to be of fabulous wealth, his sailing orders stated that the first object of his voyage was 'to convert all infidels to Christianity'.

Of more immediate importance in the eyes of Europe was the Spanish army, which was the best in the world. Trained and organized on the lines laid down by Gonzalo de Cordoba, 'the Great Captain', at the beginning of the century, the famous Spanish infantry had never yet been beaten in a pitched battle. The army attracted the best elements in Spain and the Spaniard made a good soldier. A man who could put up with the climate of northern Spain with its 'nine months winter and three months hell' could stand anything. The Spaniard is naturally abstemious, he is steadier, less volatile than the emotional French and Italians; and as long as he was paid regularly the Spanish soldier could be relied upon whatever the situation. In Spain, unlike other countries, the infantry was the senior arm and it was largely composed of battle-trained regulars, the 'Soldados Viejos', but even the bluest blood in Spain thought it an honour to serve on foot. Nobles and hidalgos, peasants and writers fought in the infantry 'for God and the King'.

The supreme self-confidence of the Spaniard made him proud; he was Spanish and Catholic and therefore represented the highest aristocracy in the world. He became the prototype of the gentleman, of exquisite manners, cultured, brave, devout. The world sent him her choicest goods: tapestries from the looms of Flanders, paintings, perfumes and the most cunning work of goldsmiths from Italy, precious metals from the New World and spices from the East. Spain's universities were the centre of European learning, while Madrid became more than a capital, she became a world centre for business and the arts. This feeling of superiority percolated through all classes of society. A mule driver was as jealous of his honour as a Duke; and every Castilian considered himself a noble, though his nobility might, for the moment, be dormant. Even craftsmen carried swords and insignificant clerks demanded to be addressed as 'Don'. Grandees and labourers, beggars and soldiers, artists and merchants all carried themselves with a swagger just because they were Spanish. Not Spaniards, but Auvergnat peasants from France polished the boots, cleaned the knives and held the horses of the hidalgos of Madrid. The faith of Spaniards in themselves and their religion led them on to incredible acts of bravery and endurance. The men who followed Pizarro through the jungles of Peru, who marched with Cortez over the mountains of Mexico or with de Soto through the swamps of Louisiana; the stubborn infantrymen who held out at Mers-el-Kebir against untold thousands of Infidels; the men who conquered at Lepanto, were no chance heroes thrown up by opportunity. They represented the average Spanish man. He had so often accomplished the impossible, that no matter what he undertook, he felt that success was inevitable.

This brilliance of Spain's position and the majesty of an empire that spanned the world were focused in that retiring black-clad figure hidden away behind piles of papers in the Escorial. No man in Europe ever approached the prestige enjoyed by Philip the King. His wild Conquistadores who overran whole empires conquered them by his leave and in his name; his viceroys round the world derived their authority from him. He could terrify them in audience and his icy coldness and the fixed stare of his unwavering blue eyes could reduce men who had won continents to babbling incoherency. Philip was the apex of the vast, highly-centralized organization that controlled the Spanish Empire. His asceticism and holiness only enhanced his prestige because they appealed to the streak of fanaticism in the Spanish character. He was a man of few words who always preserved the dignity of his great position—His Most Catholic Majesty, King of Spain. He was in his stall in church raptly following the service when the news of the victory of Lepanto was brought to him. Beyond whispering some instructions to a page he made no sign of having heard, and continued with his devout attention to the priests at the Altar. Only when the service was over did the choir break into the swelling paean of the 'Te Deum'. Philip had given honour for the victory to Whom he considered it was due.

In spite of his oddities—or perhaps because of them—Philip was the most popular monarch that Spain had ever had. After thirty years on the throne he was respected and liked as an institution, even if he were not exactly loved by a people who seldom caught a glimpse of their King. In spite of their sturdy independence, the Spaniards were intensely loyal to Philip, they would make any sacrifice for him because they considered him worthy of it. He was a Spaniard and a Catholic so that when he decided on the conquest of England there was a wave of almost delirious enthusiasm over the whole country. The project was regarded as another crusade. Its religious purpose—the conversion of another heretic country—the very difficulty and magnitude of the whole conception appealed to the spiritual and devotional side of the Spaniard. In every church in Spain Mass was being offered for the success of 'La Felicisima Armada'. The aristocracy of Spain left its estates, its private quarrels and its love affairs to ride off along the dusty road to Lisbon. The humbler sort followed them. Poets dropped their quills and disappointed lovers their guitars to join the expedition. Spain had not risen with such unanimous enthusiasm since the campaigns against the Moors.

CHAPTER XII

Delay at Lisbon

*

Spain was committed to an undertaking beyond her powers, for which she was fitted neither by temperament nor tradition. The ordinary Spaniard was a landsman who disliked the sea and could not be induced to serve upon it; he had no interest in the Navy, his heroes were victorious soldiers; and if the idea of invading England appealed to him it was because he thought of it as another glorious military adventure, ignoring the fact that England could only be reached by sea. For all her colonial possessions Spain was still at heart a continental power. She looked upon the fleet as an army afloat and fighting at sea as another form of land warfare to be conducted, inconveniently, in ships, when the battleground of the famous Spanish infantry would be transferred from land to water. This frame of mind was carried to extremes afloat where the soldiers were senior to the sailors who were regarded as troublesome necessities, treated as drudges and given no proper accommodation on board their own ships. Spanish Admirals had none of that sea sense which led Drake instinctively to pursue the same strategy on the coast of Spain which Sir Edward Howard with another English fleet had used off the coast of Brittany seventy years before. The greatest colonizing power in history despised the fighting service that alone could preserve her overseas possessions which depended on sea communications. In peace or war Spain had no permanent organization to administer a navy; there was not a drydock in the country and except for the galley arsenals, no Royal Dockyards. Apart from the Portuguese galleons which she had acquired in 1581, Spain had no regular fighting fleet.

For some months after Drake had returned to England, the only man capable of organizing the invasion was in the Azores to cover the passage home of the great Eastern carracks and the Indian treasure fleet from an attack which never came. One by one the carracks lumbered home and eventually the treasure fleet got safely through to Spain with a richer cargo than usual. While Spain was receiving this transfusion of riches without which she could not finance her project, the only English ships in Spanish waters were the *Spy* and *Makeshift*, two small pinnaces. Parma was busy in the Netherlands where peace talks were in progress at Ostend, for the Queen was always ready to negotiate and King Philip hoped that the talks would delay England's preparations. But while he kept the English Commissioners talking Parma was busy widening canals and waterways to accommodate his concentration of barges, flat-bottomed boats and horse transports, and his soldiers were cheerfully laying odds that they would be in London before Michaelmas.

The King of Spain was grimly determined that his Armada should sail in September, and with Santa Cruz away at sea, he sent the most brilliant officer of his Court to hasten things at Headquarters in Lisbon. This was Don Alonso de Leyva, a versatile cavalryman and the very pattern of Spanish chivalry. He had resigned his high office of Captain-General of Milanese cavalry to serve in the Armada for which he supplied his own ship and paid all his own expenses. But neither this officer nor his master the King could make the unwieldy machine move any quicker because the trouble lay in the machine itself. The arming and equipping of a fleet is not a matter for amateurs, and Spain had no permanent officials who had become expert through experience. An official was liable to be switched from one task to another, finding himself one day in charge of victualling and on the next responsible for the mounting of cannon, with no real experience of either. A veteran of Lepanto who had failed as a dramatist, one Miguel de Cervantes—he had yet to write *Don Quixote*—was suddenly transferred from his job of requisitioning wheat in the plains around Ecija and put to storing ships in the port of Seville. But with creaks and groans the concentration which Drake had interrupted went slowly forward: the Andalusian Squadron put out hesitantly from Cadiz, the Neapolitan contingent emerged from the Mediterranean, Oquendo and his Biscay ships rounded Finisterre, but had then to drop down to San Lucar for stores; and at the end of September with a fleet of storm-damaged ships Santa Cruz himself returned to Lisbon. He was met at the entrance by a galley carrying a messenger with instructions from the King not to disembark his men, but to be ready to sail at once for England. The answer which this official received from the weather-beaten Admiral has, regrettably, not been preserved in the Spanish archives.

The Marquis of Santa Cruz, accustomed like all seamen to facing realities afloat, brought in with him from the Azores a cold blast of common sense. He sent a deputation up to the Court to explain that it was late in the year to sail, that the force was not yet concentrated and that many ships were unseaworthy. King Philip sent the deputation back with peremptory orders to get to sea. Now Santa Cruz knew what he was talking about. He had made a personal study of the problem of invading England and had first suggested it in 1583. He had studied the winds and the weather to be expected and knew that even if everything went well it would not be an easy undertaking. But for once in his life the King was in a hurry. Courier after courier galloped down to Lisbon with letters of advice, with questions, warnings, demands and orders to get to sea. Santa Cruz was doing his best, but sail he could not. He was fighting a losing battle against Spanish inefficiency and although the Biscay Squadron joined his flag in October the fleet was not ready to sail. Stores and equipment had gone astray, there was a shortage of provision casks and far too many ships were unseaworthy. The Admiral refused to sail until these had been refitted, but the King urged him on and complained that he was too dilatory. Santa Cruz replied that he could not work miracles.

In December the Admiral decided to put the facts squarely before the King in an official memorandum. He wrote that it was his solemn duty to advise his master to postpone the sailing date until March. This would avoid the winter Atlantic gales and the fogs and thick weather to be expected in the Channel. He ended by declaring that notwithstanding this advice he was prepared to sail and give his life if Philip so ordered. It was the blunt warning of a seaman with no illusions, and King Philip at last saw reason. The Expedition would sail in March. A month or so after this decision was made Santa Cruz fell ill, and the King had to consider the appointment of a relief. Then on February 9th there occurred the first of that series of disasters which dogged the Armada—Santa Cruz died. After escaping the hazards of the sea and coming safely through fifty years of battles in the service of his Sovereign, the gallant old Admiral died quietly in his bed from an attack of typhus fever. The son of a seaman, he was the outstanding naval figure of his generation in Spain and carried as much prestige in the eyes of his countrymen as if he had been a soldier. The whole country was shocked, while a mood of gloom and dismay swept over the fleet at the loss of a commander-in-chief it trusted and admired. At Lepanto he had commanded the Neapolitan galleys; he had fought in the Mediterranean and the wide Atlantic; he was at the capture of Tunis and was the victor of Terceira in the Azores. He had never lost a battle, and they called him the 'Never Vanquished'. With his departing spirit went the last hope of success the Armada might ever have had. In all Spain the one man who appeared unperturbed was the King whose only comment was that God had been kind in that it had happened now and not when out at sea. Then he called for his Secretary and dictated two letters; one was a duty letter of condolence to the Admiral's son, the other was to Don Alonso Perez de Guzman, Seventh Duke of Medina-Sidonia, known as 'the Good', appointing him as the new 'Captain General of the Ocean'.

Everybody was astonished and concerned, but no one more than the unfortunate nobleman himself who was resting tranquilly on his pleasant country estate at San Lucar near Cadiz when the shattering news reached him. De Guzman was a mild and popular country gentleman of thirty-eight, short, broad-shouldered, a good horseman, brave and God-fearing. He was only interested in his estates and wanted nothing more of life than to be left alone to watch his oranges ripening in the sun. He was unfitted for high command and he hastened to inform the King's secretary of this fact in a letter which protested his unworthiness. He suffered from colds and was quite certain that he would be seasick; he had no ready money (a Commander-in-Chief paid his own expenses); he had never met his officers; he knew nothing of the sea or war. 'So, Sir', he concluded his pathetic letter, 'in the interests of His Majesty's Service, I submit to you for communication to him, that I do not understand it, I know nothing about it, have no health for the sea or money to spend upon it.' This letter was only the answer to Philip's warning while Santa Cruz was ill and the courier with it crossed a royal courier bearing the order appointing him Commander-in-Chief, which the King had sent off as soon as he learned of the death of Santa Cruz. The Duke saw that there was nothing to be done about it, the King had made up his mind, and with the high sense of duty of a grandee of Spain, de Guzman accepted the post with the statement that he had satisfied his conscience by confessing his incapacity.

The Duke of Medina-Sidonia has been variously described as a fool, a coward or both. He was neither. He had been suddenly pitchforked into a job far beyond him, as he was the first to point out. But once in it he did surprisingly well considering the state of his command when he took over and the nature of the task he had been given. No man on either side could have succeeded in it, not Santa Cruz nor Drake·himself. As for cowardice, his flagship was always where the fighting was hottest and during the long engagement in the Channel he often turned to meet the enemy unsupported. He was not an inspired leader of men; but when he personally was given the whole blame for the disaster, he was being made the scapegoat for the inefficiency of Spanish administration and years of neglect of the Navy. No fighting service which in peacetime does not have the backing of public opinion can be expected to perform marvels on the outbreak of war.

The problem of the High Command was not an easy one. The Spanish Admirals of squadrons were a turbulent lot, touchy on questions of honour, jealous of their precedence, and even Santa

Cruz with his immense prestige had trouble in keeping the peace amongst them. The appointment of one of their number to the Supreme Command would have been resented bitterly by all the others; while not even the King could possibly have expected a soldier to serve under the command of a sailor who had not the aura of a commander like Santa Cruz. If it were not Santa Cruz, it could be no other sailor. So Philip had no choice; he knew all about the personal feuds, the jealousy, rivalries and the intrigues going on at Lisbon and he thought that only a grandee of very high social position (which counted for much in those days) would be able to take charge.

Alonso de Guzman held the oldest dukedom in Spain. His ancestors had distinguished themselves in the fighting against the Moors and from the tenth century it had provided a succession of illustrious servants to the State, generals, viceroys, statesmen. And in St. Benedict it had produced a saint. The seventh duke had an impressive string of titles and was a Knight of the Golden Fleece; moreover he had recently acted with energy ashore when Drake attacked Cadiz. On breeding and form, therefore, Medina-Sidonia was the selection; the King himself, or so he thought, could provide the knowledge and experience. All arrangements had been made, everything had been foreseen, so what did it matter if this reluctant nobleman were inexperienced in the art of war? The King sent him many friendly letters of advice and encouragement. He reminded the Duke of the services of his illustrious ancestors, and regretted that he himself was prevented from accompanying the Armada only by his many duties at home. Then the King added in his own handwriting, sprawled right across the page: 'I am quite confident that, thanks to your zeal and care, you will succeed very well. It cannot be otherwise in a cause so entirely devoted to God as this is. There is no reason for you to trouble about anything but the preparations of this expedition.' Medina-Sidonia tried one last throw: he asked if he might present himself at Court, but he was told to go to Lisbon at once. 'If you fail you fail,' wrote the King magnanimously, 'but the cause being the cause of God you will not fail. Take heart and sail as soon as possible.'

DELAY AT LISBON

The Duke at first showed more procrastination than diligence and lingered on at San Lucar as if he were awaiting some miracle that would relieve him of his awful responsibility. But instead of a reprieve there came a gentle, understanding letter from the King which ended with a broad hint in the Royal hand, 'I can but think that this letter will find you nearer Lisbon than San Lucar'. After that there could be no escape. So, apprehensive, uncertain of himself and hating the whole business, the new Captain-General of the Ocean made his way to Lisbon to take over the supreme command of the 'Enterprise of England'.

CHAPTER XIII

The Great Armada

*

'In the year 1588 there sailed from Spain the greatest
Navy that ever swam upon the sea'
FRANCIS BACON, *Considerations touching a war with Spain*

It was raining when the new Commander-in-Chief arrived in
Lisbon at the beginning of March. He might have expected,
from the King's urgent orders to be gone, to find a fleet ready
to sail, waiting only for its new Commander to hoist his flag and
give the order to weigh and proceed. But even to his landsman's
eye there must have been something most unready about the
great forest of masts clustered out in the stream off the city, for
no sails were yet bent on the bare and dripping yards. The fleet
had hardly recovered from the shock of Santa Cruz's death; there
had been no work done and it had rained steadily ever since
that day a fortnight before. The men were in low spirits, they
had been preparing for too long and there had been many post-
ponements. On top of that, a number of ships had dragged and
others had lost their anchors and cables in the worst spring
weather that had been known in years.

Medina-Sidonia might have been excused for being more des-
pondent than his men for he had never wanted the job and had
done his best to get out of it. But he set to with energy. The first
thing he did was to make a personal inspection of every ship in his
command, either lying out in the stream, or, as too many were, in
dockyard hands alongside the wall. Whatever ship he boarded,
whether she were at anchor or echoing to the ring of caulkers'
hammers and reeking with the smell of hot pitch as she lay alongside, the tale of woe was the same: there was much sickness;

desertions were frequent; stores and ammunition were low; the water was foul; the food was going bad. An epidemic of typhus fever was racing along the overcrowded, dark and gloomy mess-decks of the fleet so that Medina was already short of men. At the first review of his troops ashore, out of a roll of some 22,000 nearly 5,000 were reported as 'dead, fled, or sick'.

He poured out his troubles in long letters to the King. He blamed the inefficiency and dishonesty of rascally contractors, the weather, shortage of money and the muddle caused by Santa Cruz's death for the new delays. But he forgot to blame Drake, who was the real culprit. The raid of the year before had strained an administration, already weakened by inefficiency and dis-honesty, almost to breaking point. Those dull weeks of patrolling by Drake's light craft when they had brought coastal traffic to a standstill and destroyed all those stores were now having their effect. That was why water casks leaked, why stores were short, why everything was late, why the standing rigging in many ships had not been renewed and there was a shortage of shipping.

There was also the usual shortage of money—Parma's army was eating up incredible sums every month, quite apart from the Armada—and the shortage was serious, so serious that Philip actually stopped all work on the Escorial and his other palaces. But lack of money has never yet deterred a country set upon war; nor caused a State once engaged to give up the struggle. The King would find the money somehow. Between them, he and Medina could seize or charter ships, could impress more men to replace the wastage, they could furnish new stores and provisions, they could and did hurry on the preparations; but what no one could do was cure the weakness inherent in the Spanish Navy itself. This weakness lay in the failure to appreciate that the broadside gun had brought about a radical change in naval tactics; the galley still dominated Spanish thought, which had not ad-vanced since Lepanto (an all-galley battle). The offensive power of the galley was directed in the way she was going, by ramming with her beak or firing a gun in her bows; galleys attacked in line-abreast like a squadron of charging cavalry, and the aim was to board the enemy and fight him hand to hand. The fire power of

'The Battle of Lepanto—a land battle afloat'

the broadside ship was directed at right angles to the line of advance; she had to approach within range then wheel to bring her guns to bear and the formation best adapted to this manœuvre was line ahead. They had not yet perfected this in England but the rudiments of the line-ahead formation was to appear in the English Channel. The Spanish aim was to send a swarm of ships against the enemy, batter him with close-range guns, then board. There was even the idea that there was something unsporting about gunnery, that boarding was the only honourable method of fighting at sea. The cannon was looked upon as an 'ignoble arm, all very well at the beginning of the fray and to pass away the time until the moment came for engaging hand to hand', when the Spanish tercios would, of course, come into their own. Spanish ships, therefore, were armed in the main with short-range, heavy-shotted pieces to batter the enemy and carried hooked grappling irons at the yardarms to fasten in his rigging at close quarters.

As hand to hand fighting and not a gun duel was the object, seamen were of secondary importance and not enough of them were carried to manœuvre the unhandy ships under sail. The Spanish fleet flagship, the *San Martin*, of 1,000 tons carried 300 soldiers and only 177 sailors; the English flagship of 800 tons carried 300 sailors and 125 soldiers, and if it had not been for the space occupied by Medina-Sidonia and his staff the *San Martin* would have carried more than 400 soldiers. Therein lay the essential difference between the fleets. The English looked upon their ships as weapons to be manœuvred; the Spaniards used theirs as vehicles for infantry. English ships had no ladders on the upper deck and strong doors in the bulkheads pierced by 'murdering pieces' in case they were boarded, which they did not intend to be. King Philip knew all about the English long-range tactics: 'above all it must be borne in mind', he warned Medina, 'that the enemy's object will be to fight at long range in consequence of his advantage in artillery'. He made a last-minute effort to obtain and mount long-range guns, but it was too late and the Armada sailed without them. 'Therefore, the aim of our men', the King laid down, 'must be to bring the enemy to close quarters and grapple with him.' But he does not explain how his Commander-in-Chief was to get within grappling distance of an elusive enemy in superbly-handled ships.

The time had passed for trying to alter the basic principles of Spanish tactics. 'The chief point is that the Armada should start', the King wrote to Medina, underlining the words in the dispatch with a stroke of his own pen. He suggested March 31st as a suitable sailing date but April came in with its softer weather and still Medina showed no signs of moving. On April 6th the usual convoy of galleons left Lisbon for the West Indies, unescorted, for the warships were required for fleet duties, and now the entire resources of the ports could be concentrated on getting the Armada ready for sea. The King changed the day to Palm Sunday, but Palm Sunday came and went and the balmy spring days drifted by with that huge fleet still swinging round its anchors on the placid waters of the Tagus, with Medina pressing on the work and Philip attending to countless petty details by day and getting up from his bed every night in the Escorial to pray to God. There were the usual religious processions and services during Holy Week and Easter when little work was done, until on April 25th, St. Mark's Day, it really did seem at last as if something were about to happen.

Long before dawn parties of soldiers from every ship were being pulled ashore; twelve hundred soldiers smartly dressed in their best clothes with arquebuses brightly polished, landed at the quays of the city on that cool spring morning. As they marched away to form guards of honour in the great squares before the Viceregal Palace and the Cathedral, the sun came up behind them and the fleet burst suddenly into colour as every standard and ensign, flag and streamer that the ships had in their lockers were hoisted to greet the day. For an immense standard especially designed and embroidered for this operation alone was to be presented with solemn ceremony to the new Commander-in-Chief. When the first stroke of six boomed out from the Cathedral tower, the Viceroy of Portugal, the Cardinal Archduke, nephew to the King, rode out of the Palace in his cardinal's robes of scarlet with the Duke of Medina-Sidonia on his right hand. The leaders of the expedition, veteran soldiers and sailors and all the

228

gentlemen volunteers, cadets of every great family in Spain, poured after them in a glittering cavalcade. The sun shone down on hose and doublet, it picked out the vivid colours of rich velvet cloaks, it winked back from damascened breastplate and set ablaze the jewels in plumed cap and ceremonial sword-hilt as the procession clattered through the empty streets to the Cathedral.

When High Mass had been sung, the Viceroy led the Duke up to the High Altar and lifting up a fold of the standard which had been lying on the altar during Mass, placed it in the hands of the kneeling Commander-in-Chief. As he grasped the heavily embroidered folds, the troops in the streets and square outside fired their heavy muskets in a salute which was echoed a second later by the thunderous roar of the guns of the fleet. The Duke handed the standard to Don Luis de Cordova, his standard-bearer, and walked out of the Cathedral followed by the gay procession which had been swollen now and toned down by the sombre habits of monks and friar and secular priests. The Duke led the way to the landing place where his barge was waiting for him. Another salute roared out as he was pulled off to his flagship and in the drifting smoke the standard was reverently hoisted at the main of the Royal galleon, *San Martin*. When the light spring breeze shook out its heavy silken folds, the wondering crew saw that it bore on one side the embroidered figure of Christ crucified, on the other the Blessed Virgin.

By this ceremony, so much in keeping with the religious aspect of the expedition, so full of the medieval pageantry of Spain, the Duke officially assumed command of the Armada, which was never known as 'Invincible'. Philip sometimes referred to the whole expedition in his dispatches as 'The Enterprise of England' and it was called *La Felicisima Armada*, the 'most happy fleet'. In official correspondence it was normally referred to as *La Armada Grande*, or the Grand Fleet, a term that we often used ourselves in the eighteenth century, and the name under which that mighty company of ships based on Scapa Flow in the 1914 war fought under Sir John Jellicoe.

The Armada, then, consisted of 130 ships, not all of them warships, manned by 8,000 sailors and carrying 19,000 soldiers, but with the gentlemen adventurers, the priests who sailed with the fleet, and the unfortunate slaves who sweated at the oars of the galleys, some thirty thousand men were waiting for the expedition to begin.

The Armada was divided into territorial squadrons. The fighting nucleus of the fleet was composed of the two squadrons of Portugal and Castile acting as two divisions in one large squadron. The 'Armada' of Portugal, of ten royal galleons and two pinnaces, flagship the *San Martin*, wearing the flag of the Commander-in-Chief, was really the old Portuguese Royal Navy. The Armada of Castile of ten galleons of the Indian Guard, four ships from New Spain and a couple of pinnaces, was under the command of Don Diego Flores de Valdés. But this officer sailed with Medina-Sidonia in the *San Martin* because Philip had given orders that de Valdés should advise the Duke in everything that had to do with manœuvring the fleet. It was a curious appointment because he became a sort of chief of staff, with extraordinary powers. This de Valdés was an unpleasant individual with a bad temper and jealous of all the other Admirals. Although he knew a lot about ship construction and surveying and had served for many years at sea, he had a bad fighting record; but quite recently he had managed to catch the King's eye which had brought him this appointment. Meanwhile the 'Admiral of the Armada', or, as we should call him today, the second-in-command, was Recalde. After this came the armed merchantmen in four squadrons of ten ships each: the *Biscayan* under Recalde, the *Andalusian* under Pedro de Valdés, the *Guipuscoan* under Oquendo and the *Levant*, of Italian 'argosies' or merchantmen, under Don Martin de Bertendona.

For all their great experience of the sea these officers were not at home upon it and their conduct of operations did not come as part of their second nature. Recalde, perhaps, was the finest seaman; he had served in the Indian Guard, under Santa Cruz in the Azores campaign and ashore as Superintendent of the Galley Arsenals. Oquendo had distinguished himself at Terceira where he had 'handled his ship like a horseman'. Pedro de Valdés had also gained his experience with the Indian Guard and in the war

A contemporary painting of the Armada by an unknown artist

against Portugal. De Bertendona had commanded at home in 1583 while Santa Cruz was in the Azores. These were stout seamen who had served their King faithfully for many years, but all suffered from the same defect. They had served under Santa Cruz and had absorbed his ideas. Now Santa Cruz had two great sea battles in his career, Lepanto and Terceira. At Lepanto the only vessels engaged were galleys, while at Terceira he had won a comparatively easy victory by charging down on the enemy with a superior fleet and boarding. He and his school imagined that galley tactics used with galleons would give them victory over the English fleet.

Although the Spaniards should have learned their lesson at Cadiz the year before when they saw how English galleons, even with the conditions against them, dealt with galleys, they included four Neapolitan galleasses and four Lisbon galleys in their fleet. They thought, perhaps, that they would come in useful when the wind dropped, but the fact is Medina-Sidonia collected every single ship that would float for the expedition. Perhaps the feeling of mere numbers gave him confidence. The galleasses were powerful fighting ships, but with their low freeboard they were unsuited to average Atlantic weather; they were essentially Mediterranean craft, survivals from the past, from Lepanto and even further back, from Salamis. They had auxiliary sail power of two square-rigged masts, but their main motive power was oars, and in smooth water, under the whips and curses of the petty officers, the 300 unfortunate slaves could be forced to drive them along at an astonishing speed. They were a compromise between the galley with its offensive power directed only forward and the galleon with its fire on the beam, for they carried guns on the broadside which interfered with the unfortunate rowers and were not a success. They were commanded by a stout old veteran called Hugo de Monçada and stayed with the fleet.

In days when ship to ship signalling was primitive or non-existent, urgent orders had to be passed by boat and for this despatch work there was a light squadron of small ships under Hurtado de Mendoza. He commanded twenty-two 'zabras' and 'patches'; the zabras were sloop-rigged Biscay smacks, while the pataches were larger, being used normally as coastguard cutters and tenders and were equivalent to our pinnaces. This squadron was not meant to take part in the fighting.

The last squadron of the fleet was non-combatant. It was a collection of storeships gathered together from all over Europe. Some were Spanish, some Italian, others came from Rostock in the Baltic and Hamburg. They were not fighting ships; they were heavy, clumsy, slow merchantmen—'tramps' we should call them today—and they should never have been included in the fighting fleet. They only slowed it up and added to an already unwieldy mass of ships. There were twenty-three of these 'hulks' or 'urcas de cargo' and they carried an astonishing miscellany of stores and spares. In a modern invasion fleet this squadron would have formed a 'slow convoy' which would have sailed on its own and not as part of the main attacking force. But here they were with their 8,000 leather bottles, 5,000 pairs of shoes, 11,000 pairs of sandals, 20 spare gun carriages, 3,500 cannon balls, 40 artillery mules, their wagons, limbers and harness, their 7,000 arquebuses and 10,000 pikes. They carried the heavy transport and artillery of the expedition, as well as sappers' tools and stores, which included stocks of wood and iron for erecting palisades and forts ashore.

The Enterprise of England was a vast undertaking, and under the minute and detailed scrutiny of the King everything had been foreseen. If the expedition were successful a civilian organization would be needed to administer the occupied country; therefore an Inspector-General with a staff of fifty, and nineteen officers of justice sailed with the fleet. One hundred and eighty monks and friars were embarked, largely to administer to the spiritual needs of the soldiers and sailors, but also to spread the Word on landing. It was obviously considered that spiritual needs were likely to be more urgent than physical because the hospital staff for 30,000 men was a mere handful of eighty-five. No, nothing had been forgotten, not even 200 English flags for use on arrival, an item which particularly infuriated Drake when he heard of it.

If anything were to happen to Medina-Sidonia the supreme command would fall upon the military commander of the expedition, Don Alonso de Leyva, who sailed in his own ship, *La Rata Santa Maria Encoronada*. Under his especial charge, the King had placed the noblemen and gentlemen volunteers of whom 'there were so great a multitude, that scarce any family of account, or any one principal man throughout all Spain, that had not a brother, a son, or a kinsman in that fleet: who all of them were in good hope to purchase unto themselves in that navy, invincible endless glory and renown'. Many other volunteers were scattered round the fleet, ranging from the Prince of Ascoli, reputedly a son of the King on the wrong side of the blanket who had embarked with his thirty-nine servants, to a poet and playwright who was in some trouble over a lady, Lope de Vega, who sailed as a shipmate of his brother. Others again were attracted either by the chance of serving their religion or for the mere joy of striking a blow at England, like certain Irish gentlemen of means; while, tempted, perhaps, by the promise of loot, one anonymous German accompanied the expedition.

Such was the Great Armada, still lying off the city of Lisbon on April 30th when the Venetian Ambassador reported to his government: 'Here in the churches they make constant prayers; and the King is on his knees two or three hours every day before the Sacrament. Everyone hopes that the greater the difficulties, humanly speaking, the greater will be the favour of God.' In the intervals between his devotions and the attentions of his doctors who were continually bleeding and purging him for his gout, Philip somehow found the time to go into every detail connected with the expedition. Medina-Sidonia had to send full statements of all stores and supplies to the Escorial and even his own orders to the fleet were annotated by the King who was concerned about the personal behaviour of his soldiers and sailors. For an undertaking which was almost a Crusade, it was only natural that the King should open the orders to his Commander-in-Chief in an exalted vein: 'In the first place, victories are God's to give, and His to take away, as He sees fit. But the cause you are defending is so peculiarly His as to give us hope of His help and favour if it is not made unworthy by our sinfulness. For this reason you must take particular care in the Armada against sin of any kind.'

Medina-Sidonia, who felt that he needed all the help he could get, gave effect to this general directive by issuing the following orders to his command:

1. All from the highest to the lowest are to know the reason which moved His Majesty to undertake this expedition in the service of God and the restitution of many people to the bosom of the Church. Therefore all officers are to see that their subordinates come aboard confessed and communicated.
2. No one is idly to make use of the name of Our Lord or Our Lady or of the Saints. Less sinful ejaculations will be punished by stoppage of wine.
3. Gambling especially at night is prohibited.
4. No one is to offer or receive as an insult anything which happens on board his ship. All private feuds are considered to be at an end.

And, if that were asking too much, the wise precaution of:

5. No one is to wear a dagger.
6. As it is an evident inconvenience, as well as an offence to God, that public or other women should be permitted to accompany such an Armada, I order that none shall be taken on board.
7. At sunrise every morning the ships' boys will call out the morning salutation at the foot of the mainmast; on the approach of night they will sing the 'Salve Regina'.
8. The password will be changed daily: on Sunday, Jesus, and then in rotation, the Holy Ghost, the Holy Trinity, Santiago, the Angels, All Saints and on Saturday, Our Lady.

After the preamble he came to the operational section. On leaving Lisbon course was to be shaped for Finisterre and after that for the Scillies; the rendezvous was to be Mount's Bay. The orders then go into all the usual details of signal procedure, station keeping, the care of arms, precautions against fire, and the whole were to be read to the ships' companies three times a week. The religious preamble to operation orders was nothing unusual in those days; the orders for most English expeditions start in much the same way, though referring, of course, to a Protestant God. The sea held so much of mystery and the unknown that the seaman was perforce God-fearing under his rough exterior. Medina-Sidonia's orders were eminently sensible and good. He cannot have been quite the fool that he has been made out to be; even if they were produced for him by his staff, it was his name that was signed at the foot of them.

The rations and the allowance of wine were laid down. Each man received about a bottle of sherry, Condado or Monzon a day, but only half a bottle of Candia wine, because it was so strong, and this order the King underlined himself. The rations were for each man 1½ lb. of biscuits per day, and on Sundays and Thursdays 6 oz. of bacon and 2 oz. of rice; on Wednesdays and Saturdays 6 oz. of cheese and 3 oz. of peas or beans; on Wednesdays, Fridays and Saturdays 6 oz. of fish: oil and vinegar were also issued. These rations were not as good as the English rations in the same campaign; not that it made much difference, for on neither side did the men get the rations to which they were entitled.

The situation before King Philip was this: in the Low Countries under Parma he had a powerful army containing some of the best troops in the world who, as Parma reported, were full of confidence; but although this concentration on clear days could almost see the coast of England, it was quite useless until it had crossed that narrow strip of water which separated it from its objective. The Navy of England had command of the Narrow Seas and until it had been deprived of that command Parma could not move. The only way to gain that command was to drive off the English fleet and this King Philip hoped to do with his Armada now at Lisbon. The Armada was expected to perform two separate functions: it was a fighting fleet and it was a convoy carrying troop reinforcements. Six thousand picked Spanish infantry were embarked who would land under Alonso de Leyva for Parma's command. Parma was to be in charge of landing operations while Medina-Sidonia was to be supreme at sea. 'As soon as you receive the order from me which will reach you separately, you are to sail with the whole Armada, making for the English Channel, and pass through it until you reach Margate Cape where you will join the Duke of Parma. You are to remove any obstacles and make secure his passage across the Channel.'

That is clear enough, the main obstacle being the English fleet. This was not so easily removable and there were no ports suitable as operational bases for ships drawing thirty feet on Parma's side of the Channel. The Armada could not back and fill indefinitely in the Narrow Seas, even if it had gained a victory over the English. The King's letter goes into considerable detail, he had provided pilots who knew the Channel and the Duke was to keep to the English side. He warns Medina not to separate his force and even instructs him how to send a messenger overland through France to advise Parma of his arrival at the entrance to the Channel. The letter is full of good sense and advice, but at the back of the King's mind there seems to be the thought that the mere appearance of the Armada will give him all he wants: 'It is understood that you will fight only if you cannot otherwise make secure the passage across to England of the Duke of Parma.' What he thought the English fleet would be doing during this operation is impossible to guess, but he seems to have been under the impression that Medina-Sidonia would find the English fleet divided. After more words of encouragement and advice on what he should do if he met Drake, which was to avoid action unless he were too closely pursued, the King ended with the solemn words: 'I will commend you to God that He may guide you in that cause which is His.' The orders were dated, 'Madrid, April 1st 1588'; they were signed, 'I, the King'.

In both the King's directive and Medina-Sidonia's general orders the name Drake appears again and again. If Drake is here; if Drake intends this or does that; King Philip, Medina, the Pope, kings, ambassadors and spies all use the word Drake when they are referring to the English Navy, which in their eyes, he personified. The name of Drake recurs like a knell in letters, dispatches, conversations and orders—it was his hour.

Just when everything was ready there was some trouble with the soldiers over the application of Order No. 6, the one to do with women (public or private). It was found on counting them that over six hundred ladies were cosily installed round the fleet. Medina was taking no chances; he not only had them taken ashore but thrown clean out of Lisbon and the neighbourhood into the bargain. This did not at all suit the soldiers, who raised a great outcry, until they were comforted with the report that there were ripe and comely wenches in England.

By May 11th every man had been shrived and had received a certificate to that effect; the last gentleman with his numerous servants and piles of baggage had embarked; the last stores had been struck down below; the last mule had been swayed, struggling and kicking, over the side; the last woman had been rowed, protesting, ashore and the fleet dropped down to Belem at the mouth of the estuary, some three miles from Lisbon. Everything was as ready as it was ever likely to be and Philip cancelled all audiences and refused to see anyone while he waited impatiently for word that the Armada had gone. But, as Medina-Sidonia piously reminded him on May 14th, 'God ordains all things and He has not seen fit to send us weather for the sailing of the Armada; it is as boisterous and bad as if it were December. But everything is ready and not an hour will be wasted.' Lest the King should be unappreciative of his efforts he adds the little reminder: 'It is two months ago today that I came to this city and I leave it for others to tell Your Majesty how much has been done.' His Majesty well knew how much had been done because he had done most of it himself.

At last God ordained that there should be a favourable breeze. On the evening of May 29th the wind blew steadily and gently from the north-north-west and as the sun came up on May 30th the *San Martin* fired a gun, the signal to weigh. All ships acknowledged by sounding a flourish of trumpets and hoisting their colours. The capstans groaned as the crews heaved round to their Mediterranean chanties. Lumps of grey Lisbon mud dropped back off the anchors into the water with a plop as the great sails slowly filled and displayed their coloured paintings of saints or the great red St. Andrew's Cross of the Burgundian Saltire. All

237

through that brilliant summer's day the long procession of ships moved majestically out to sea; one by one they dropped down the river: *St. Martin, St. Philip,* the *Magdalen, St. John the Baptist,* the *Trinity, Our Lady of the Rosary,* the *Holy Cross,* the *Holy Spirit,* the *Crucifixion, Our Lady of Guadaloupe.* There was as much pageantry as if the ships were knights entering the lists. Trumpets were sounding; music was stealing across the still water drowning the monotonous chant of the leadsmen in the chains; and every flag and ancient, every silk streamer and pensail, blazoned with the arms of nobles or of cities, fluttered languidly out in a mass of colour in the light breeze. Each squadron sailed under its own flag: the dragons and shields of Portugal; the castles of Castile; the flowered cross and luces of the two Sicilies; the cross and foxes of Biscay; but the national flag under which the Armada fought, corresponding to the English St. George's Cross, was the flag of Burgundy, a white flag with a 'saltire raguled red'—or red St. Andrew's Cross. While they cautiously felt their way past the shoals at the entrance with the handier galleys towing the unwieldy galleons round awkward corners, the sun rose high and brought out crowds of local folk to watch the Grand Fleet leaving harbour. The Portuguese were glad to see them go, for the country was nearly bankrupt through having had for so long to supply this huge concentration of ships and men. But the nobles and the volunteers, the soldiers and the sailors recked little of that. The sun was shining; the bands were playing; they were off on their great adventure for God and the King. In a long line the stately vessels moved slowly out to sea, they glided past the white Tower of Lisbon, past the monastery built to mark the place where Vasco da Gama spent his last night ashore before sailing for India. And as they passed below him the Cardinal Patriarch on the heights over Belem blessed them one by one. For two whole days the long procession continued, until on the evening of May 31st, when the sails of the leading ships were black against the setting sun, a courier who had been waiting, leaped to his horse and spurred furiously to the Escorial to inform the King that his Enterprise of England at last was under weigh.

CHAPTER XIV

From the Tagus to the Lizard

*

Now that they were out at sea, the thrill of departure over, trumpets silent, the gay flags back in their lockers, those who sailed in the Armada were jolted into reality, and they found little of glory or romance in what they now had to face. A light northerly breeze carried the fleet of overcrowded vessels down to leeward; the galleons tacked out and in but lost ground on each tack and the remainder of the fleet had to stay with them. Although the galleons were crowded with the finest soldiers in the world they carried too few sailors to work them smartly even in a light wind. Every day the Duke sent a dispatch boat into Lisbon with a report for the King and this varied little in its daily tale of woe. The water casks were leaking and what remained was foul; the biscuit was mouldy; the meat, fish and cheese putrid and they had to throw them overboard. Then the north wind freshened and soon the Duke was reporting from as low down as Cape St. Vincent. After his Armada had been a fortnight at sea, therefore, instead of reading dispatches from the mouth of the Channel as he had hoped, King Philip was receiving reports from the latitude of Lisbon that the ships' companies were suffering from dysentery. The pilots of the fleet were now begging the Duke to put in somewhere for fresh water, and the King's daily reports were urgent requests for fresh supplies to be sent out to the fleet.

At last on June 10th the wind shifted to the south-west, the galleons squared away before the wind and for the first time the Armada began to make headway in the right direction. Up in England they did not yet know for certain that the Armada was

239

at sea, but they were soon to have a report from an eye-witness. Shortly after the shift of wind a Hamburg sea captain, Hans Limburger, who had sailed from Cadiz with a general cargo, saw ahead of him a vast array of ships spread over the sea. As he slowly overtook the Armada he watched the magnificent sight for a whole day, but he had the heels of the fleet and next morning he was alone. A patrolling English warship picked him up at the mouth of the Channel and took him into Plymouth where he was well entertained for three days before being given a safe conduct and sent on his way. The local correspondent of the banking house of Fugger, wide-awake as always, interviewed Captain Limburger on his arrival at Hamburg and reported to his head office that the English 'rejoiced that the Armada was at sea'. The correspondent then added an item of local news which had puzzled him but which gives us four hundred years later an indication of what sort of summer they had up there in 1588. 'On two consecutive days the sun and moon have been quite bloody,' he wrote, 'what this signifies the merciful God alone knows.' He thought it a portent of terrible loss of life in the anticipated fleet action. Although he ended with the strictly non-committal prayer, 'May God defend the Right', in a postscript he left no doubt where his sympathy really lay. Adding that he had confirmation of the sailing of the Armada from Cologne, he concluded, 'May God grant it all prosperity'.

When those words were written the Armada was in Corunna, and if it was not exactly prospering at least it had escaped premature disaster. As the fleet came up to Finisterre conditions had become impossible; five hundred men were down with stomach trouble and more were reporting sick every day. The provisions then remaining could not have supported a campaign which might turn out to be a long one; and once past Finisterre the last chance would be gone of obtaining fresh supplies. The Duke summoned a Council on board the flagship to consider the situation. The Admirals were decided to a man that the Armada could not proceed with things as they were and advised him to detach a squadron to land the sick at Ferrol just round the corner and bring out stocks of fresh provisions. Although this was the obvious thing to do the Duke was doubtful. It meant going against the King's positive orders not to stop anywhere or to separate his forces, and no man in Spain, least of all one of high rank, would lightly disregard the orders of Philip the King. While the Duke was wondering what to do the weather decided for him. On June 19th the wind suddenly shifted and it came on to blow hard. The Commander-in-Chief with the Squadron of Portugal, the galleys and some of the larger galleons made in for Corunna, leaving the rest to follow. This providential alteration in the weather provided the excuse which saved the Armada from guttering out like a spent candle before even it had reached the Channel.

The full strength of the gale scattered the ships caught outside and during the next few days they came limping one by one into harbour, one dismasted, many leaking and all with sick and exhausted crews. And when the dismal procession stopped after about a week, a third of the force he had started with was still adrift. No news had been received of these missing ships, when the Duke sent off a gloomy and defeatist report to the Escorial. After describing the victualling situation he came to the condition of the fleet, 'The men are out of spirit: the officers do not understand their business; we are no longer strong', and he went on to advise the King to make the best terms he could and call the whole thing off. It was the sort of dispatch calculated to bring a Commander-in-Chief his dismissal by return, but instead of the sack Medina-Sidonia received a long letter of comfort and encouragement consisting of pages of reasons why the King was convinced the enterprise could not fail. He was absolved of all blame for what had happened so far, and it was only towards the end that the King was other than coaxing. Suddenly he exhorts the Duke, 'Stir yourself then to do your duty, since you see that, pressed as I am by financial and other difficulties, I am resolute to overcome them all with God's aid.' The King was as good as his word, and this time he did not leave everything to his Commander-in-Chief. He would have no more slackness or dishonest contractors which, he felt, had been as much to blame for the state of the fleet as the Duke. King Philip sent his secretary, Andres de Alba, from the Escorial down to Corunna with authority over the local officials, Medina-Sidonia and the Governor of Galicia included. He had full power to requisition supplies and take whatever steps he considered necessary to send out the fleet well victualled and in a seaworthy condition. With the arrival of this official things started to happen.

The harbour of Corunna is an estuary of the sea into which a peninsula curves out like a protecting arm to form a safe anchorage. The old walled town on the tip of the peninsula had supplied many ships and seen them sail away: Phoenicians, Romans, lateen-rigged Moors, Venetian wool galleys on their way to England, even French and English privateers, but never in its long history had such a fleet lain at anchor under its battlements. Now lumbering oxcarts and trains of pack-mules crowded its narrow streets, squads of apprehensive recruits tramped over the cobbles, while cloaked, bejewelled hidalgoes clinked their spurs on last-minute shopping expeditions. All round the shore of the bay ships lay awkwardly on their sides being caulked and tallowed. The local fishermen had never toiled so hard and long, and lowing herds of cattle were driven in from the surrounding pastures to provide fresh meat. Meanwhile the invalids all recovered in hospital, the water casks were repaired and filled and a stock of fresh provisions was struck down into every hold. Then, to crown all, the missing ships came sailing in apparently none the worse. Some had been as far as the Scillies, one or two into Mount's Bay, but none had been lost or was even badly damaged. Now that all ships were in company, and thanks to the way in which de Alba had carried out the instructions of the King, the morale of the Armada recovered. It had been generously supplied with victuals of good quality and the men knew it. In every way it was in better shape than it had been on sailing out of Lisbon, but much time had been used up and not many weeks of summer remained. Only one thing was left to do before leaving. Tents were set up on an island in the harbour with an altar in each. Next morning in orderly succession the boats of the fleet moved to and fro across the harbour landing all ships' companies until every man of the Armada had been given Absolution and had received the Blessed Sacrament. 'This is great riches', the Duke wrote to his King, 'and the most precious jewel I carry with me. They are now all well, content and cheerful.'

Fortified and refreshed, at dawn on Friday, July 22nd, the Armada sailed from Corunna. No Cardinal was there to bless them on this occasion, only the townsfolk gazed down from their city walls in wonderment on that long procession of ships sailing out into the Atlantic. It was a quieter departure than from Lisbon and many of those who now looked back from the crowded decks at the old walled city with the green hills beyond were having their last sight of Spain. By the evening of July 23rd, Cape Ortegal was astern, and for once the omens seemed favourable. As the great stern lantern was lit in the flagship the Armada picked up a moderate wind from the southward and the fleet followed as she headed out across the Bay. The weather was fair, the sea slight. The Commander-in-Chief was under orders to proceed up Channel, keeping to the English side, and to fight only if he could not otherwise secure the passage of the Duke of Parma's army. He was to stop nowhere on the way. These orders did not satisfy Admiral Juan Martinez de Recalde, a tough old seaman from Bilbao who knew Ireland and the Channel. He had been long enough at sea to realize that the Armada could not fight a campaign without an advanced base. With that freedom which King Philip allowed his subjects he had written to the Escorial from Corunna to ask that the orders might be modified to allow Plymouth or Dartmouth to be captured on the way up Channel, but the King had ignored the suggestion. 'To invade by sea on a perilous coast, being neither in possession of any part nor succoured by any party may better fit a prince presuming on his fortunes than enriched with understanding. Such was the enterprise of Philip II upon England in 1588', was Sir Walter Ralegh's lofty comment on Philip's strategy.

With a fair wind the fleet sailed on towards its doom. At dawn each morning the ships' boys gathered at the foot of the mainmast to sing a morning salutation, and as the sun went down they sang the 'Salve Regina', an antiphon five hundred years old even in their time. For three days the Armada made good progress across the Bay until on the night of Monday 25th the Duke with all his fleet in company had reached the entrance to the English Channel. Next morning there were all the signs of a change in the weather. Puffs of air blew from the northward, the sky was overcast, a silvery sea was calm but there were heavy showers of rain. By Wednesday the wind had backed and it was blowing a gale from the west with a high sea running which broke into the stern galleries of the galleons. The fleet was hove to and lay head-to-wind for an anxious and uncomfortable Thursday. On Friday the wind had dropped, but a long swell coming in from the wastes of the Atlantic made the crank overmasted galleons almost unmanageable. As the sky cleared and a light wind came out of the south-west, a look-out in the maintop of the *San Martin* reported that some forty sail were missing. Being unable to ride such seas the galleys had made off for the coast of France before they were swamped. They took no further part in the proceedings. The other missing ships were only a few miles farther down to leeward and after the Duke had picked them up the Armada sailed on over a silent, empty sea. The pilots made their position to be in 50° N. and at noon on Friday the Armada picked up soundings at fifty-six fathom.

Here was Medina-Sidonia at last in enemy waters, but there was nothing to show it, neither sail nor sight of land. He made the signal for the Armada to assume its battle order which had been worked out months before in Lisbon by his Council of War. Their deliberations resulted in a formation to be expected of a body made up of soldiers, and sailors drilled in galley warfare. It was a compromise between the 'Eagle formation', which had been used with success in galley battles since the days of Themistocles, and the customary order of march of a military column venturing into hostile territory. The result was an elaborate formation that called for exact station keeping, but it was flexible and the only thing wrong about it was that it had been devised to deal with a situation that did not exist. Its strength was in the head because the Duke was under the impression that a comparatively weak enemy detachment was in Plymouth while the main body of the English fleet was far ahead guarding the Narrow Seas, whereas it was the other way about and the main concentration was by now

Look-out vessels (Frigates and Feluccas) 2 Miles in advance

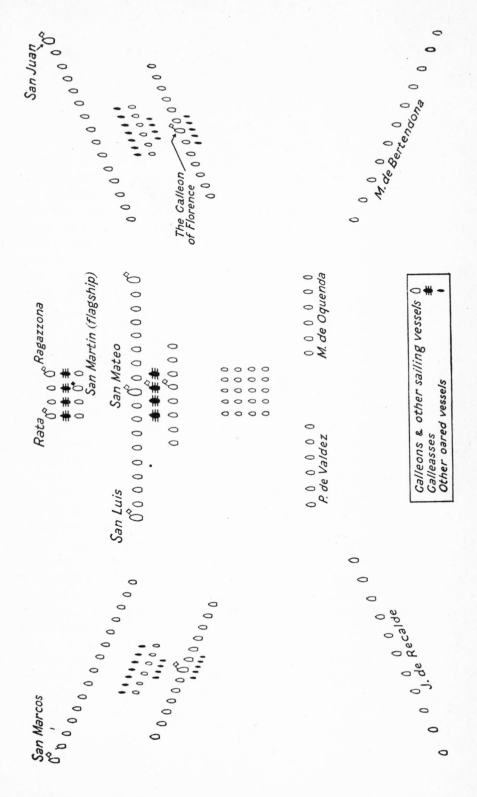

San Juan

San Marcos

Rata · Ragazzona

San Martin (flagship)

San Luis

San Mateo

The Galleon of Florence

M. de Bertendona

P. de Valdez

M. de Oquenda

J. de Recalde

Galleons & other sailing vessels	
Galleasses	
Other oared vessels	

in Plymouth. When the complicated movement had at last been completed, a light screen of pataches and lateen-rigged gallizabras sailed two miles ahead of the fleet, as it were a cloud of scouts and skirmishers. The flagship, closely attended by two galleasses, led the main body, the two strongest squadrons, those of Castile and Portugal in line abreast disposed on either beam. Half a mile astern, sandwiched between the two fighting halves, the vulnerable portion of the Armada was stationed, the store ships and lightly-armed transports. To protect these on either quarter, and to form the rearguard for the whole, two squadrons of galleons sailed in port and starboard quarterline. As evolved in Lisbon the formation looked on paper something like the drawing on p. 245, but to an observer at sea level the formation might very well give the impression of being crescent-shaped from whatever quarter he observed it.

Once formed in battle order the Armada sailed on through a grey and lifeless sea. There was a hush that afternoon over the flagship: the water made only a gentle rippling down the side and even the sailors talked in whispers as they moved every now and again to trim the sails. Then at four in the afternoon the pilot high up on the poop saw that the horizon was no longer a straight unbroken line, a blue irregular shape was rising slowly from the sea. It was the coast of England. The Commander-in-Chief hoisted his great personal standard which had been consecrated in Lisbon so long ago, the guns fired a salute and the ship's company knelt in thanks to God for having brought them this far. And as the Spaniards gazed at that fabulous coast they observed smudges of black smoke rising at intervals along the land and knew them to be alarm beacons. Braced for what might come the Armada sailed quietly on. As night fell the coastline grew blurred to become one with sea and sky; and by the time the ships' boys gathered at the foot of the mainmast the port horizon was dotted with points of fire.

CHAPTER XV

In the Channel

*

1. *'Beyond the Beacons'*

The Spanish Commander-in-Chief and his staff gazed at that fringe of twinkling fires without a notion of what was really happening in the realm that lay beyond or that the information provided by the King would turn out to be wrong in almost every particular. King Philip, normally so cautious and sane, inclined to examine a problem with maddening deliberation before reaching a decision, seems to have lost his sense of proportion over anything which had to do with the invasion, to become credulous and wildly optimistic. Part of his trouble was that for the last four years there had been no Spanish Ambassador in London to keep him accurately informed of the state of the country or the temper of its people. He had not heard, therefore, of the great surge of patriotism over England which swept away all differences and united Englishmen under their Queen— nor, if he had, would he have been inclined to believe it. Lacking authentic information Philip listened to malcontents and *émigrés*, to anyone with a specious tale so long as it supported what he wanted to believe.

After dealing with a pro-Spanish Scot, the Earl of Morton, King Philip believed that he could get Scotland to come in on his side, but Morton was arrested on his return and Scotland remained neutral. The Jesuit Parsons, out of touch with the feeling in his own country, convinced Philip that the Catholics in England would revolt. The Catholics sprang to arms but not on the side of Spain. One of the most uncompromising of these Catholics had been at Southampton on a summer's morning thirty-four years before, almost to the day. A Spanish fleet had just arrived bring-

247

ing Prince Philip of Spain to wed England's Queen, Mary Tudor. Dressed in a new suit of black velvet and gold, young Sir Anthony Browne awaited the Prince as his Master of Horse with a gift from the Queen of a white charger; and later the two young men rode off to Winchester. Created a Viscount for his services under Queen Mary, he had been fearlessly outspoken in the House of Lords attacking Queen Elizabeth's policy towards her Catholic subjects. But when the news reached Cowdray down in the woods of Sussex that another Spanish fleet was on the coast Sir Anthony called for his horse and armour, and rode off with his son and grandson at the head of 200 retainers to join the Standard of his Queen at Tilbury Fort. Although Philip had lived amongst them he had never been able to fathom the English, and it was beyond him now to imagine the feeling in that puzzling island. Even with the record of Edmund Campion before him it seems never to have struck him that men, whatever their religion, might glory in being English. A Venetian in Paris writing at about this time to his Government would have given him a better picture: 'The battle will be bloody for the English never yield,' he wrote, 'in this present case they would count themselves victorious even if they died to a man along with the enemy, provided they could save the Kingdom.' The Catholics were loyal, the Northern border was quiet with an amenable neutral beyond it and after a generation of peace at home and abroad England was strong, united and prosperous.

The peril of invasion was so familiar in the southern counties that the precautions for dealing with it had come to be accepted as part of everyday life. England had no standing army for the defence of the realm; she relied instead upon a militia composed of her citizens. The burden of this fell upon everyone: the humbler sort served in the ranks, the people of property provided the arms and equipment according to their means. Although every able man in the land was liable for compulsory military training, in practice the quota of trained men demanded of a locality could normally be met from volunteers helped by a form of selective conscription. The average Elizabethan poked fun at the militia, grumbled when 'pressed' and dodged it when he could, but he

(*a*) Lord Howard of Effingham. Lord Admiral

(*b*) Sir Francis Drake

(*c*) Sir John Hawkins

THE ADMIRALS WHO BEAT THE ARMADA

accepted the principle and saw no curtailment of his personal free-dom in this national duty. In the rural districts defence was a local matter, the affair of the hundred, the village or the parish: a man drilled with his neighbours under an officer he knew, with arms provided by the squire. Nothing could have been better suited to a self-reliant people with a liking for running their own affairs. The whole organization was amateur but it was not alto-gether haphazard if the reports can be believed of the Muster Masters who inspected the shires in the early spring of that year.

The scare of 1586 had resulted in discipline being tautened and the training and organization overhauled. Every holiday and Sunday afternoon since then had seen awkward-looking country-men, variously armed, gathered for drill on field or village green; and as subordinate officers knew where every man 'in an instant could be called and had' not many succeeded in dodging it. The tall strong men carried pikes, the nimble fellows muskets; the remainder were armed with bows and arrows or bills, which were the billhooks they used on weekdays, fastened to the ends of poles. That unpopular weapon, the arquebus, was replacing the bow and by this time most had gained sufficient confidence through practice not to 'wincke or pull their heades from the piece' on firing, while some were fair shots. Miscellaneous parts of ill-fitting, dented armour were handed out to those who would wear it; but no one would use the uncomfortable 'morions' or steel casques lately issued from the Tower of London.

The militia were a scratch lot but their spirit was high. That summer the tinkers were hawking a new ballad round the country districts all about the great doings of Sir Francis Drake at Cartha-gena and Cadiz, from which the country folk had formed a poor opinion of Spaniards. They were cheerfully confident that they could deal with any invader, and it is possible that if there had been a landing they would have given the Spanish tercios a rougher passage than they bargained for. At likely landing places stakes had been driven into the beaches and covering trenches had been prepared for the defenders. And if the Spaniards did succeed in landing the orders were drastic: all crops in the path of the advancing enemy were to be burned, the cattle driven and bridges destroyed. The enemy was to be harassed by sniping and alarms day and night; small parties were not to give battle on their own but were to join the nearest English concentration. The orders for alarm were obviously framed to prevent people from rushing madly about trying to stop the invasion single-handed and for this reason no beacon was to be fired except on the order of a Justice of the Peace.

The beacon fires which Medina-Sidonia was staring at were the antennae of a warning system that had been carefully worked out. By the firing of certain beacons inland the men of those counties could be directed to reinforce concentrations where needed. Somerset men could be sent to Dorchester to await orders, those of Wiltshire to Southampton, while the bands of Kent and Essex could aid each other across the bridge of boats at Gravesend—all at the firing of the appropriate beacons. There was no wild panic, therefore, when the Armada was sighted off the Lizard because people knew what to do. Each man trudged off to his mustering place, where by the light of blazing torches he was issued with armour and weapons, to march off with his companions, singing through the night.

As the threat of a landing in the west receded, to disappear when the Armada moved up-Channel, so detachments of County Militia marched across the breadth of England for Tilbury and the defence of London, the heart of the realm. Squire and yeoman, merchant and artisan, they marched in companies each with its banner carrying the device of country gentleman or town borough. These men from the farms and villages or thriving provincial towns thought themselves fine fellows, to judge from the report of one onlooker who saw them marching through London 'with cheerful countenances, courageous words and gestures, leaping and dancing'. The City Fathers, however, treated defence as a serious matter: all citizens had to carry arms and every householder had to keep a number of filled leather water buckets in his home or shop in case of fire. The large number of foreign craftsmen in the City was also a problem and the roads were patrolled because the authorities were not certain of their attitude if there were a landing and also because they would be attacked in the event of trouble by the London mob which hated strangers. In supplying troops London excelled all other parts of England, and during the past months her trained bands had spent many boring hours at pike drill on Mile End parade ground. Ten thousand of them now, well drilled and disciplined, equipped by the City Livery Companies marched down to the great camp at Tilbury. The armour did not fit, weapons were out of date, the food at the camp ran out; there was muddle, but no dismay—now that the hour had come the mood of England was one of gay defiance.

2. 'Parma in Dunkirk'

On the night of his arrival on the coast of England Medina-Sidonia wrote a letter to his King which was a sort of private postscript to the official dispatch. Although this was headed 'in sight of the Lizard', like almost every other letter he had written since leaving the Tagus it breathed perplexity and misgiving. His trouble now was that he had not had a word from Parma, although he had warned him of his coming. So he had decided to wait off the Isle of Wight until he knew what Parma intended. Also he had not been able to pick up any information on the way because he had not fallen in with a single ship during the voyage. The ominous glow of the beacons, the eerie silence, and the strangely deserted sea were getting on his nerves. 'We are', he wrote, 'groping in the dark.' Quite how much in the dark he really was the Duke did not know. The position at that time was this: The Duke with the Armada was off the Lizard; 400 miles on at the far end of the Channel the Duke of Parma with the Spanish Army waited at Dunkirk; and somewhere in between was the English fleet.

Medina-Sidonia cannot be blamed for feeling worried: he could not invade on his own because he was only bringing stores and reinforcements, and Parma could not move without the protection of the Armada; but it had never been laid down how or where they should meet, nor was either commander aware of the intentions of the other. It was hardly the way in which to stage an invasion. To add to the confusion Medina-Sidonia thought that he would be able to anchor and water his fleet on the Flemish coast and was proceeding on that assumption. As he made his way along that dark tunnel of an English Channel he thought all the time he could see a faint glimmer of light at the far end, that his troubles would be over when he reached Dunkirk—he even thought that Parma with his soldiers in rowing boats could reinforce the Armada. A succession of letters from Medina-Sidonia containing these quaint ideas were no comfort to Parma who had enough troubles of his own.

He had chosen Dunkirk as his invasion base because it was the nearest port to the Nore that was offering—he had spun out the peace talks hoping to capture Ostend before they were over, but he had failed, and Dunkirk was not an ideal base. The harbour could not take ships of any size, certainly not Medina's galleons, and even with his small vessels Parma could only get out at spring tides. Every time he looked out to sea, there, hovering to pounce were the sails of blockading enemy squadrons: Sir Henry Seymour with fifteen of the Queen's ships from the Downs or twenty Dutch warships based on Flushing. Only if the wind blew from the west were these squadrons driven off their station, but when the wind was westerly Parma himself could not get out. The Duke of Parma was beginning to regret that he had ever endorsed the idea of invasion: in the abstract it had appeared attractive: his army of superlative troops would have no trouble with the inexperienced English army; but he was not the last commander to have it borne in on him that no troops, even the finest veterans in the world, could conquer England by sitting on that side of the Channel. With great energy he had concentrated a large army; using the inland waterways of the area, he had accumulated stores, horses and artillery. To transport them he had collected small sailing vessels and rowboats, and for his cavalry he had built flat-bottomed boats with ramps, which in appearance were like the small infantry landing craft used in the late war. But how to get this collection over to the mouth of the Thames? 'Most of our boats are built only for the rivers and cannot weather the sea', he wrote in exasperation after one of Medina-Sidonia's letters, 'as for fighting, they cannot; they can only carry over the men in perfectly fair weather.' As far back as May Parma had been complaining of the shortage of money, and Spanish infantry were at their best only so long as they were paid regularly. But now there was no money to pay them, sickness had reduced their numbers and their morale had so far gone that a reliable spy could report to Burghley that they were 'in utter misery'. All in all, the more Parma saw of the invasion now that it was imminent, the less he liked the look of it.

Watching events from his station in the Downs as Seymour's Rear-Admiral, Sir William Wynter thought no more of Spain's invasion chances than did Parma himself. Judging from his experience of what had been required for the Leith Expedition in the time of King Henry, he considered that Parma would need at least 300 vessels of sixty tons to ferry across his army with all its equipment and stores; and that if Parma did get to sea the prevailing westerly wind of that summer would force him to make for the Isle of Sheppey or the Kent coast. All this he wrote to Walsingham in a letter which was a masterly review of the situation. He disapproved of Howard's fleet being 'shut up' in Plymouth because the wind that brought the Spaniards on would keep the English in. Having given Walsingham the benefit of his shrewd good sense and experience the old Admiral dropped a hint that a buck from Kent would made a welcome addition to his table.

Parma did not have anything approaching three hundred vessels and he could not find seamen even for those he had collected. The problem facing him had no solution; he could only get out of Dunkirk on two days a month at spring tides, and then only if the wind were in the east and light; but this wind would bring the blockading squadrons down on him and at the same time stop the Armada which would be working its laborious way up-Channel. And even if it did get as far as the Flemish coast, it could not back and fill indefinitely until Parma got out. The whole scheme was impracticable. But the real bar to an invasion and what decided the whole matter was not the wind, the tide or the trouble Parma was having over his army, it was the main English fleet, her ships, the finest and best equipped in the world according to a Frenchman of that day, and the fighting qualities of the officers and men. These were at Plymouth about to make contact with the Armada.

3. *'Howard at Plymouth'*

The English fleet, like the Armada, had a nobleman of high rank as Commander-in-Chief, and for the same reason: he had to be someone whom a difficult lot of subordinates would naturally obey. But whereas King Philip's choice had fallen upon an individual who had the rank but not the qualities for a leader, there was at hand in England the man ideally suited to this office. On December 21st, 1587, Charles, Lord Howard of Effingham, was appointed Commander-in-Chief—and from that moment seamen and gentlemen volunteers accepted him as their natural commander. The great thing about Howard was that he had the confidence and natural authority of a man whose position was assured —he was Lord Admiral, cousin to the Queen and her friend—so that he could give his whole mind to beating the Spaniards.

His first act was to inspect the ships at Queenborough, going over them thoroughly from truck to keel, crawling through noisome compartments down below to satisfy himself on the state of their timbers, and the fleet quickly realized that Howard was no titled figurehead. He might have the stately presence and courtesy of a man who had spent most of his life at Court, but there was little of the Navy, its strategy and problems that he had not studied since he had become Lord Admiral. He had not spent his life at sea, more important, he knew how to handle and use those who had. He composed the differences between Wynter and Hawkins, recognizing the worth of each, and he stopped in time what might have been a violent quarrel between Frobisher and Drake. If he held councils of war, it was not because he was ignorant or helpless; he was conforming to the usage of the Navy, and when he summoned his commanders for consultation, he listened to their views, made his decision and stuck to it against Queen and Council if need be. No one else in the fleet or realm could have handled the seamen and volunteers so that the fleet fought as a coherent body and not as a collection of brilliant individuals; yet he managed this without blunting the fine edge of their skill or daring. It was Howard's battle, and he won it.

Although the great gun had its influence on the result, the prime factor of victory was English skill in the difficult art of seamanship, for it was that which gave the guns their target. English seamen had learned the art in a hard school: among the fogs and blizzards of the Arctic, in the steaming heat off Darien; in the baffling calms and currents of the Guinea Coast or through the endless fury of Atlantic gales—and here they were in from the seven seas as officers of the Queen. This generation of seamen did not create the Royal Navy—England was a great sea power before the Norman Conquest—but it was the first to employ the tactics which were to govern sea warfare for the next three centuries. The tactics of the short Armada campaign were rudiments of what was to come, hazy and unformed as yet, but the pattern was there. We can see each captain working instinctively to gain the windward position as their successors were to do all through the sailing era. They made a rough attempt at the line-ahead formation because by this they could best employ their guns on the broadside; and, as a corollary, they divided the fleet into manageable squadrons half-way up the Channel, and fought in squadrons for the victory of Gravelines. Here were the first attempts at that discipline under sail which other English seamen were to bring to finished perfection.

The seamen who found themselves using these tactics were individualists who looked upon each other as equals, and would only have obeyed the orders of another when they felt like it. Drake, the greatest of them, flew his flag as second-in-command in the *Revenge*; Fenner commanded the *Nonpareil*, and, scattered round the fleet in Queen's ships or armed merchantmen, were many of the great company who had sailed with Drake round the world or in and out of the Caribbean. John Hawkins, the creator of England's fleet, flew his flag in a reconditioned galleon named, appropriately, *Victory*, while his son Richard had been promoted to the command of the Queen's ship *Swallow*. Frobisher, fearless in battle but still of an uncertain temper, commanded the *Triumph*, a monster of 1,000 tons, which had only been commissioned for the emergency, and Fenton, once of the tiny *Gabriel*, now commanded the *Mary Rose*.

The oldest and most experienced naval officer of them all, Sir William Wynter, was seeing the last of his sea service which he had started as a boy nearly forty years before. He knew more about fleetwork than any of them: he had served in every fleet which had been assembled during that time and now, as a Rear-Admiral, together with three of his sons and a nephew, he was serving in the greatest that had ever sailed for England. His squadron was based on Queenborough, and though he had been much put out at having to miss taking the waters at Bath as was his custom, he was delighted with the *Vanguard*, and was gentleman enough to write to the Council praising those ships built by Hawkins which he had once condemned. In every age the Navy has had its William Wynters, valiant, quick-tempered, pigheaded at times, but generous and fair-minded, masters of their profession.

Back from his Arctic voyages, unassuming and retiring as ever, John Davis commanded the *Black Dog*, twenty tons, to act as pilot in the Channel for the Lord Admiral. There is no mention of Davis or his vessel in dispatches, nor is there of another Arctic voyager, William Borough, who had been Drake's unfortunate second-in-command on the Cadiz expedition. He had command of the only galley in English service, the *Bonavolia*, which was employed as a guardship on the Thames with undefined duties. It was his intention if Parma approached to precede him up-river, 'shooting off great ordnance to give warning to the country and army at Tilbury', until he reached Gravesend where he proposed 'to stay and stop a gap with the galley between two blockhouses to impeach their passage higher up the river'. But as things turned out Borough was called upon to do nothing more heroic than accept this slighting command without a fuss and he put his time on the Thames to good use. All his life he tried to make navigation more scientific and therefore safer—he had written a book on the Variation of the Compass, he had worked out azimuth tables for the sun—and now, characteristically, he spent the weeks of waiting in making an accurate survey of the mouth of the Thames. William Borough was not one of England's romantic heroes, but a navy always needs his like, and as much as the heroes he was a typical product of his time. So too was an officer in a minor command at Plymouth, though it is surprising to find him in any command for he had once been presumed to have come to 'a miserable end'.

This was William Coxe of Limehouse, the mutineer who had been the cause of Captain Barker's head being sent by courier to Truxillo. After that voyage Coxe had been arrested and thrown into prison, which Hakluyt naturally thought was the end of him. But Coxe bobbed up again for Gilbert's tragic voyage when he sailed as master of the *Golden Hind* and though the discipline on that expedition was lamentable, over-awed perhaps by the God-fearing and efficient Captain Hayes, Coxe behaved himself. No more is heard of him after that until 1587 when he reappears, as Captain of a pinnace this time, employed on intelligence work on the Biscay coasts of France and Spain. He obtained detailed information of the Armada, its size and how it had been provisioned and altogether did so well that one of his reports found a place in State Papers with Drake's interpretation of the intelligence received. Coxe was now at Plymouth in command of the *Delight*, 100 tons, and he is one of the few men other than senior officers mentioned by name in accounts of the fighting.

'There is here the gallantest company of Captains, soldiers and mariners that ever was seen in England; it were a pity they should lack meat when they are so desirous to spend their lives in Her Majesty's service.' Such was the acid postscript to the first letter Howard sent to Burghley after assuming the command at Plymouth. The Lord Admiral had arrived, eager to be off at once to pursue the offensive on the coast of Spain; but store ships expected from the Thames before this had not yet arrived and the general victualling situation was serious, yet—'God send us a wind to put us out, for go we will though we starve', the Admiral decided, and sail he did: only to be driven back to Plymouth from the mouth of the Channel by one of the strong westerlies of that boisterous summer. His letter had been addressed to the Lord Treasurer, the official he considered to be ultimately responsible for the supply of provisions, but the lack of them in the west was not entirely the fault of Burghley. The Queen was the chief culprit: for inscrutable reasons of her own she refused to sign victualling orders to supply the Navy with more than a month's provisions at a time. The officers of the victualling department could therefore never build up a reserve, they could only begin to collect supplies when the victuals of the fleet were nearly finished.

If this policy was designed to keep the fleet at hand it certainly succeeded, and that may have been her intention, for the Queen hated the thought of her fleet being anywhere but in home waters. Her two contributions to naval strategy at this time show how little she understood the proper function of the Navy. The first, to 'Keep an eye on Parma' is understandable because of a hostile army just across the way; but the second, that Howard should 'ply up and down in some indifferent place between the coast of Spain and this realm to cover all approaches', is ridiculous, or as the Admiral bluntly put it, 'a thing unpossible'. Apart from the difficulties caused by the Queen's policy, there were others due to the weather, the prevailing conditions and the emergency. An endless succession of westerly winds that summer prevented or delayed the passage of store ships round from the Thames; there was no method of storing food and there was such a concentration of men and ships in the west as had not been dreamed of, camps of the Militia eating their heads off and thousands of seamen in the Sound always clamouring for more. In those days beef could only be stored on the hoof and grain in barns; the beasts had to be killed and salted, the grain milled and baked into biscuit before the ships could be victualled.

The fleet in the west all that summer was short of food and under-nourished men who had been on board for months were going down with scurvy; the longer the Spaniards delayed their coming, the worse became the condition of the English fleet. There was much sickness, there were desertions, and it was only due to Howard's masterly handling of the situation that there was not worse. Only a week before the Armada arrived Howard wrote to Burghley: 'I thank God we are not troubled with any mutinies, nor I hope shall not; for I see that men kindly handled will bear want and run through fire and water'. In all his letters to the Council and the Queen he was urgently concerned for the welfare of his seamen, but he allowed nothing to stop him—not even the Queen herself—from carrying out what he and his council of sailors thought was the correct strategy, to attack the Spaniards on their own coast.

Four times the English fleet tried to sail south, but were baffled each time by contrary winds. At the fourth attempt a southerly wind took them down across the Bay until they were nearly in sight of the Galician mountain tops—then the southerly died away and the wind turned foul. As so many of his ships were 'but meanly victualled' Howard could not afford to hang about off the Spanish coast so he returned to Plymouth. He arrived on July 12th and immediately started provisioning. He had lost so many men through sickness after this latest foray that he had to pay off four ships to find hands to bring the others up to complement, but without a pause the work of provisioning kept on by day and all through the night by the fitful glare of blazing cressets. While the men of the fleet sweated and toiled the pinnaces were out on their patrols, casting westward to the Scillies and over to Ushant—the sea was not quite as empty as it had appeared to Medina-Sidonia—and at 1 a.m. on the night the Duke had been writing to his King of the deserted sea, a Captain Fleming in the *Golden Hind* pinnace sighted the Armada off the Lizard. Captain Fleming put his helm up and raced back to Plymouth. The wind which had driven Howard back had brought the Armada out and Medina-Sidonia now had the English in the very position in which they had hoped to catch the Armada. Despite the conditions afloat, disease and a shortage of food, the English fleet was in a condition to face whatever might come, for its spirit, under Howard's inspired leadership, was high. 'There shall be neither sickness nor death which shall make us yield until this service be ended', he wrote on July 17th, 'I never saw nobler minds than we have here in our forces.' The noblest belonged to the Lord Admiral of England.

4. 'The Fleets in Contact'

Captain Fleming reached Plymouth with his news at four in the afternoon of the same day, to see the fleet still provisioning with yards rigged as derricks and working parties ashore from every ship. Many of the smaller vessels were berthed alongside in an inner harbour known as Sutton Pool, others lay in the Cattewater, while the *Ark*, the *Revenge* and the larger vessels were anchored between St. Nicholas (now Drake's) Island and the shore. The wind was blowing from seaward across the Sound, penning the ships in harbour; and during the next few hours the fate of England rested not upon valour but upon discipline and seamanship, for if the Spaniards had come sailing in with a fair wind nothing could have saved the fleet. Because it was a routine operation no one thought to write for posterity a graphic description of the fleet's exodus; we do not know, therefore, how the alarm was given, what signals were made nor exactly by what methods the ships got themselves out—but get out they did. There can have been no panic, not much confusion but there was no doubt a good deal of robust language; each captain knew that he had to get to sea and it was most probably left to him to get there as best he could. Provisioning ceased; and boats which only minutes before had been loaded with beef, beer and biscuit were now employed laying out anchors, taking cables to buoys or towing their ships. It was a blustery afternoon with cloud scudding across a leaden sky, and the Mayor and citizens of Plymouth up on the Hoe saw no fine pageantry that day, no brave show of flags and streamers, no trumpets, no orderly procession of stately vessels. They saw what must have seemed to the landsmen amongst them a scene of wild confusion—but it was not. It was a grim and purposeful business where each man knew his job as the ships moved off in any order, the crews straining desperately to get them out into the Sound. All through that Friday evening and short summer's night they warped themselves clear of the harbour and on Saturday morning they beat out of the Sound 'very hardly the wind being at South West'. By noon Howard had fifty-four ships with him out by the Eddystone and at three o'clock through haze and drizzle he sighted the Armada.

The Spaniards were some twenty miles off to windward, creeping past Fowey, and in the Spanish flagship at this moment a Council of War was debating whether or not to attack the English squadron supposedly in Plymouth. In the end it was decided to

The Armada approaching Plymouth. Note Howard leaving harbour and his course straight out to sea. The chart shows two operations; the stragglers beating to windward by night and their junction with Howard next morning

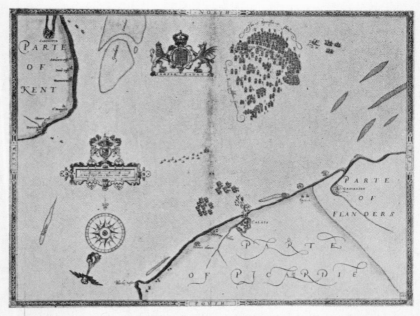

Chart of the Armada off Gravelines. It also shows Howard attacking the galleass at Calais and then sailing to join the battle

carry out the King's instructions not to attack any port until they had effected their junction with Parma. Howard and his ships were not sighted. At nightfall the Duke of Medina-Sidonia anchored his fleet with orders to expect attack at daylight. As the night dragged on the look-outs in his port wing ships were puzzled by what they took to be a small detached squadron between themselves and the shore. The sails of ghostly ships glimmered feebly in the moonlight for an instant then disappeared as they sailed on; and for hours the Spaniards watched the light of the leading vessel making long zigzags in towards the land and out again, but they did not move to investigate. These phantoms were some of the ships which had been late in getting out of Plymouth Sound beating laboriously to windward. Meanwhile, by the light of a fitful moon Howard boldly led the bulk of the English fleet straight out to sea across the bows of the Armada, leaving Plymouth uncovered. At daybreak on Sunday, July 21st, he went about on to the port-tack and there ahead and to leeward of him was the Spanish fleet, immense, hazily unsubstantial in the early morning light, moving up-Channel with ponderous grandeur. This was Howard's moment, and all that happened in the next ten days stemmed from the advantage and position he had gained by the dawn of that Sunday morning.

The mists and shadows of night dissolved under the rising sun, the sea took on its sparkle and as the English closed in so the indeterminate mass of enemy shipping slowly resolved itself into a formation of orderly columns, which from being mere lines were soon made up of individual ships. The crew of the *Ark* at the head of the English line began to note details: towering superstructures, blazoned sails and unfamiliar flags, sinister grappling hooks ready at the yardarms; decks crowded with soldiers. They were impressed and perhaps a little awed, but on the whole it was what they had expected to see. The last thing the Spaniards thought daylight could bring was an English fleet upwind approaching from seaward. At the first shock these ships seemed to have materialized from nowhere and the Duke and his officers thought they must be a fleet out of Dartmouth. Nor were the Spanish seamen comforted at the sight of vessels heeling gently in the breeze as they sailed along in rough formation of line-ahead. They were the first foreign seamen to see an English column in line of battle bearing down to the attack. Realizing that he had been outmanœuvred and that he would not be able to avoid a fight, the Duke of Medina-Sidonia hoisted the Royal Standard of Spain at the fore of the *San Martin*—the signal for general action.

While his ships were acknowledging by running up their own flags of combat—the castles of Castile on a red ground—a diminutive vessel suddenly darted ahead of the English line and made straight for the Spanish fleet all by herself. When she was about musket shot off she fired the first round of the campaign at the nearest enemy vessel, turned and rejoined. She was the Lord Admiral's pinnace the *Disdain*—her name was a lucky chance—'giving defiance to the Duke of Medina-Sidonia'. After this formality Howard led the English line across the rear of the enemy and attacked his weather division, which happened to be Recalde's Biscayan Squadron. The English line sailed past the end of the column firing broadsides in succession, then turned to fire the other broadside—pouring in such a rapid concentration of fire as had never been known at sea. It is hardly to be wondered at that the first ships ever to face this ordeal should have crowded away upon their centre as a flock of sheep flinches away from the sheep-dogs. But that stout old seaman Recalde was not to be daunted; he hauled into the wind at once and held his ground, only to be surrounded and in serious trouble. Whereupon the Duke led other galleons to his rescue, the fleet flagship at one time being hotly engaged by three English vessels. There was a short and violent engagement, with the English flitting about always out of reach and firing their murderous broadsides. One Spanish ship the *Nuestra Señora del Rosario* had her foremast sprung in collision and another ship was badly damaged by gunfire, but at last the wounded vessels were gathered in to the cover of their own close formation and with its lines still orderly and intact, the Armada held to its course up Channel.

As Howard had no intention of becoming involved in close-quarter, ship to ship actions by sailing in among the body of the enemy he hoisted the signal to break off the action. He lay with his ships a little to windward watching the enemy drift slowly to leeward past the entrance to the Sound, a sight which a much-comforted Mayor of Plymouth witnessed from that natural grandstand the Hoe. The Duke chose this moment to hold another of his councils in the great cabin of the *San Martin* and with the distant view of Plymouth through the stern windows growing fainter as they talked, his Captains were urging him to capture a port. It was madness to think of sailing through the Channel without one, and de Recalde who had reconnoitred these waters privately, insisted that it should be one as far west as possible. But which? Plymouth was astern. Dartmouth too small to take the fleet, why not Torbay; but the Duke would only consider the Isle of Wight and he would not promise even that, so strictly did he consider himself bound by the orders of his King.

Howard was up to windward collecting his scattered fleet and after ordering Drake to send off a pinnace to warn Seymour in the Downs, he sat down to give the news to Walsingham. 'I will not trouble you with any long letter', he started off, 'we are at this present otherwise occupied than in writing.' And as if to give point to his opening he devoted a bare eleven words to the action just fought: 'At nine of the clock we gave them fight which continued until one.' But the meat was in the postscript: 'Sir, for the love of God and our country, let us have with some speed some great shot of all bigness; for this service will continue long.' And having given the Council something to keep them busy, the Lord Admiral relapsed into a silence which he did not break for eight days.

There was not so very much that Howard or anyone else could say about the fight that Sunday morning because its results were mainly psychological. It had been an inconclusive action which left both sides with the vague feeling that they might have done better. The English were surprised by the solid resistance of the Spanish formation and saw little prospect of breaking it to deal with the enemy piecemeal. They had fired off an alarming amount of ammunition and had taken no prizes. The Duke of Medina-Sidonia could do nothing about the nimble enemy ships so well handled; he could not force a victory without boarding and there was little prospect of that, meanwhile his soldiers were being massacred while achieving nothing. But his objective was to join Parma, and this was a great moral handicap. The English had started on his tail to the westward of him and his course took him always away from them. This gave the Spaniards the feeling that they were retiring all the time while the English felt as if they were in chase of a retreating enemy. As the fleets moved up Channel the Armada saw a continual stream of small craft sailing out from every little port along the coast; a traffic which made it look as if Howard were being incessantly reinforced, while the Armada was all alone on an unfriendly sea.

That Sunday afternoon was one of councils: they were held in the great cabins of both fleet flagships, they debated the same issue and arrived at the same answer. The question, depending on the flagship, was where should or would the Spaniards make for next; the answer was, the Isle of Wight. Any expedition against England had to have a secure anchorage in the Channel as an advanced base: the waters sheltered by the Island were the nearest point to Parma and the last place on either side of the Channel sailing eastward which could accommodate a large fleet. The Duke of Medina-Sidonia had been persuaded of this, the English knew it already; only King Philip failed to appreciate the need. The two Commanders-in-Chief being at one about the Isle of Wight, the Armada shaped a course a little north of east and proceeded at its average speed of about two-and-a-half knots. It was only by spreading just enough sail to give him steerage way that the Duke was able to maintain the military precision of his formation with ships keeping their 'dressing' and squadrons their distances like foot soldiers on parade. The Armada led off in fine style but as the wind freshened off the Start, the Duke was pained to observe the flagship of the Andalusian squadron suddenly break ranks and drop out of position, making signals of distress. This was the *Nuestra Señora del Rosario*, flagship of Don Pedro de Valdés, and her trouble was the foremast damaged that morning which had now broken off short and fallen foul of her mainmast. In rising wind and bad light the Duke with two other vessels to help failed to take Don Pedro in tow. He could not risk detaching a squadron or the confusion of halting the Armada; it would be cheapest in the end to lose her. He detailed a galleon, a galleass and a pinnace to stand by the derelict while the Armada sailed on.

Knowing that he could overtake the enemy when he felt like it, Howard decided not to give chase until he had collected and re-formed his fleet. The cruising order for the night was given out with Drake in the *Revenge* as guide of the fleet. At midnight Howard gave the signal to make sail, the *Revenge* lit her great poop lantern and the English fleet set off in chase. One ship was missing, the *Margaret and John*, 200 tons, of the Levant Company, and her captain was giving a demonstration of how a single ship on her own instinctively did the right thing. At about five o'clock that afternoon she had sighted a little stationary group of enemy ships and bore down to investigate. 'At the sudden approach of our ship', said Captain Fisher in his report, 'a great galleon, a galleass and a pinnace all forsook Don Pedro, leaving him to the mercy of the sea.' They most probably took the armed merchant-man for a scout ahead of the main fleet. The *Margaret and John* had a crew of ninety men—the Spaniard mounted forty-six guns and had a company of 300 soldiers and 100 sailors. The Londoner lay off to windward until dark when she crept in to have a closer look at this towering great ship. As the Spaniard showed no sign of life the *Margaret and John* fired a mixed volley of small arms and arrows into her stern galleries to see what would happen. At this the Spaniard woke up and let fly with two heavy guns, the *Margaret* gave her a broadside, retired to a safe distance and continued her watch. In the middle of the night, seeing vessels of her own fleet passing her Captain Fisher decided to rejoin the flag and report his derelict.

While the *Margaret and John* had been watching Don Pedro, the English fleet had been following the *Revenge*, when suddenly her light went out. At this some captains hove to, others shortened sail, but the *Ark* with the *Bear* and *Mary Rose* in company held on after the enemy and were soon far ahead. No one knows the true cause of Drake's singular behaviour—his own explanation is unconvincing—but its consequences against a more skilful enemy might have been serious. At dawn the Lord Admiral in the *Ark* found himself with Berry Head abeam, the *Revenge* nowhere in sight and only the masts showing of his fleet hull down astern. But less than a mile away and to leeward was the whole Armada. Soon a small merchantman under full sail came racing up from astern towards the flagship. It was the *Margaret and John* with her account of the enemy derelict; but as Captain Fisher was making his report to the Admiral a pinnace came alongside the *Ark* with the news that Drake in the *Revenge* had taken possession of Don Pedro's flagship.

Howard may have been puzzled but he took all this very calmly and does not even mention the incident of Drake's defection in his 'Relation of Proceedings'. He had his eye on something more important just then, the movements of the enemy. He was relieved to see that the Spanish fleet was continuing eastwards and not altering in towards Torbay. The Duke of Medina-Sidonia had missed another chance of taking a suitable anchorage, and as the Armada streamed away towards Portland Bill Lord Howard shortened sail to allow the remainder to rejoin.

While Drake, some miles astern, was accepting the surrender of Don Pedro de Valdés in the grand manner, the Lord Admiral was on ahead in close touch with the enemy, where he too picked up a prize, and with no formality. She was the *San Salvador*, an 800-ton Biscayan ship which had been abandoned after an explosion on her upper deck, and she did not look to be much of a prize. But when Captain Fleming towed her with his pinnace into Portland next day it was found that her contents below the main deck had not been damaged. As Captain Fleming groped round her hold he was not interested in the pipes of wine, the casks of meat gone bad, or even the solitary German woman he found there—he was after cash. But this had all been removed, and instead he came upon some booty of more value just then than the riches of the Indies: one thousand iron shot of assorted sizes and two hundred barrels of high-grade powder. Without waiting for the shore officials to make a proper inventory he loaded the ammunition into a coasting vessel and sent her out after the Admiral. She found him at Calais, by which time the English had been reduced to firing ploughchains for want of round shot.

IN THE CHANNEL

After dropping the *San Salvador* and seeing that he need fear no attack from a disorganized enemy fleet that forenoon, the Duke of Medina-Sidonia took the opportunity of reorganizing his own fleet so as to allow Recalde's ship to make good defects. He combined and reinforced the two wings of the rear half of the Armada to form one unit of forty-three fighting galleons under Don Alonso de Leyva; a manœuvre which took a little time, for the Duke used a clumsy though effective method of getting his ships into position, and once in, of keeping them there. The sailors had nothing to do with it, the whole affair being a military operation. A pinnace full of officers of the Provost's Corps went round placing each ship in her exact position with instructions to hang the senior military officer of any ship which got out of station. From the Lizard to Calais, a distance of about three hundred miles, the Armada progressed up Channel in perfect order; it fought three battles on the way but its formation was never broken. Meanwhile the Duke himself in the *San Martin* sailed at the head of the Armada leading it across Lyme Bay, the coastline hazily indistinct on his port hand. The mass of Portland Bill, long visible, loomed ahead, a narrow spit seemed to run out joining it to the land, they were beyond the white chalk face of the Bill, and another bay opened up curving round to the eastward with low, green hills running down to the sea.

All day the English had been closing on the *Ark* with her Royal Standard at the main, and around her now, but spread out in no proper order, was her brood of nimble, deadly galleons. When the sun went down the wind died abruptly to a flat calm, leaving the fleets only just out of range motionless upon a darkening sea. They spent the night in full view of one another under the moon, drifting listlessly with the tide now to the westward of the Bill then back again but never far from its shadowy mass. Presently it seemed to be growing larger, but it was only the dawn bringing out its detail in the slow brightening to full daylight. And with the sun came the light airs of a summer's morning, but these were from the north-east and the first move the Duke observed that morning was the English slanting in towards the land to win back the weather gauge. At once the great Standard was hoisted

267

in the Spanish flagship as he stood away on the same tack, and the battle of Portland was joined.

'This fight was very nobly continued from morning until evening,' wrote Howard in his *Relation*, and he has very little more to say about it except that it was often at close quarters. The fact is, the English fleet being in no formation at the start, fought haphazard in groups where and as the necessity arose, while the Spaniards preserved their formation. Frobisher was cut off and in trouble, but after a brilliant defence against the galleasses was rescued by Howard. During another stage of the battle the Duke of Medina-Sidonia showed what he was made of. His flagship the *San Martin* found herself detached with no ship in close company and the *Ark* and six galleons bearing down on her. Instead of running the Duke came up into the wind and all alone withstood the attack, suffering terrible punishment as the English broadsides poured in. The great Standard, consecrated in Lisbon, was cut in two, his rigging was soon in tatters and his ship was so badly holed that she was making water fast, but other Spanish galleons gathered round their Admiral and the danger was over. It was a day of incidents, one causing another as Spaniard and Englishman—invisible from the land under their pall of billowing smoke—fought with all the tenacity and courage of which those two nations are capable. There was no real pattern to the fighting which moved slowly eastward as the wind had veered through south to south-west; and by about five in the afternoon when both sides had had enough, the action was called off. The Duke fired a signal gun, and still in its formation, the Armada continued majestically up Channel. With the shift of wind the English were now back in their habitual position to windward, as it were herding this monstrous enemy fleet along past their own shores.

The Battle of Portland may have been 'managed with confusion enough'—as a contemporary neatly put it, but it had important results. Next day Howard and his Admirals sat in Council on board the *Ark*: so far, try as they might, the fleet had not been able to inflict any real harm on the Armada. It had suffered damage and casualties, but the English attacks had always broken on its rock-like defence, and the basis of that defence was the superb

way it maintained formation. Here it was nearing the Isle of
Wight, and nothing done to stop it, with Parma not so far ahead.
And as they debated, the key was given them by the enemy.

Organization could only be met by better organization, and
there and then they drew up the dispositions employed in the
next two engagements. They realized that they would never get
anywhere so long as ships were free to roam about during an
engagement, joining in where they thought fit and attaching
themselves first to this commander then to that, so that groups
of ships were of different sizes and uncoordinated. The fleet was
formed into four squadrons, each composed of a proportion of
Queen's ships and armed merchantmen. Howard commanded the
first squadron and after him the Admirals of the others chose
themselves: Drake, Hawkins, and after his conduct at Portland,
Frobisher—all, except the Lord Admiral, professional seamen.

Because of the qualities of his ships and their crews, Howard
could always dictate his own time for battle, and on July 25th he
took a breather in order to replenish with food and ammunition.
The fleet had never been adequately victualled with two months'
provisions on board and as a result the men had been on short
rations since the spring; and now England's fleet, though in touch
with the enemy, had to rely on driblets picked up along the way to
keep going. It was the same with ammunition; the original outfit
was too small because no one had dreamed that ships would fire
away so much under the new conditions of fighting, so Howard
had to collect what powder and shot he could on his passage up
Channel. He had sent the pinnaces on ahead to requisition from
the local authorities along the coast, and as these were asked for
more than they could supply from the resources of their ports,
they went to neighbouring inland towns and scoured the countryside. They sent out replacements for the sick, they collected beef,
bread, beer and vegetables, took over stocks of powder ear-
marked for the militia, and where they had no round shot called
in all ploughchains from the Dorset farms and sent them out
instead. These petty officials, perhaps because they could see the
Armada, acted with speed and energy with no regard for regulations.

After a busy day taking in stores, when a south-westerly breeze got up in the late afternoon, the big ships cast off their victuallers and made sail after the enemy. Howard was convinced that the Duke meant to take the Isle of Wight: and it was a fact that Medina-Sidonia had come as far as he intended to go until he had established communication with Parma. The Spaniards wanted to stay where they were, the English intended at all costs to keep them going—the next would be a crucial engagement and both sides knew it. Just before dawn next morning the fleets were becalmed a few miles south of the Isle of Wight off Ventnor between St. Catherine's Point and Dunnose.

It was the Feast of St. Dominic, and as the Duke who was of the same family can only have expected, its dawning found him with the advantage. For there was not a breath of wind, conditions which gave his galleasses their chance, while the English ships could not move. But that calm was only the temporary calm of a summer's morn and with the sun the breeze returned. To the Duke's surprise in the grey light of early morning he saw the English moving in to attack two of his ships which were separated from the rest, the *Santa Ana* and the *San Luis*. Howard in the *Ark*, his kinsman Lord Thomas Howard in the *Golden Lion* and Hawkins in the *Victory* in tow of their own boats moved slowly over the still waters as the tow-ropes slackened then tautened with a jerk. To the rest of the two fleets it looked a hopeless task, but once started the galleons were kept on the move and the oars of the boats dipped and rose until arquebus fire from the two Spaniards made them cast off. The two enemy ships were severely handled until the galleasses suddenly came to life and foamed down to the rescue, and after a sharp fight the two Spanish galleons were rescued.

Meanwhile Frobisher in the *Triumph* was in much the same predicament. He found himself becalmed in the middle of a number of the enemy and the Spaniards thought they had him, but eleven pulling boats of his own squadron took him in tow and when a lucky puff of wind came along he moved off, leaving the Spanish ships as if they were at anchor. Then the wind came from the south-west and the character of the engagement altered.

The English could now use their skill and mobility. If the Duke of Medina-Sidonia lacked many of the qualities of his kinsman the Saint, physical courage was not one of them, for at a critical juncture after the wind had arisen, he prevented what might have been a disaster by inviting the concentrated attack of an enemy squadron on his flagship the *San Martin* to allow a section of his fleet to rally. This was at a stage in the action when Drake and Hawkins were doing their best to shepherd the Armada on to the Owers, a dangerous bank which lay to the north-east. However, the Duke recognized the danger in time, made the signal for breaking-off action, assumed his position as guide of the fleet, and weathering the danger under his lee made off to the eastward with his Armada still in good order. The English at once took up their normal position to windward.

As the fleets were breasting the west-running stream they made slow progress, and it was not until three o'clock in the afternoon that they had disappeared from view into the summer haze over the Channel. The Duke had not obtained his anchorage, but the Armada, still a coherent fighting force, was sailing in perfect order towards its junction with Parma. The English had not yet succeeded in breaking the formidable enemy formation, but they had inflicted more damage than they had received and above all the island was now to leeward and out of danger. The engagement was a draw which each side felt that it had won, yet the sequel was disastrous for Spain.

Whenever the Duke looked over his shoulder there were the ships of England, menacing and watchful—'infernal devils' he was calling them by now—and he had despaired of ever being able to compete with those superbly-handled galleons. At this stage the Duke had lost confidence in himself and in his fleet, and a commander's mood quickly permeates his command, be it army or fleet. His passage so far up Channel had been one long mental agony, but now he thought he could distinguish that faint glimmer of light at the end of the tunnel—the army of Parma which was not far off. Parma, he felt, could help him in his trouble and relieve him of some of his responsibility. Now at last he deliberately disobeyed the orders of his King: instead of keeping to the

English side he crossed over the Channel towards Calais. At the same time he sent a pinnace off to Parma with an impossible lot of demands, for flyboats, for oared gunboats, for ammunition, but what he really craved was moral support. While this pathetic appeal was on its way to Dunkirk, Walsingham got a letter from Seymour in the *Rainbow* at Dover where he had just received the news of the engagement off Plymouth. 'I am most glad of this most happy beginning of victory obtained of Her Majesty's enemies' was his immediate reaction, though he cannot have had much of a notion how that victory could be completed, 'but most sorry that I am so tied I cannot be an actor in the play'. He was not to be disappointed for long: as he had no idea how far the Armada had reached by now, he and Wynter sailed along to Dungeness, only to receive peremptory orders there from the Queen to return and lie off Dunkirk. They obeyed unwillingly and made back for the Downs to revictual, but they had only just anchored when a pinnace came racing up before the wind. She was from Howard with orders that Seymour should sail at once and join the main fleet. With no hesitation they ignored the Queen, made the signal to weigh and with only three days' victuals on board beat to the southward to join the Lord Admiral.

While Seymour and Wynter were on their way back to the Downs—Wynter only slightly mollified by the splendid buck that Walsingham had waiting for him at Dover—the main fleets were lying becalmed in mid Channel. No one was gloomy in the *Ark* that forenoon, least of all the Commander-in-Chief. He had lost no ships and few men; twice the enemy had been prevented from gaining a foothold on the English coast; his orders were on their way to Seymour and he knew that he would shortly be joined by some of the finest ships in the Navy. No, all that bothered Lord Howard were the companies of useless musketeers which the Queen had suddenly sent down to the fleet: he could not think what on earth to do with the fellows, he had no room for extra soldiers and certainly he could not feed them. But instead of worrying he decided to provide a little diversion for the fleet and summoned a number of senior officers to the flagship.

One after the other Lord Thomas Howard of the *Lion*, Lord

Sheffield of the *Bear*, Captain Beeston of the *Dreadnought*, Martin Frobisher from the *Triumph* and John Hawkins of the *Victory* boarded the *Ark*, while the rest of the fleet looked on, mightily interested to know what it was all about. As the officers stepped on to the poop, there was the Lord Admiral, tall and imposing, with his officers and gentlemen volunteers drawn up behind him. Presently the Lord Admiral drew his sword and knighted the officers one by one: Howard and Sheffield, both gentlemen volunteers who had been up with the *Ark* all the way; George Beeston, a regular naval officer who had commanded the Channel guard over twenty-five years before; Frobisher, the tough adventurer who had lately distinguished himself; and Hawkins, member of the Navy Board who had produced the ships which lay all around —none better in the world as Howard had often told the Council. Knighthood was a decoration, not a step in rank, which could be conferred by a commander-in-chief in the field, 'for such a one is the true judge under the prince of the behaviour of honourable men'. Howard was also a shrewd judge of the common sailor, for each man in those five ships would feel as if he himself had been singled out for reward; while the fleet as a whole would appreciate the gesture of holding an investiture in full view of the enemy.

When the wind came at five o'clock that afternoon the English crews had seldom moved more smartly to make sail after the Armada. There was a feel of autumn in the air, from the look of the sky it seemed as if the weather were breaking up, and for the first time since the enemy had arrived in the Channel it came on to blow hard. Through an uncomfortable night of squalls and a bumpy sea the chase went on and when dawn broke yellow and threatening the Spaniards saw the English ships still there, swinging to and fro only a mile away.

In the afternoon when Medina-Sidonia sighted Calais he had quickly to decide what to do next, and as he came abreast of the town he made a decision which proved to be fatal. He anchored. By a very smart evolution, for he cannot have been expecting it, Howard did the same, bringing up short at his usual distance to windward. The Duke sent off one of his secretaries to Parma, and the Governor of Calais paid a call to offer the facilities of the port and also a warning that the Duke had chosen a dangerous anchorage. It was too late to do anything about that even if he had been able to, and now came something else to add to the Duke's anxieties: another enemy fleet slanting across the Channel to join with Howard. With their habitual ignorance of English dispositions the Spaniards took the ships to be a squadron under Hawkins. It was Seymour and Wynter with their force from the Downs. The Queen's ships were leading: first the three flagships, all modern vessels: the *Rainbow*, *Vanguard* and *Antelope*, then five lesser ships and four attendant pinnaces. Astern of them came the vessels from the Cinque ports and east coast towns, bringing the whole force up to some forty sail. The moral effect on the enemy of its arrival at this juncture was considerably heightened by Wynter. Apparently feeling skittish at his first sight of the Armada, 'very round and near together not far from the shore" the old Admiral took the *Vanguard* in towards it and gave the rear Spanish ships a broadside as he sailed by to anchor with the remainder of the force. Soon after they had anchored, Howard sent his pinnace over to the *Vanguard* for Wynter and during the evening in the great cabin of the *Ark*, the Lord Admiral discussed the situation with the most experienced officer in the Navy. Wynter at once suggested the use of fireships against the Armada, and Howard's manners were too polished for him to inform the old seaman that a good many other people had already had the same idea. Instead he said that he would call a Council about it next day.

There was a great deal of coming and going in both fleets all through that Sunday, starting at dawn when a messenger from Parma arrived on board the *San Martin*. This officer had been sent on ahead when the Armada was nearing Plymouth and the news he had brought to Medina-Sidonia was too bad to be true. The Commander-in-Chief of the invasion force was not even at Dunkirk, he was at Bruges, his troops were not ready and could not be embarked for at least a week, but he was leaving at once for the coast. It was quite impossible to send ammunition vessels or flyboats out of Dunkirk: he could not help the Duke in any way at sea. Medina-Sidonia had been making for a light which was

The fireships at Calais

out when he reached it, and while he was digesting this, the flag of Council went up in the *Ark*. It was decided to make an attempt with fireships that very night as wind and tide would be favourable, and all ships in the Armada had let go a second anchor. There was no time, therefore, to fetch suitable craft across from Dover; orders were given for eight of the 'worst and basest' vessels with the English fleet to be fitted out as fireships at once, leaving their stores and guns in them if necessary. Medina-Sidonia could find little for his fleet to do to remove the general gloom or the uncomfortable feeling of impending danger, in what form they knew not. During the forenoon he sent his victualling officers ashore with plenty of money to buy fresh vegetables, but in the words of one of his own officers 'in a great watching we continued on Sunday all day long'.

At about four in the afternoon, a small episode did nothing to hearten the Spaniards when suddenly they saw a small pinnace leave the English fleet. She raced down between their lines making straight for the fleet flagship the *San Martin*. She fired four shots into the astonished flagship, then went about and returned to her own fleet with only one shot through her topsail. The Spaniards could not think what all this was about, but they could not help admiring the seamanship. 'It was much noted', said one of them, 'for its daring impertinence, and more than ever we saw how by the use of very good and very light ships, it was possible for them to come and go any way they pleased, the which we could not do.' Most probably she had taken that run down, not to impress the Spaniards, but to see how the tide was setting and to find out the best point from which to release the fireships.

So that dismal Sunday wore on into a dark and moonless night, with the nerves of the Spaniards getting more and more on edge, but nothing happened. At midnight the tide turned, and now wind and tide were both in the same direction and the cables of the Spanish galleons were bar taut as the tide went sluicing by, but still all was quiet. Then at two in the morning, when the eyes of the Spanish look-outs were smarting from peering into the wind, they suddenly saw two suspicious-looking fires over in the English lines, fires which grew rapidly larger: then six others and in a moment eight fireships with their sails set were racing down on them, 'spurting fire and their ordnance shooting which was a horror to see in the night'. It was the horror which finished the Spaniards; fireships are frightening, but determined men can generally divert them to go clear. But the picture uppermost in Spanish minds that night was the holocaust of Parma's soldiers at Antwerp in 1585 when the Dutch sent floating mines down the Scheldt to blow up a bridge. The Duke gave the order to slip their cables and the Armada then panicked. The English could see little, but clearly there was wild confusion as ships lying ahead to wind tried to make sail and get clear in the dark. When the dawn came the anchorage was empty except for a galleass threshing about in the shallows like a wounded whale. The Armada with its formation broken at last was lying scattered to the northeast a few miles away off Gravelines.

By an extraordinary chance Medina-Sidonia had brought his fleet to the exact position for a junction with Parma's flotilla.

CHAPTER XVI

Gravelines and After

*

The one man on the Spanish side who did not lose his head that night was the Commander-in-Chief: the orders he gave were correct but they were not carried out. He had placed one of the best officers from his flagship in charge of the patrol boats which had been warned what to expect, but when these failed to tow the fireships clear because they had not the nerve to go near them, the Duke was forced to take the fleet clear instead. He had given the order to slip and buoy cables, intending to anchor again when the scare was over; and when the fireships had gone past and were burning themselves out in the distance, the *San Martin* with a couple of other galleons had let go a sheet anchor about two miles from Calais. The remainder of his fleet had been unable to obey the signal to anchor because their spare anchors were stowed away far below and they had drifted off in a body to the north-eastward. They were now trying to haul to the wind somewhere off Gravelines, therefore the Duke weighed at daylight to run down to leeward and reform his fleet. But not on that day or ever again was the great Armada to assume its orderly military formation. All the Duke was able to do before the enemy were upon him was to collect his best galleons round him, and he was trying to sort these out when Howard gave the signal to weigh and make sail after the enemy.

The disabled galleass still floundering about the anchorage without a rudder was the *San Lorenzo*, flagship of Don Hugo de Monçada, and in Spanish eyes the finest ship afloat. Howard delayed to finish off this vessel while his other squadrons were racing for the main Spanish fleet. Howard sent the pinnaces and ships' boats of his squadron at the galleass which ran aground, but the English small craft were kept at bay until de Monçada was killed by a musket shot when the resistance collapsed. The slaves and crew promptly jumped into the sea and the English swarmed on board. The first man over her side was William Coxe of the pinnace *Delight*, and with someone like him in the lead the *San Lorenzo* was gutted in short time; and so thoroughly that nothing of any value was left for the hopeful citizens of Calais who had been waiting in a little crowd on the beach for the battle to finish before they too went on board. The galleass quickly settled into the Calais mud and became a total wreck.

The other English squadrons were already in action, and the decisive engagement of this campaign, indeed of the whole war, had begun. The Battle of Gravelines opened at nine in the morning of July 29th, 1588, and continued with hardly a lull until six in the evening: it was fought under a grey sky beyond the shoals along the coast of Flanders and in sight of Parma who had just arrived at Dunkirk. He can have known little of what was going on in the thick cloud of smoke which hid it, how superbly the Spanish soldiers and sailors were fighting and dying; but from the way a ship would occasionally emerge, pause for a little, then loose her sheets and go tearing in again, and that the ship was always English, he must have gathered that his chances of invasion were fast disappearing in that struggle off shore. The battle was fought out between the Queen's ships and the best galleons of Spain; but it had no pattern. No diagrams and track charts record each subtle move for posterity to argue over. There was nothing subtle about it—it was a slogging match. The Armada was out of formation: the English saw their chance and went bald-headed for the enemy—no long-range shooting this time. They would finish things at close quarters. Drake in the *Revenge* with Fenner in the *Nonpareil* were the first to attack, closely followed by Hawkins in the *Victory* with Fenton in the *Mary Rose*. They were soon in the thick of it where round shot were flying about like musket balls. The *Revenge* was frequently holed above the waterline. These two squadrons were to windward, shepherding the Armada towards shoal water, and a contemporary mentions old George Beeston in the *Dreadnought* as doing as well as anyone at the start of the engagement. As the *Vanguard* came on sailing free, her gunners with their slow-match burning, 'The enemy were in a proportion of a half-moon, their Admiral and Vice-Admiral in the midst and on each side their galleasses, armados of Portugal and other good ships. My fortune was to make choice to charge their starboard wing without shooting off any ordnance until we came within six score paces of them and some of our ships did follow me.' Then Admiral Wynter opened fire and for the rest of the action he was within hailing distance of the enemy. Howard joined the battle in the early afternoon and at once the thrusting William Coxe who was up with the leaders took his *Delight* into the fighting where a pinnace had no business to be and he was killed.

The Queen's ships were moving targets; the Spanish galleons, each fighting on her own, drifted slowly to leeward. Time after time the English vessels came in to fire a broadside; circled to fire the other, hauled to the wind to reload in seven minutes then sailed in again to repeat the dose.

'I saw myself in that day', said the Chaplain of one Spanish vessel, 'in such sore straits that it was a miracle of God we escaped; for twice the ships were scattered and could not help one another, the enemy's galleons came together and charged us in such numbers that they gave us no time to draw breath.' The decks of the galleons were a reeking shambles but all through that inferno the priests and friars went about absolving the dying until they too were dead, the scuppers literally ran blood, while down below carpenters were feverishing plugging shot holes to keep their vessels afloat—but no Spanish ship struck her colours or even contemplated surrender. The *San Mateo*, a Portuguese fighting galleon carrying the Tercio of Sicily, the flower of the Spanish Army, cut off by an English squadron, 'was a thing of pity to see, riddled with shot like a sieve; all her sails and rigging were torn and destroyed; of her sailors many perished and of her soldiers few were left in the galleon.' But with that few Don Diego Pimentel fought proudly on; when an English vessel called upon him to surrender the Spaniards left alive shouted insults at the English and dared them to try boarding.

279

GRAVELINES AND AFTER

But close fighting was not in Howard's plan, his ships continued to profit by their mobility, and the Spanish galleons never had a chance to use those menacing grappling irons. The battering went on with such fury that Spanish veterans said afterwards that compared to Gravelines Lepanto was a picnic. All day the English kept to windward, shepherding the enemy towards the shoal water of the Zeeland Banks, and in the early evening when the Armada had been split up into isolated groups of damaged vessels the Queen's ships were poised for the kill. At this moment the English saw a squall racing towards them across the water; they left the guns, all hands were piped to shorten sail, they came up into the wind and hung there in a deluge of rain, while the squall swept over them. When it cleared after a quarter of an hour, a large Biscayan had foundered, but the remainder of the Armada in running before it had amazingly regained some sort of formation. The squall marked the end of the fighting that day, for the good reason that the English fleet had fired away all its ammunition. Not only was there no powder at sea, but none was left in the magazines ashore. By six in the evening of July 29th England had no gunpowder, and the Armada, such as it was by now, was still in being. That evening Howard chose to break his long silence with a letter to Walsingham. It was a modest letter not at all in the exultant vein of a Commander-in-Chief who had won a decisive victory. 'All day until this evening late we have chased them in fight and distressed them much; but their fleet consists of mighty ships and great strength; yet we doubt not by God's good grace to oppress them.' Then, lest there should be any doubt who had been doing the fighting, he adds, 'There is not one Flushinger or Hollander at the seas.' Howard could measure victory only in prizes taken or ships sunk, and it is doubtful if he ever did realize all that had been achieved at Gravelines. Nor, for that matter, did any of his Admirals except the experienced old naval officer, William Wynter.

When the squall had passed the Lord Admiral reformed his fleet to take station for the night on the weather quarter of the Armada. The wind freshened, the seas grew ominously short and steep telling of shallows ahead. According to Father Geronimo they recognized these signs well enough in the Spanish fleet, where, he says, 'hardly a man slept that night; we went along wondering when we should strike one of those banks'. The *San Mateo*, the *San Felipe*, and another galleon did strike them during the night. They were captured by the Dutch, but later sank under tow at the mouth of the Scheldt. Don Diego Pimentel survived and was taken prisoner. Whenever the Spaniards, hoping for a break in the weather, looked back to windward, there, as it had been now these ten days past, was the English fleet. They saw its lights and preferring what lay ahead drove on to destruction. All, that is, except the Commander-in-Chief. In the grey light of early dawn, the *San Martin* with a couple of other galleons in company hauled to the wind while the remainder of the Armada drove down to leeward, and all alone faced the English fleet. The Duke of Medina-Sidonia and his officers confessed and received Holy Communion, and were now ready to meet their fate like Christian soldiers.

Of all the Armada only Don Miguel de Oquendo, the hero of Terceira, and Don Alonso de Leyva, the high-born cavalier, had been able to stay in company with the *San Martin*. Like their Commander-in-Chief they could hope for no more than death in battle, but fate did not even grant them that. For as the Spaniards stood peering into the wind at the enemy they saw that the English galleons were holding off, and it was not long before they realized why. Their own agitated pilots were gesticulating at the shore and at the leadsmen in the chains who were chanting 'eight fathom'. The Queen's ships drew more water than Spanish galleons, and all they could do now was to watch the enemy driving on to be shattered on a lee shore. After Gravelines, the enemy ships, full of holes and with masts and yards badly hurt, were in no condition even to try beating off a lee shore. With daylight when they could see around them, the situation was even more terrifying. 'It was the most fearful day in the world', wrote a Spanish captain, 'for all the people were now in despair of a happy issue and stood waiting for death.' The sing-song reports from the chains were like the tolling of a funeral bell, 'seven

fathom . . . six fathom . . . five fathom.' The sea was dis-
coloured, the foam on the breaking waves a brownish scum. They
must be skating over the shallows now, ahead were the sands and
death. But, 'being in this peril with no hope of remedy', wrote the
Duke afterwards, 'God was pleased to change the wind to WSW'.
This apparent miracle has a prosaic explanation. As the centre of
a disturbance passed over that area the wind backed a couple of
points. At the last moment, straining and labouring, the Armada
was just able to claw off the lee shore into deeper water.

Their miraculous escape revived the spirits of the Spaniards
for the time it took them to lumber slowly round on to a safe
course, but it was a beaten and demoralized fleet which now stood
away to the northward. The Duke was on his way home, Parma
and the invasion forgotten. Although his ships were not battle-
worthy a Spanish Council of War had considered trying to fight
their way down Channel and the factor which decided them
against it was not the condition of the ships but the attitude of
the men. They had had enough; their officers could no longer
answer for them. 'Once let us get home', it was being said openly
on the mess decks, 'and we shall not again meddle with the
English.' Far from the wind 'delivering' England from invasion,
it was enabling a beaten fleet to run from victors who could not
finish off the job because they had no more ammunition. The only
way the Duke could reach home now was northabout round the
Orkneys and his pilots accordingly shaped a course to take them
up the centre of the North Sea. The relative position of the two
fleets was still what it had been all the way from the Eddystone,
the English to windward and in chase, but now the Armada really
was on the run.

Howard was shadowing with the main English fleet, having
detached Seymour to victual then resume his station off Dunkirk;
orders to which Seymour had objected strongly, but he obeyed
Howard as he would certainly not have obeyed any seaman. As it
happened his blockade was no longer necessary for Parma had
struck camp and marched away leaving his invasion craft to rot at
their moorings. While he and his soldiers marched south, the
Spanish galleons wallowed and laboured northward as wind and

sea increased. For three sleepless days and nights the English followed. Then early on Friday, August 2nd, the wind started to blow from the north-west, a direction which prevented the Duke from making the coast of Scotland and carried him instead out towards the Shetlands. Howard's men were almost starving by now, many were sick; at noon, therefore, he put his helm up and turned to the southward leaving the Armada to drive on into the northern mists. And so, says Francis Bacon, 'This great preparation passed away like a dream. The Invincible Navy neither took any one barque of ours, nor yet once offered to land, but after they had been well beaten and chased made a perambulation about the Northern seas, ennobling many coasts with wrecks of mighty ships.'

Six days later the Armada was sighted by an English fishing boat in the Fair Island Channel sailing along with a south-easterly wind between North Ronaldshay and Fair Island. So far the Armada was having a run of luck with the weather: snatched from the Walcheren Sands, a soldier's wind had taken it up the North Sea to find a breeze which would carry it away from the Orkneys, the North of Scotland and the Outer Hebrides. Most rare in that part of the world, this south-easterly wind held steady for days until the Armada was well clear in 60° N. 'But', wrote one in that fleet, 'our route outside Scotland is very long. Pray God we come safe home. I am very hungry and thirsty; for no one has more than half a pint of wine or a whole one of water each day, and the water smells worse than musk. We have 400 leagues still to go.' They were out by the Rockall Bank with no warm clothing; they had scurvy and dysentery and hundreds of wounded with their wounds uncured. Their food was going bad even in the Channel, yet after Fair Island they had thrown all their horses and mules overboard to save water; the new water casks embarked at Corunna had been stowed on deck and shot to pieces at Gravelines. The wonder is that any Spaniards at all managed to reach Spain alive. The Armada had kept fairly well together until now—one ship, the flagship of the transports had been wrecked on Fair Island, where her captain and company spent a miserable winter before being repatriated in the following year—but otherwise the fleet had had a good run. After reaching 60° N the Duke gave the order for ships to proceed independently back to Spain; two days later they were hit by a westerly gale and after that there are no details from any ship of the voyage itself.

While the Armada was approaching Rockall Howard was writing to the Queen from Dover, 'With great grief I must write unto you in what state I find your fleet in here. The infection has grown very great and in many ships, and now very dangerous; and those that come in are soonest infected; they sicken one day and die the next.' An epidemic of typhus was ravaging the English fleet and men whose resistance was low through scurvy and short rations were dying like flies. The contagion had reached the fleet from the shore at Plymouth, but it did not break out with violence until soon after Howard left the Armada to turn south. Only 600 men had been lost in the fighting, now as many thousands died of disease in a matter of days. The sick were sent ashore but nothing was ready for them, no lodging, no medical aid, no proper food—they died in the streets and in the gutters, like dogs. 'It would grieve any man's heart', wrote Howard, 'to see them that have served so valiantly to die so miserably.' Howard and his Admirals dipped deep into their own pockets without being able to do much to relieve the general distress—only the Crown could do that. But the Crown did not: the danger had passed and England forgot the men who had saved her. Most of the fleet was paid off, which flooded the ports and adjacent countryside with the sick and hungry. There were no pensions, widows starved and men who had fought off the Armada were now presented with licences permitting them to beg for a living. England was a poor country and the prolonged emergency had almost emptied the Exchequer.

Neither fleet at this moment was in very good shape. The English fleet, though temporarily out of action, was in its Home ports; but more seamen could be found at a pinch to man ships which were unharmed and seaworthy. The Armada was far from home on the unfriendly sea where no help could reach and salvation depended upon its own efforts. The Duke's pilots wisely kept the *San Martin* far out to the westward, dipping her main-

yard under in the tremendous swell. Every day she buried over
the side a few more of her company; but each day also she was a
few more precious miles to the southward. She was one of the
lucky few: many a vessel which followed her example by keeping
out was never heard of again. The roll would become heavier
and heavier with a sickening lurch at the end. Each time she
would take longer to recover until at last she stayed there, while
cannon, crew, stores and everything movable all mixed together
slid with a terrifying roar to leeward. Then silence; very slowly
she rolled over until masts and yards and high poop had disappeared. A few heads would bob about in the water for a short
time. Then the seabirds would soar up and wheel away on the
look-out for another ship. No one has ever learned what happened
to thirty-five of the ships which sailed from Corunna. They just
disappeared—a quarter of the Armada.

Apart from those vessels which foundered out in the lonely
deeps of the Atlantic—a large number turned in towards Ireland,
where their doom was almost as certain. Some could not help it,
they were blown there because they were not in a state to hold
on to the southward; others were so desperate for water that they
went in to find it, whatever the risk. The coast of Ireland was a
lee shore full of rocks and hidden dangers, the pilots had no charts
or any knowledge of those waters, and most of the ships which
did reach the coast drove ashore because they could not anchor.
Altogether seventeen ships were wrecked and over five thousand
Spaniards lost their lives on the coast of Ireland. The loss occurred up in the north of the man whose death, so it is said, the
King felt more keenly than any other in his Armada—Don Alonso
de Leyva, the flower of Spanish chivalry. His *Rata Encoronada*,
waterlogged and helpless, was blown into Killybegs harbour.
De Leyva and most of his company got ashore where they were
hospitably received by the O'Neil, one of the greatest Irish chieftains. The authorities at Dublin, when they heard of this, threatened the O'Neil, whereupon de Leyva, characteristically, refused
to be a danger to his host and set off for Scotland in a patched-up
galleass which was in the harbour. Coasting along the shores of
Donegal he had rounded Malin Head and was nearly up to the

Giant's Causeway when the ship was dashed to pieces on a rock. With him died those young cadets who had joined at Lisbon so eager 'for endless glory and renown'. The place where they died is known today as 'Spaniard's Rock'; their bodies were washed ashore to lie in unmarked graves.

One by one the galleons drove ashore all down the Irish coast from Donegal to Kerry. Some were smashed to pieces on the rocks, others beached on a shelving shore, but for most of their companies death came soon. On one beach five miles long in Sligo Bay an English officer counted eleven hundred corpses spewed up by the sea, soldiers and their officers, nobles of ancient lineage and humble Biscay fishermen—all equal now in death. From vessels which missed the rocks and somehow beached themselves, famished and half-drowned Spaniards staggered through the breakers only to be knocked on the head by wild Irish tempted by the sight of gold chains and rings. The local chiefs hurried down to stop the slaughter when they learned of it and gave shelter to many sick and starving survivors; but the English authorities were not so humane. This sudden influx of Spaniards created an awkward problem: the garrison being thin on the ground feared that when the Spaniards had recovered they might reinforce the rebellious Irish, and orders went out accordingly for the survivors to be hunted like felons and executed when caught.

And here Captain Christopher Carleill comes into the story again. He was now on garrison duty in Northern Ireland and so missed all the excitement his old shipmates of the Caribbean had in the Channel. One day fourteen Spanish soldiers, miserable and in rags, gave themselves up to him, begging him as a fellow soldier to spare their lives. That was his wish but the orders were strict, so he sent them to the Lord Deputy with a letter about their case asking him for clemency. The Lord Deputy, described by a contemporary as 'sour of soul and severe' would not hear of mercy and sent them back to Carleill with instructions that they should be hanged at once. This brutal order was too much for Carleill, who had come to know and appreciate the average Spaniard during his long stay at Carthagena three years before. This was no way to treat prisoners of war, so instead of hanging them out of hand, he decided to give them a chance—if they survived the crossing to Scotland, good luck to them. He bought them passages in a Scottish fishing-boat and with new clothes on their backs and money in their pockets sent them off, 'putting everything to the decision of the elements'. Few English officers had the courage or humanity of Carleill, scores of shipwrecked Spaniards were hanged as soon as they were captured, but the Irish chieftains managed to smuggle a few out of the country. It was only months later when these reached Spain that the King learned any details of the tremendous disaster in Ireland.

Meanwhile, out in the region of 15° W the Duke of Medina-Sidonia, unaware of the tragedy in progress far to leeward, travelled south without sighting the coast of Ireland. The *San Martin* and eleven other galleons which had followed a similar course weathered Cape Clear and ten of them dropped down into the Bay. The exception was a transport which turned in too soon and sailed up Channel under the impression that she was on her way to Spain until she was disillusioned by hitting the Bolt Tail in Devon. For the others the wind began to lose its piercing keenness and there was warmth again in the sun. Then each in turn sighted the mountains of Spain, blue in the distance, and the battered ships limped singly into port as the wind took them, to Corunna, Santander or San Sebastian. They were home after a long nightmare and there to prove it were trees heavy with fruit, grapes ripening in the sun, the flowered creeper on a whitewashed wall. The Duke arrived at Santander on September 22nd, and dispatched his sad but incomplete report on the fate of the Armada next day. Most of the ships which had returned were dismasted and nearly all the sailors dead; what had happened to the rest of his fleet he did not know. In his own flagship 180 were dead, the rest down with fever and only two of his personal attendants were left alive.

The King received the news of the disaster with calm and dignity, but he acted promptly. Instead of blame and recrimination he sent down food and money, clothes and medicine to the Biscay Coast. He organized hospitals and awarded immediate pensions to the known widows and orphans. It was only by degrees that the full extent of the disaster filtered through to Spain. And before they knew of it, Oquendo and Recalde, worn-out, ill and with nothing to live for, died soon after they had brought their ships home. Their Commander-in-Chief had a sympathetic answer from the King, and returned overland to San Lucar. Philip never gave the Duke any blame for what had happened, perhaps because he came to realize that most of it attached to himself. Philip II of Spain had his moments of great-ness as a monarch and as a man, and this was one of them. He complained neither of God on Whose behalf he had launched the Enterprise, nor of the man to whom he had entrusted it, for to do so would not befit a Christian king. Instead he ordered a Mass of Thanksgiving for those who had returned and Masses through-out Spain for the repose of the souls of those who had not. One hundred and thirty ships and 30,000 men had sailed out of Lisbon with flags flying on that sunny May morning; sixty-five battered hulks with 9,000 sick and dying men struggled back to Spain before the autumn equinox. 'The uncertainty of naval enterprises is well known', the King wrote to his archbishops. 'We are bound to give praise to God for all things which He is pleased to do.' This was the King's last word on the subject, and who shall gainsay him.

King Philip was right in taking the broad view, but even so he did not reach the heart of the matter. The failure of the Ar-mada was not due to weather, certainly not to any lack of courage in those who took part, not to organization or to leadership. But neither was it due to the uncertainty of naval enterprises—the cause of failure lay deeper. The Armada sailed in the wrong century. It was contemporary with the partition of the world, an 'army by sea' adrift in a new era. Hawkins, Drake and the English seamen had changed the form of sea warfare; and though the last 'army by sea' fought with medieval dedication and courage it was routed inevitably by the first of the oceanic navies.

BIBLIOGRAPHY

*

Original Documents
(N.R.S. pubd. by Navy Records Society. H.S. pubd. by Hakluyt
    Society)
    Naval Accounts and Inventories of the reign of Henry VII
                                          N.R.S.
    Letters and Papers relating to the War with France, 1512–13
                                          N.R.S.
    The Ordinance Book of the Merchants of the Staple
    Spanish Documents concerning English Voyages to the
        Caribbean   H.S.
    Spanish Documents relating to English Voyages to the Spanish
        Main   H.S.
    'More Light on Drake', Spanish Documents from Pacific
        colonies   H.S.
    'A Brief Summe of Geographie'. Barlow, Ed. Taylor   H.S.
    The Three Voyages of Sir Martin Frobisher and State Papers
                                          H.S.
    Papers relating to the Navy during the Spanish War, 1585–7
                                          N.R.S.
    Fighting Instructions, 1530–1816   N.R.S.
    'The Autobiography of Phineas Pett'   N.R.S.
    The Fugger News Letters, 1568–1605, Ed. von Klarwill
    Voyages and Works of John Davis   H.S.
    'The Monson Tracts', with appendices   N.R.S.
    'The World Encompassed'   H.S.
    State Papers relating to the defeat of the Spanish Armada,
        2 Vols.   N.R.S.
    Calendar of State Papers: Spanish
                           Venetian
                           Rome
                           Elizabeth (Dom. and For.)

BIBLIOGRAPHY

Calendar of Treasury Papers, 1557–96
Phillipps Transcripts N.R.S.

Other Authorities
Hakluyt's *Voyages* H.S.
History of England—Trevelyan
Social History of England—Trevelyan
The Navy of Britain—M. Lewis
Shipwright's Trade—Abell
The Royal Navy. A History—Clowes and others
The Ocean in English History—Williamson
Tudor Geography—Taylor
The Administration of the Royal Navy—Oppenheim
England's Quest of Eastern Trade—Foster
The Portuguese Pioneers—Prestage
S. Francis Xavier—Broderick
Indian Ocean—Villiers
Shakespeare's England—Oxford University Press
Camb. Mod. History, Vol IV, Chapters IX and XV
The Reign of Elizabeth—Black
Short History of the Royal Navy (1217–1688)—Hannay
Statesmen and Sea Power—Richmond
Elizabethan England—Tenison
The Navy as an Instrument of Policy, 1558–1727—Richmond
Mary Tudor—Prescott
The Age of Drake—Williamson
Hawkins of Plymouth—Williamson
Drake and the Tudor Navy—Corbett
History of Iberian Civilization—Oleveira
History of Spain—Bertrand and Petrie
The Golden Age of Spain—Davies
Travel and Discovery in the Renaissance—Boies Penrose
The Spanish Story of the Armada—Froude
English Seamen of the Sixteenth Century—Froude
La Armada Invencible—Duro
Considerations touching a War with Spain—Francis Bacon
Howard—J. Knox Laughton

BIBLIOGRAPHY

Nine Vanguards—P. K. Kemp

'Was the failure of the Armada due to Storms?'—Rose (Proceedings of the British Academy)

British Flags—W. G. Perrin

'Mariner's Mirror'—'Armada Guns'—two articles by M. Lewis

INDEX

293

INDEX

INDEX

INDEX

INDEX

INDEX

INDEX

INDEX